Bertino Rodmann
Gypsy Jazz Guitar

Volume 1
– A Tribute to Gypsy Jazz –

Introduction into the style of Jazz-Manouche

© 2011/2013 by **Alfred Music Publishing GmbH**
alfred.com
alfredverlag.de

All Rights Reserved!
Printed in Germany

Cover art design: Bertino Rodmann, Thomas Petzold
Engraving: Bertino Rodmann, Helge Kuhnert
Production: Thomas Petzold
item-#: 20157US (Book / CD)
ISBN 10: 3-943638-34-0
ISBN 13: 978-3-943638-34-9

CD-production: Bertino Rodmann
Guitar: Bertino Rodmann
Guitar: Matthias Hampel
Bass: Jonas Lohse

Copyrights images:

Coverphoto: Leo Eimers Guitars ('Mod. Pizzarelli')
Page 12, 13 right © 2010 *www.eimersguitars.com*
Page 13, left: courtesy of Francois F. Charle (Paris)
© 2011 *www.rfcharle.com*
Page 8, 14, 40, 74 and 76 © 2011 Bertino Rodmann,
www.jazzmanouche.de
Page 15 mid left, courtesy of Wegen Picks
© 2011 *www.wegenpicks.com*
Page 15 bottom, courtesy of Dugain Picks,
© 2011 *www.dugainpicks.com*
Page 27 and 30 courtesy of Baro Winterstein,
© 2010 *www.marodrom.com*
Page 141, © 2009 Hinrich Wulff Photography,
www.hinrichwulff.de

translation by Bertino Rodmann and Leonie Hughes

Introduction into the style of Jazz-Manouche 3

"The one who never learned to listen,
will never learn how to play ..."

(Benny Goodman)

Contents

Preface .... Page 8

Introduction
- The Guitars .... Page 12
- The Strings .... Page 14
- The Picks .... Page 15

PART 1 – RHYTHM GUITAR
- Rhythm-Exercises – Introduction .... Page 17
- Finger-Exercise 1 with Extended Chromatics .... Page 18
- Finger-Exercise 2 .... Page 22

Rhythm Exercises – Lesson 1
- Rhythm Excercise 1 – Comping Straight Quarter-Notes .... Page 23
- Rhythm Excercise 2 – Comping Eighth-Notes .... Page 24
- Rhythm Excercise 3 – Comping Eighths with Added Dead-Notes .... Page 24
- Rhythm Excercise 1/1 – Comping 'La Pompe' .... Page 24
- Rhythm Excercise 1/2 – Comping Valse .... Page 25
- Rhythm Excercise 1/3 – 'La Pompe' (Csárdás) .... Page 25
- Rhythm Excercise 1/4 – Extended Comping 'La Pompe' .... Page 25
- Rhythm Excercise 1/5 – Comping Extended 'Swing-Pompe' .... Page 26
- Rhythm Excercise 1/6 – Comping 'Staccato Eighths' with added Dead-Notes .... Page 26

Rhythm Exercises – Lesson 2
- *Minor Swing* .... Page 27
- The Blues Cadence .... Page 27
- Exercise 2/1 ('La Pompe'-Rhythm, Example: *'Minor Swing'*) .... Page 28
- Chord Substitution .... Page 30
- Exercise 2/2 ('La Pompe'-Rhythm, Example: *'Minor Swing'*) .... Page 32
- Gypsy Chords .... Page 34
- Lesson 2/3 (Chord Substitution, Example: *'Minor Swing'*) .... Page 35
- Lesson 2/4 (Chord Substitution 2, Example: *'Minor Swing'*) .... Page 37

Rhythm Exercises – Lesson 3 – Songs for practise
- Lesson 3/1 – *'Minor Swing'* (Django Reinhardt/Stephane Grapelli) .... Page 41
- Lesson 3/2 – *'Douce Ambiance'* (Django Reinhardt) .... Page 44
- Lesson 3/3 – *'Good times (Schukar ziro)'* (Bertino Rodmann) .... Page 51
- Lesson 3/4 – *'Blues en mineur'* (Django Reinhardt/Stephane Grapelli) .... Page 55
- Lesson 3/5 – *'Valse à Bertino (Le grand escalier)'* (Bertino Rodmann) .... Page 59
- Lesson 3/6 – *'Blues Clair'* (Django Reinhardt) .... Page 67
- Lesson 3/7 – *'Swing 48'* (Django Reinhardt) .... Page 70

Introduction into the style of Jazz-Manouche

PART 2 – SOLO GUITAR
- Introducing Solo Guitar .... Page 74
- The Right Hand Placement .... Page 74

Solo / Lesson 1 – Picking Technique
- Picking Technique... Page 75
- 1/1 – Reststroke Picking .... Page 77
- 1/2 – Up and Down Reststroke Picking .... Page 77
- 1/3 – Sweptstroke Picking .... Page 78
- 1/4 – Arpeggio Picking .... Page 78

Solo / Lesson 2 – Scales (Part 1)
- 2/1 – Simple Pentatonic in Am .... Page 79
- 2/2 – Pentatonic in Am with added sixth (Am6) .... Page 79
- 2/3 – Minor scale in Am with additional 6th note .... Page 80
- 2/4 – Major scale in D .... Page 80
- 2/5 – Seventh scale over E7th .... Page 80
- 2/6 – Diminished scale over E7th .... Page 81
- 2/7 – A7th scale over A7 .... Page 81
- 2/8 – Gmaj7 scale (F# locrian) .... Page 81
- 2/9 – G major scale (Django style) .... Page 82

Solo / Lesson 3 – Arpeggios
- 3/1 – Am arpeggio .... Page 82
- 3/2 – Am6 arpeggio .... Page 83
- 3/3 – Am6 arpeggio (variation) .... Page 83
- 3/4 – G major arpeggio .... Page 83
- 3/5 – G major arpeggio (variation) .... Page 84
- 3/6 – G major arpeggio (D shape) .... Page 84
- 3/7 – C minor arpeggio .... Page 84

Solo / Lesson 4 – Solo-Licks (excerpts from 'Minor Swing')
- 4/1 – Lick 4/1 (*Am6*) .... Page 85
- 4/2 – Lick 4/2 (*Dm6*) .... Page 85
- 4/3 – Lick 4/3 (*E7*) .... Page 86
- 4/4 – Lick 4/4 (*Am6*) .... Page 86
- 4/5 – Lick 4/5 (*Am6 / Dm6*) .... Page 87
- 4/6 – Lick 4/6 (*E7 / Am*) .... Page 87
- 4/7 – Lick 4/7 (*Am6 / Dm6*) .... Page 87
- 4/8 – Lick 4/8 (*Dominant-7th over F7/E7 to Am6*) .... Page 88

Solo Transcriptions for Practice
- Excercise 4/9 – '*Minor Swing*' (Django Reinhardt/Stephane Grapelli) .... Page 88
- Excercise 4/10 – '*Blues en mineur*' (Django Reinhardt/Stephane Grapelli) .... Page 95
- Excercise 4/11 – '*Douce Ambiance*' (Django Reinhardt)... Page 100

Solo / Lesson 5 – Tips & Tricks

- Lick 5/1 – 'Trill'-Effect .... Page 105
- Lick 5/2 – Arpeggio in Am .... Page 105
- Lick 5/3 – Arpeggio in Am (2) .... Page 106
- Lick 5/4 – Gypsy-Lick (*Gm6 over C7*) .... Page 106
- Lick 5/5 – Lick in D-harmonic minor + Arpeggio in Dm .... Page 106
- Lick 5/6 – Lick in D-harmonic minor over dominant-7th-chord (*A7*) .... Page 107
- Lick 5/7 – 'Trill'-Effect (2) .... Page 107

Solo / Lesson 6 – Scales (Part 2)

- 6/1 – Minor pentatonic scale in C minor .... Page 108
- 6/2 – Minor-Pentatonic-scale in C with added *Blue Note* (add*b5*) .... Page 108
- 6/3 – Minor pentatonic scale in C (over three octaves) .... Page 109
- 6/4 – The blues scale in C .... Page 109
- 6/5 – The harmonic minor scale in A .... Page 110

Solo / Lesson 7 – The Use of Scales and Arpeggios in Gypsy Jazz

- 7/1 – Cm6 arpeggio in Django style .... Page 111
- 7/2 – Gm scale in Django style .... Page 111
- 7/3 – Dm6 arpeggio in Django style .... Page 111
- 7/4 – Dm arpeggio in Lollo Meier style .... Page 112
- 7/5 – Diminished scale in Lollo Meier style .... Page 112
- 7/6 – Harmonic minor in Django style .... Page 112
- 7/7 – C major arpeggio in Django style .... Page 113
- 7/8 – Arpeggio Repetitions in Django style .... Page 113
- 7/9 – Chord Substitution in Django style .... Page 113
- 7/10 – Arpeggio sequences in Romane style .... Page 114
- 7/11 – Combination of scales and arpeggios in Lollo Meier style .... Page 114
- 7/12 – Diminished scales in Stochelo Rosenberg style .... Page 115
- 7/13 – Cm6 arpeggio in Django style .... Page 115

Solo – Transcriptions for Practice (2)

- Excercise 8/1 – *'Blues Clair'* (Django Reinhardt) .... Page 117
- Excercise 8/2 – *'Good times (Schukar ziro)'* (Bertino Rodmann) .... Page 120
- Excercise 8/3 – *'Valse à Bertino (Le grand escalier)'* (Bertino Rodmann) ... Page 123
- Excercise 8/4 – *'Swing 48'* (Django Reinhardt) .... Page 132

Epilogue .... Page 139

About the Author .... Page 141

Glossary .... Page 142

Sources / Thanks .... Page 145

CD-Tracklist .... Page 146

Introduction into the style of Jazz-Manouche

"There is two kinds of music, the good and the bad. I play the good kind".

(Louis Armstrong, 1941)

Preface

My passion and love for the music of *Gypsy Jazz* (or *Jazz-Manouche* as it is known in France), has been growing for many years.

I shall tell you how I first became interested in this type of music and why I am so fascinated with it, so that you as a learning guitarist can begin to understand the depth of feeling and respect that I have for *Gypsy Jazz*.

Where did it all start?
My career as a musician started with a dream in the early 1970s when I bought my first guitar. The first music that I began to play was the music that I listened to, the music that was 'in' at the time. It was a mixture of blues music, people such as the great **B.B.King, Muddy Waters** and **Rory Gallagher**, and early rock music, such as **Led Zeppelin, Deep Purple, The Animals, Eric Clapton, Santana** and many more.

After just a few months of playing guitar, I started playing in bands and my repertoire constantly changed and developed over the years. *Pop, Funk, R&B, Reggae* and *dance music* were just some of the styles that were added over time.

By 1982 I had collected some 10 years worth of knowledge about music and playing the guitar itself. I'd tried out many different styles, had played in a lot of bands, supported live projects and worked in recording studios. However, I began to feel bored by what I was playing – always playing the same three chords (as in blues or some rock songs) wasn't my cup of tea. I began to feel that many of the songs I played were too easy and didn't present a real challenge for me anymore.

So it was around this time that one day I was at a friend's house. He was a collector of records and owned more than 3000 LPs. We would often sit together and play our new favorites to each other. All of a sudden he asked me "Hey **Bertino**, do you know this one?", whilst showing me a five record set which was a 'Best Of' album of **Django Reinhardt** and the **Quintette du Hotclub de France**.

I replied, "Well, no I don't. **Django Reinhardt**? Who is that? Is that a new band?" He was absolutely flabbergasted! " You don't know **Django Reinhardt**?" he said. "My God, what kind of a guitarist are you? You have to listen to it"! He put the record on, *and yes, from that moment I was blown away!*

I had never heard anything like it before in my entire life. Melodies, like precious pearls, fell on my ears, melodies of such beauty and distinction.

I was listening to a musician who showed me all his fear and pain as well as his joy and luck – incredibly melodic and then completely detuned in the next second.

Rushing out or coming back into straight timing in one second, perfectly melodic again on the next chord. So shocked was I by the beauty of *Django's* playing, that I started to cry within the first minutes of listening.

The incredible virtuosity of this **man** ('**MANouche**' means 'human being' in Romanes, the language of the *Sinti*) and his ability to tell fairy tales and stories in his playing totally surprised me. *This guy was talking with his guitar.*

Exactly on point every second, rhythmically perfect and, at many times, absolutely beautiful and elegant – his playing rendered me speechless. *From this moment on my fascination for this powerful music was born!*

Alex Rodmann Group, 1983

Introduction into the style of Jazz-Manouche

It took a lot of hard work to convince my friend to sell me this record (which I still own today) and from that day, I started listening to nothing else, trying to learn what *Django* played. At first, I was just haplessly trying to match what he was doing, which was simply impossible for me at that time. I really had no clue what they were playing at all!

Maybe I should also let you know that when I started learning the guitar, it was at all times completely 'autodidactic'. I would listen to records trying to learn a melody, a chord or a sequence of notes. I started to play the guitar when I was 13 when a friend first showed me some basic chords that he knew and that was it. I never had an hour of guitar lessons in my entire life!

In my family we didn't have any money for music lessons or teachers so I had to take my ears and learn what I heard…and that is one thing that I strongly recommend to any musician:

listen to music every day and strengthen your ears early, don't just play notes that you read!

It's good to know about reading music, no doubt, but it is just as important to a musician to develop a feeling for a sound and its colours and to play them at the right moment.

So, I have always 'learned by doing', practising and practising for between five to eight hours in those first ten or so years – my dream back then was to, one day, become a professional guitar player.

Through all this work I had learned a great deal about music – *but this Gypsy Jazz sound was really something else! It was so completely different from what I had known and learned before with its unique melodies, chords, scales and rhythms.*

I had to start again at *absolute zero*. Hardly any of the music theory that I had learned up to that point could really help me to understand this music. But, I was determined to play it and 25 years later and after many hours of practising, I am starting to understand this great music a little better.

In the beginning, I never thought that *Gypsy Jazz* would be so complex, so difficult to play and so *incredibly challenging* for any musician. That is, difficult if you want to play it truly authentically and not sound like a group of *'dance musicians'*. Today, regrettably, many of the *Gadjo-Gypsy Jazz-bands* ('*Gadjo*'= non-Gypsy in Romanes) sound superficial.

Dealing with the tradition and culture of the *Sinti* (Manouche) took me a lot closer to understanding their music: *How did they live and what kind of impact did this have on their music?*
Why is their music like it is: at times fast and wild, others very loud and raw; soft and mellow; melancholic and full of feeling – sometimes just wonderful in its beauty.

To truly understand how this music developed, one has to look at the history of the *Gypsies*.

The oldest history documents state that *Gypsies* are relatives of *Indian people* and that they lived in northern India until the 5th Century. At this point they were already professional, famous musicians.

The *Sintis* (a north-Indian tribe) often played at the temples and palaces of the Indian *maharajas* until they fell into disgrace and had to leave the country with their families.

They escaped from India travelling at first barefoot and then using horse-drawn wagons. They made their way through what would today be called *Uzbekistan*, *Iran*, *Iraq*, *Kurdistan* and *Turkey* on route to the *lower Balkans* (*Romania* and *Hungaria*) where some of them settled. Others travelled further to *Russia*, *Italy*, *France* and *Germany* and some went on to *Andalucia* in southern *Spain*.

They had to feed their families on this long journey and so they had to make a living. They did this by playing music *in almost every country* they passed through, most of the time being hired to play music for festivities such as marriages, parties or other occasions. Their *deep musicality* and *technical fluency* helped them to pick up local music styles quickly and efficiently.

The ability to play this music and to be more skilled in it than the local musicians was their capital and crucially important for them.

Their need to make money also explains why it was so absolutely necessary for them to play an instrument perfectly and to know as many songs as possible from each country they went through.

It was during this time that the purely *oral tradition of music education* developed. Most of them could not read or write and so their musical knowledge was passed on through word of mouth from father to son, uncle to brother – sharing songs, tricks and other musical knowledge.

Historians believe that by the 16th Century, *Gypsies* had travelled and spread all over Europe to the south of Spain. It is pretty clear that they absorbed their music all the musical influences from each of the countries that they travelled; *far eastern* or *Balkan music*, *Hungarian Czárdás*, *French musette-waltzes* as well as *Italian love songs*, *Russian traditionals* and *fiery Spanish flamenco music*.

To fully grasp the music of the *Sinti* and *Roma*, and the legendary swing Jazz of the famous *Sinti* musicians like **Django Reinhardt, Bireli Lagrene, Stochelo Rosenberg** or **Tschawolo Schmitt** (and many more) who also combined all the above mentioned styles in their music, the *Gypsy Jazz* guitarist should study some of these genres (theoretically but better practically) at least to a certain extent.

> *Here's an important tip:*
> *Learn as many songs from as many different styles, countries and composers as possible! Immerse yourself in the music of other countries so that you are able to understand and adapt at least the 'basic essence' into your own playing.*

So why did I decide to write another book on learning Gypsy Jazz?

In over 40 years of my career as a musician and teacher, I have had to learn many styles of music and obtain books for each.

One student wants to learn *classical guitar,* another likes to learn *pop songs*, yet another wants to learn *blues* or *rock guitar*.

Time and time again I had requests from students that wanted to learn to play *Gypsy* and *swing Jazz guitar* and so to be able to support these students I looked deeply into the method and *Gypsy Jazz* books that were on the market.

Within my own studies on *Gypsy Jazz* I have seen many books, DVDs and CDs have been published to teach this style and more still are being produced (although sometimes their quality is another subject to discuss).

When I first became interested in *Gypsy Jazz* there was no *Youtube* or anything else to learn from. Nowadays, Youtube is great, but more often than not it's dangerous for any beginner of the style as there is too much incorrect information about *Gypsy Jazz* shown on there.

Due to the fact that this music is traditionally passed on orally through families, it has always seemed very hard, if not impossible, to learn the style authentically from a book or anything else that was available.

Moreover (just my 2 cents here!), there is a real disadvantage to learning from many of these books and DVDs as they do not show any respect for the old traditions of the *Sinti* and their commitment to playing the music in the traditional way and, in my eyes, you need this knowledge to be able to do the music justice.

Well, I'm sure all the work I did on the available material gave me many new details about the style, but I was also able to see that there was no real 'School of *Gypsy Jazz*' book to learn from like there is for other styles, such as classical guitar. Well now maybe there is!

In the beginning I felt it was an indulgence for me to teach *Gypsy Jazz* to others as I am not a 'Manouche' (Sinto) myself even if I may feel very close to the positive aspects of the traditions of the *Sinti* and *Roma*.

But still, many people asked me to teach them this style and I felt a duty to at least try to teach it, always with great respect to **Django Reinhardt** and the other great *Sinti* musicians of today.

All of this led to my decision to put together my knowledge of this music into the form of my LIVE 'Masterclass for *Gypsy Jazz* Guitar' and with great success it seems. Most of the students that took part in my masterclasses told me they were pleased they had taken part.

One of these students was a guy named **Denni** who himself is a german *Sinto* that couldn't learn the music from his relatives due to a lack of musicians within his family. After long discussions with him, he encouraged and convinced me to write this book (thank you **Denni**!) to allow other guitarists the opportunity to most authentically learn this wonderful music and to let them participate in the fascination and respect for all the great *Gypsy Jazz* musicians of now and then.

Introduction into the style of Jazz-Manouche

So, finally I wrote this book hoping that everyone who uses it will also take a piece of the respect that I have into their hearts and help keep this wonderful music alive.

This book is not meant for complete perfection and accuracy. In fact, with the great virtuosity and spontaneity of this music, that wouldn't be possible – every Gypsy guitarist is playing things a little different to another.

Instead, this book is specifically designed for beginners of the style, to give them a method and a strategy and to help them understand the pitfalls and specialities of this music a little better. It aims to be as authentic as possible by helping them with their 'first steps' into this wonderful music.

I do strongly warn people not to become complacent in this style. By the time you might be able to play quite a few of the more easy tunes such as *'Minor Swing'* or *'Douce Ambiance'* you may begin to feel like you can understand and already know everything there is to know about *Gypsy Jazz*. Be aware that this will not be true!

The types of songs in this book are the 'more easy to understand examples'. Many guitarists will already know a little about *'Blues'* music which has a pretty close relationship with the expression in these named tunes but in general *Gypsy Jazz* is much more than that. Remember that *Gypsy Jazz* (*Jazz-Manouche*) is like an unwritten language and you should as well understand and play it as such.

Knowing about *Gypsy Jazz* is not just knowing certain playing techniques. It is about the quintessence of your music, about communication with the listener, about expressing yourself through your playing.

One day, if you can achieve that, being and playing yourself, then maybe you'll be done.

Please try to always remember this and to think of it as the most important element, not only in *Gypsy Jazz*, but in all your guitar playing.

If you sometimes feel like you don't know how to progress further with this music, I would suggest going back to the source and listening closely to some old **Django Reinhardt** recordings or listen to some *Gypsy Jazz* masters like **Fapy Lafertin, Dorado Schmitt, Angelo DeBarre** or **Romane** …

Maybe you'll feel the same as I do and you'll be able to find some new inspiration or understanding and be able to widen your horizons. Then you might understand what has been said previously about these things and the never ending journey.

Now, I wish you lots of enjoyment with this book and I hope that I am able to explain its content interestingly, understandably and respectfully, especially in relation to the old *Sinti* traditions that are strongly related to this music.

Keep up the Swing!

Latscho Drom (travel well),

Bertino Rodmann

Introduction

There are several important factors that any guitarist should consider before starting to learn *Gypsy Jazz*. One of these is considering the type of guitar and strings that are best suited for this style. Sure enough, you can play almost any kind of music on any instrument, for instance, it would be possible to play Jazz on a ukulele, but this could sound comical rather than have the typical Jazz sound. It is the same for Gyspy Jazz. Better suited instruments make for a much more special sound. So we need to spend some time considering instruments and the sound they make.

The Guitars

Of course, you can play *swing* (which essentially is *Gyspy Jazz*) on a regular acoustic or Jazz guitar but you may wonder why it doesn't sound the same as the great *Gypsy Jazz* artists.

From its creation in the early twenties, *Gypsy Jazz* was played on specially designed and built acoustic Jazz guitars. They were originally made by the famous French company, **Selmer** who are still in business today but now specialize in making saxophones and clarinets.

*D-Hole of an original **Selmer** guitar 'Orchestre' model, made in 1932*

*Original label of a **Selmer** guitar 'Jazz' model, made in 1948*

These special guitars were designed for **Selmer** by an Italian guitar maker called **Mario Maccaferri**, a respected classical guitarist and student of the famous guitar maestro Segovia. **Maccaferri** immigrated to Paris and worked for **Selmer** from 1932.

These guitars were different to normal acoustic guitars because of their '*D-hole*', a big *D*-shaped soundhole, and a specially designed 'soundchamber' in the body which was supposed to greatly amplify the sound. Because of their special design, *D-hole* guitars were much louder in comparison to regular guitars. They also have a particularly strong and assertive sound, sometimes known as 'mid-and-nosey'.

In 1936, not very long after designing this special D-hole guitarmodel, **Mario Macafferri** designed another special model for **Selmer**. This new guitar, which is still famous today, was called the '*Jazz*' model but was also referred to as the '*O-hole*' guitar. It was this guitar that the great *Sinti*-guitarist **Django Reinhardt** played up until his untimely death in 1952.

Maccaferri designed the '*O-hole*' guitar because the '*Orchestre*' model still didn't fit the needs of the swing players of the time. They needed a guitar that could give a true acoustic sound with lots of power and volume to compete with the stronger brass instruments that they played with in the Jazz orchestras. Of course, at this time, electrical amplification was not yet available.

Introduction into the style of Jazz-Manouche

In the image below, you can see that the inside of the Selmer 'Jazz'-guitar was specially designed in both the bracings, but also the small O-shaped soundhole.

The sound gets 'pressed' through the *O-hole* and because of that special revolutionary new design it sounds even louder than the *D-hole* shaped 'Orchestre' models. Due to this difference in volume, the Selmer 'Jazz'-guitar was, and still is, used mostly as a solo guitar.

*'O-hole' of an original **Selmer** 'Jazz' model, made in 1939*

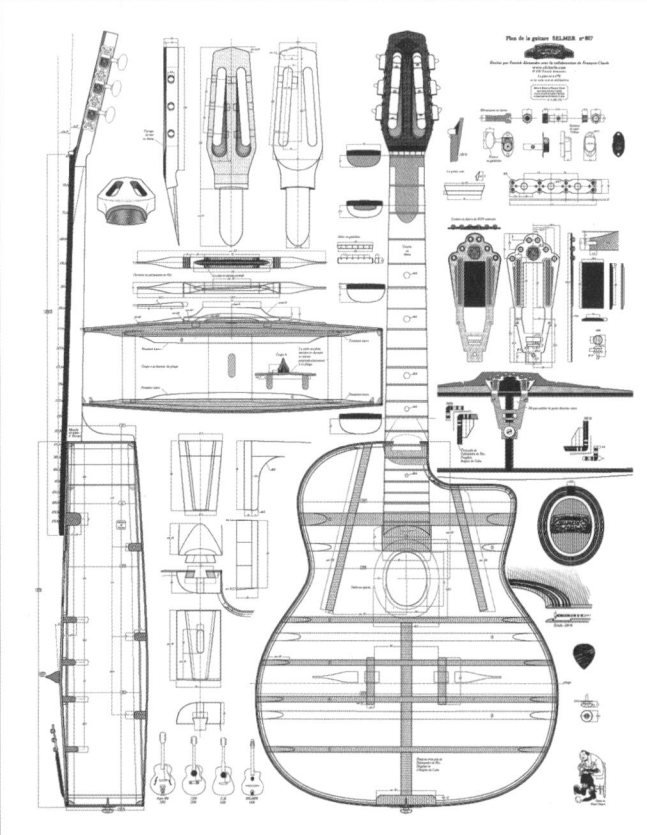

Photograph courtesy of Francois Charle, Paris

During the early 1930s to the late 1950s, there were only around 950 of these kinds of guitars built, all by hand of course. Needless to say, because of this small number, today these guitars have become extremely rare and very expensive (see the tip in the right column below).

That being said, there are many guitar makers worldwide that dedicate themselves to building more or less perfect replicas of the '*Selmer*' style guitars. The most famous of these guitar makers are: **Jean-Pierre Favino (F), Maurice Dupont (F), Leo Eimers (NL), Stefan Hahl (D), Henning Doderer (D), Geronimo Mateos (ES), Killy Nonis (UK)** and **JWC Guitars (UK)**. These all make particularly well-crafted, handmade instruments.

> *The prices of these handcrafted **Selmer** copies vary greatly. The lowest prices start at around €1,200 to €2,500, and they can go up to any price depending on your personal preferences for material and quality. This may sound expensive but when you factor in that an original **Selmer** guitar (depending upon the age and condition) will cost at least €20,000 and a good quality classical 'Masterguitar' can easily cost at least €8,000, these **Selmer** copies are actually good value.*

Companies such as **SAGA, Johnson, Aria** or **Richwood** make cheaper 'machine-made' beginner guitars so, depending on your budget, you can buy a playable guitar from around €400 up to €1500. Obviously, these cheaper guitars will not sound as good as the handcrafted ones but it is better to play *Gypsy Jazz* on a machine-made **Selmer** copy than a regular acoustic guitar.

If you are planning to play *Gypsy Jazz* more regularly, then you should definitely consider purchasing some kind of **Selmer** style guitar so that you can play it with a truly authentic sound. Once you have heard *Gypsy Jazz* being played on one of these guitars you will understand what I mean – it really is worlds apart, a completely different kind of sound!

*Left: 'Bertino'-model #001 built in 2007 by Leo Eimers,
Right: original Favino guitar of Stochelo Rosenberg, made in 1972*

My own guitars are good examples of these kind of handcrafted Gypsy guitars. Here you can see photos of them; the first built by **Leo Eimers** (on the upper left) and the second by **Maurice Dupont** (on the lower right).

You can find more detailed information on the **Selmer** style guitars on my website *www.Jazzmanouche.de* (go to 'Django and Guitars' and then 'Guitar Archive'). Another good website made by Paul Hohstetter is *www.lutherie.net/bckgrnd*.html. This one is especially about the **Selmer** style guitars.

The Strings

To be able to play *Gypsy Jazz* really authentically, another factor that needs to be taken into account is the strings that are used on these guitars. Because of the special design, the **Selmer** guitars (and their copies) will only develop their best sound with certain strings, namely silver-plated steel strings.

The French company **Savarez** was the first to create this type of string. They produce the famous 'Argentine' strings since early 1930ies and, rumour has it, **Django Reinhardt** already played 0.10 gauge Argentines on his **Selmer** guitar.

There are lots of other companies in the market today that produce these special silver plated strings: *Optima (Gypsyfire), Lezner (Silver), Golda (Wawau Adler), Galli (Gypsy Jazz), Pyramid* or *John Pearse (Nuages)* and many others.

Personally, I prefer the Argentine strings from Savarez, not just because of their reputation, but because they produce the best sound on my own guitars and last for a pretty long time.

But of course this subject is a matter of personal preference and taste. A lot depends upon the guitar and model that you are using so to get the perfect strings you will need to test some out to see which suits your guitar and your personal taste.

Maurice Dupont MD 60, made in 2006

Introduction into the style of Jazz-Manouche

   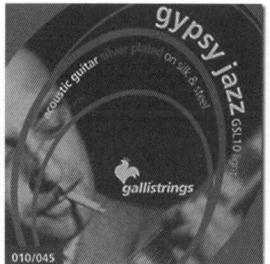 

The Picks

Finally, the last factor that you need to take into account when playing *Gypsy Jazz* is the type of pick that you use. The same as with traditional Jazz, in *Gypsy Jazz*, the pick used is traditionally very hard and thick. This is because a thick pick gives much better control according to the speed of the attack.

In *Gypsy Jazz* there are many licks, scales and arpeggios which are played very fast, so to be able to control the pick quickly is very important for the *Gypsy Jazz* guitarist.

Legend has it that **Django Reinhardt** played his guitar using a homemade pick that was actually a thick coat button made out of horn. In **Django's** time there were no professional pick makers of these special picks like there are today, so this story may well be true.

Michael Wegen (www.wegenpicks.com) is a Dutch company that make specially designed, thick picks that are used by many *Gypsy Jazz* guitarists.

The **Wegen** picks come in many different designs and shapes, colours and sizes. They have particularly good handling and make a really special sound on the guitars, hence why so many guitarists, including myself, use them.

Like with the guitars and the strings, there are many other companies that make picks that are usable for *Gypsy Jazz*, for example **Dugain, Miller, Catfish, Pickboy** and more. The material used for these picks varies from plastic and semi-precious stones to wood, horn, metal and bone.

In the end, as with the strings, whichever pick that you prefer is a matter of personal taste. Every guitarist has to choose their own pick to match their own 'sound'.

Of course, you can always play *Gypsy Jazz* with any regular thin pick. I have seen **Stochelo Rosenberg** and many other famous Gypsy guitarists play with standard thin plastic picks, yet their music always sounded like their remarkable own kind of playing.

So you can see that the music is not just dependent upon the type of materials used, but greatly on the type of musician!

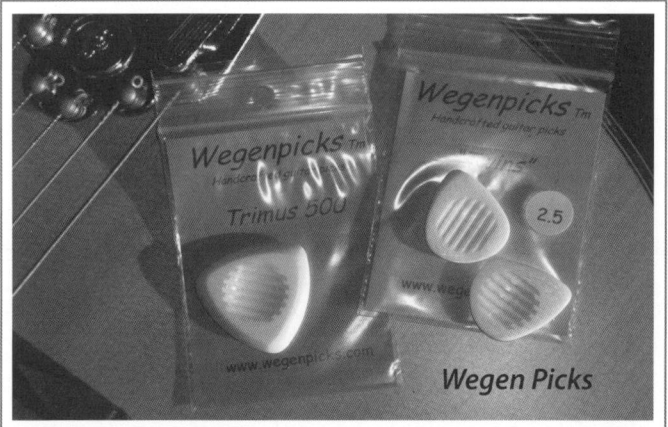

Wegen Picks

Dugain Picks

Gypsy Jazz Guitar

Part 1

Rhythm Guitar

Part 1 – Rhythm Guitar

Rhythm – Introduction

As a first step towards you mastering the challenge that is *Gypsy Jazz*, I'd like to recommend to you some important *exercises* that you can incorporate into your *'everyday practice hours'*.

I'd also like to mention at this point that all the great players that I have been proud to meet, or better yet, jam with (***Richard Manetti, Sebastien Giniaux, Wawau Adler*** or ***Fapy Lafertin***) are all practicing playing their guitar every day for hours on end! And that, of course, is one of the reasons why they are as good as they are: just training makes the master!

This is especially relevant with the very complex and, at times, difficult to play music that is *Gypsy Jazz*. In the beginning, *Gypsy Jazz* may sound easy to you, but you will soon discover that the more you delve into it, the more you realize its complexity and trickiness.

You can be as talented as you want as a guitar player – if you don't work out and practice your technique, it won't get you anywhere.

> *Important Tip:*
> *Practice every day for at least one or two hours (or more) and <u>always</u> practice everything with a metronome! This way you will achieve very good timing and precise playing which is fundamental to Gypsy Jazz. Alright then, let's start now.*

Finger-Exercise 1 (*Page 18*)

This exercise is designed to strengthen the muscles in your fingers. You will learn:

1. How to play quarter-notes in straight timing.
2. Using the whole fretboard in all positions.
3. To co-ordinate left and right hand when playing and picking straight.

> *Tip 1:*
> *Repeat this exercise at the beginning of your daily guitar-training at least for 10 – 15 minutes (without any break or letting go!).*
> *Even better, because more effective, is using it in direct combination with exercise 2.*

Finger-Excercise 2 (*Page 22*)

This exercise is designed to strengthen your ring finger and the pinkie of the left hand.
These two fingers are a little bit 'de-generated' due to them being used less by most of us. However, to play the guitar with a functioning 4-finger-set on the guitar fretboard, all four fingers need to be used with the same strength. This is why these two fingers need special training. This exercise becomes really effective if repeated in combination with Exercise 1.

> *Tip 2:*
> *Keep repeating Exercise 2 for at least 10-15 minutes, then change over to Exercise 1 for another 10-15 minutes and then again, back to Exercise 2. Try them all together for about 30 minutes at the beginning of your daily guitar practice.*

Remember: always(!) practise everything with straight metronome beats or a click-track!

Finger-Excercise 1 with Extended Chromatic

Part 1 – Rhythm Guitar

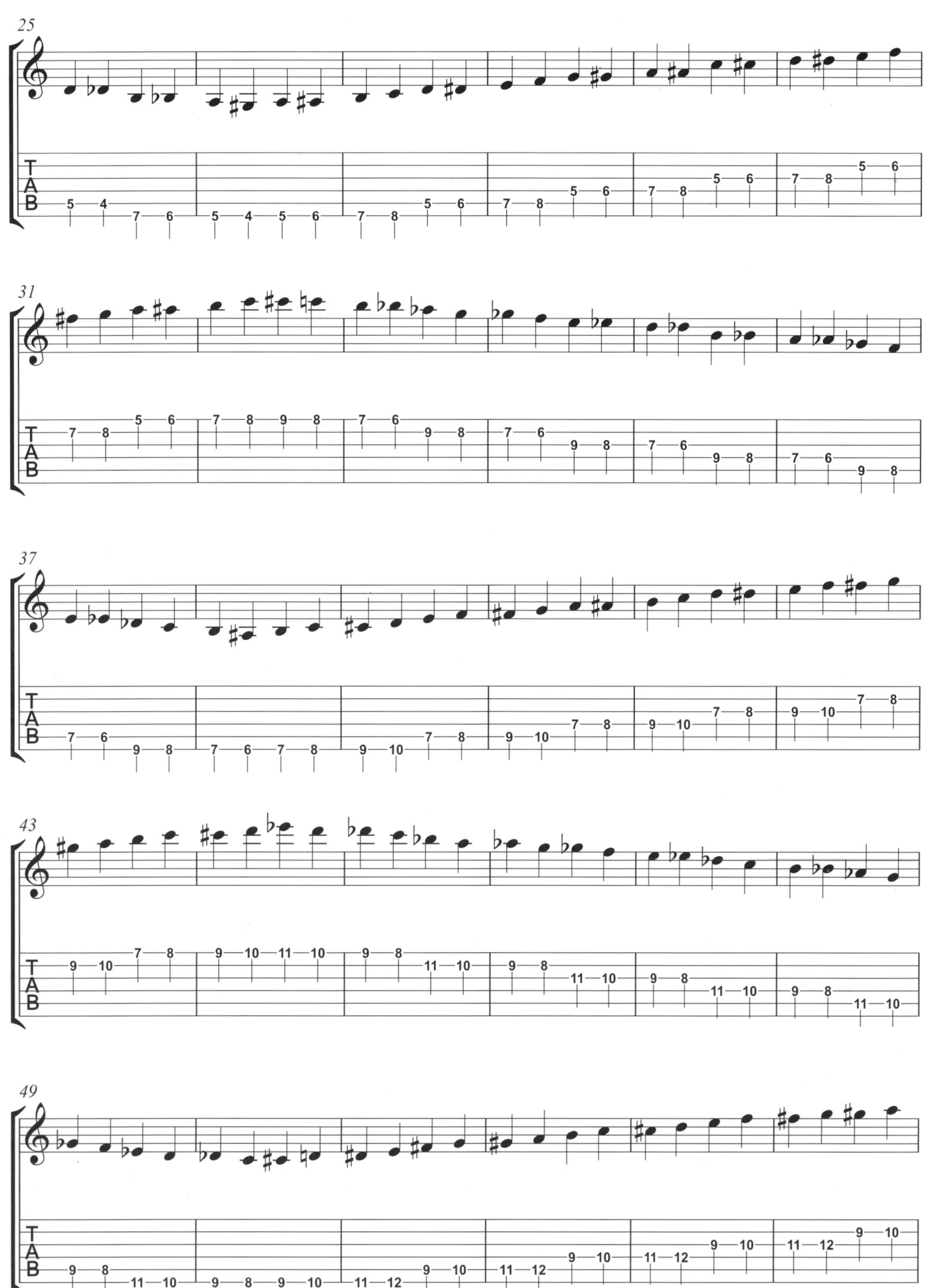

Part 1 – Rhythm Guitar 21

Finger-Excercise 2

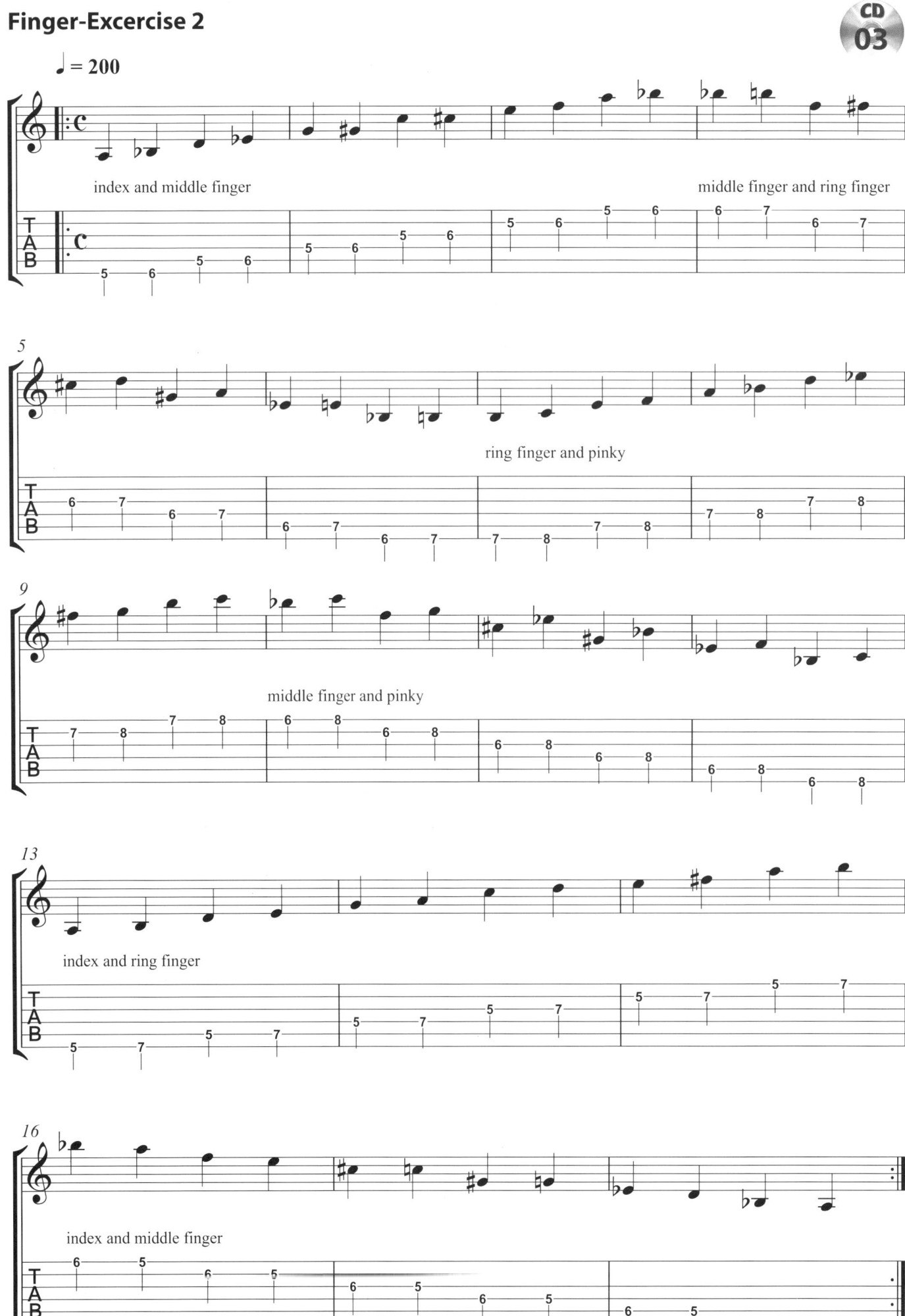

Part 1 – Rhythm Guitar

Rhythm-Excercises – Lesson 1

Many guitar players that make their debut into *Gypsy Jazz* may think that the rhythm is the easiest part of it: just a little '**boom-chick**' and it seems very easy to learn. What these players don't really know is that there are many different variations of the *Gypsy Jazz* rhythm called '*La Pompe*'. Normally these are regional differences that make the rhythm be accented and played differently.

For example, there is the so called '*Alsacian* School*' which is played by people like **Tschawolo Schmitt, Bireli Lagrene, Hono Winterstein** or **Hervé Gaguenetti**.

There is the '*Parisian School*' (played by **Django Reinhardt, Romane, Fapy Lafertin, Mattieu Chatelein** and **Angelo Debarre**), the '*German School*' (**Hännsche Weiss, Lulu Reinhardt, Wawau Adler**) and the '*Northern*' or '*Dutch School*' (musicians like the **Rosenberg Trio, Robin Nolan** or **Andreas Öberg**).

All these musicians play the swing rhythm '*La Pompe*' with completely different rhythmic accents and rhythmic specialities.

> *The Gypsies mostly start playing guitar as young children. At first they play only rhythm for at least two years before they start learning how to play any solos.*
> *One of the most important things for mastering Gypsy Jazz (Jazz-Manouche) is extremely accurate and straight timing and clear impressive **rhythm playing**.*
> *Gypsy Jazz Maestro **Romane** spends almost eight hours of his masterclasses explaining and clarifying the issue of rhythm! You can see from that how much time Sinti musicians dedicate to good rhythm playing.*
> *Remember: a really good rhythm player is always well respected amongst Gypsies!*

*'*Alsace*' is a region in Eastern **France** close to the German border.

For example, the '*German School*' rhythm is played with a harder attack and is quite jagged (a bit 'militaristic') whereas the '*Parisian School*' sounds much more elegant, more swingy and soft.
In these instances, the word 'school' is just used to distinguish clearly the differences between these regional ways of playing rhythm.

For most of the following exercises we will now use a *minor-6th chord* as a first *chord substitution*.
This means that *instead* of playing a regular *A-minor-barré chord* (left image below) we will use a typical *A-minor-6th voicing* in the style of *Django* (right image below).

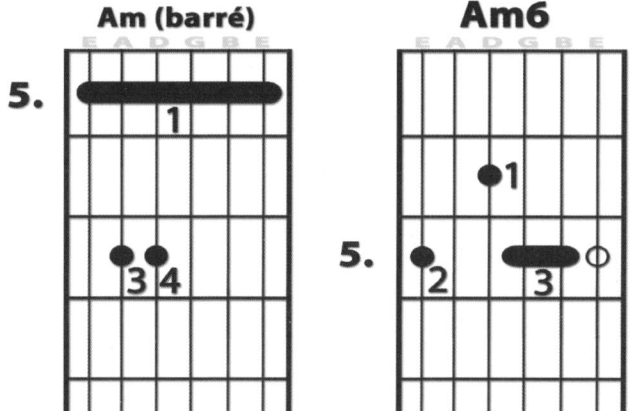

Later on in the book I will take a more detailed look at the subject of '*Chord Substitution*' (see the chapter on '*Chord Substitution*' on page 30). Let's now take a look at the rhythmic exercises.

Rhythm-Excercises

The first condition for mastering the rhythm-playing in *Gypsy Jazz* is an extremely good and straight timing and a precise beat to play a good and swingy rhythm. The following rhthym-*excercise* is designed to practise the playing of straight *quarter-notes*, a very important basic condition for a real 'swingy' *La Pompe*-Rhythm.

Rhythm Excercise 1 – Comping Straight Quarter-Notes

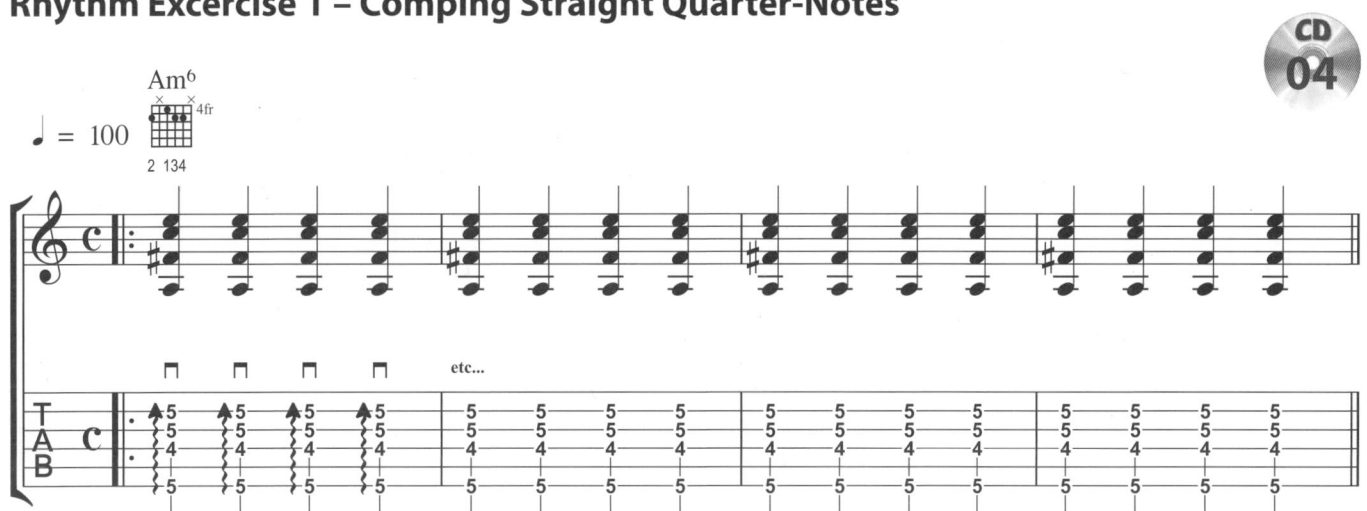

Rhythm Excercise 2 – Comping Eighth-Notes

In the second exercise we will practice the straight playing of eighth-notes. This is vital to be able to learn to play a good swingin' *'La Pompe'* rhythm later on.

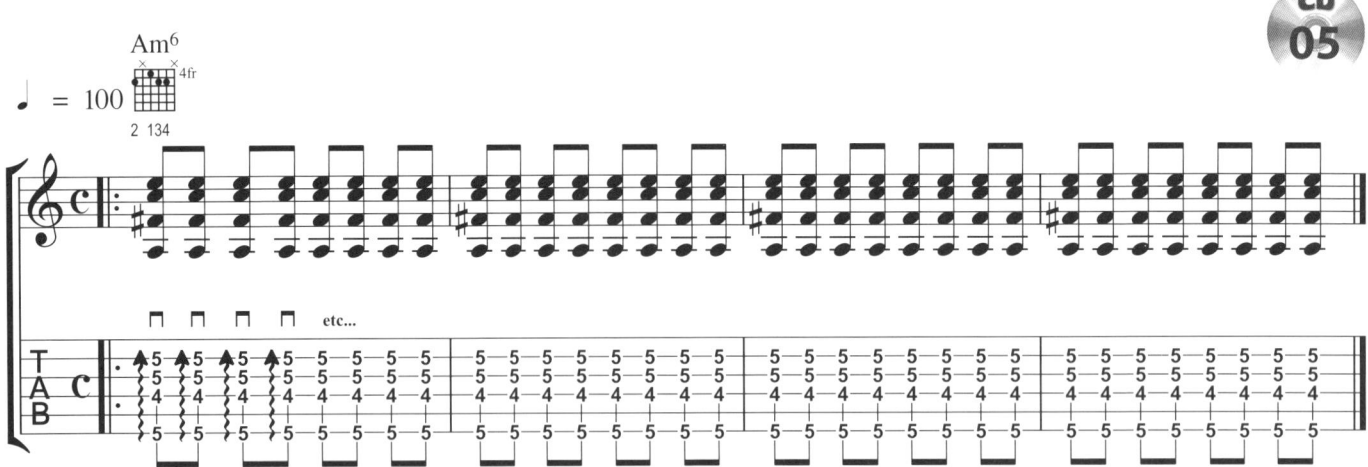

Rhythm Excercise 3 – Comping Eighths with Added Dead-Notes

This exercise is a variation of Rhythm Exercise 2 but with added muted notes ('dead-notes') (x).

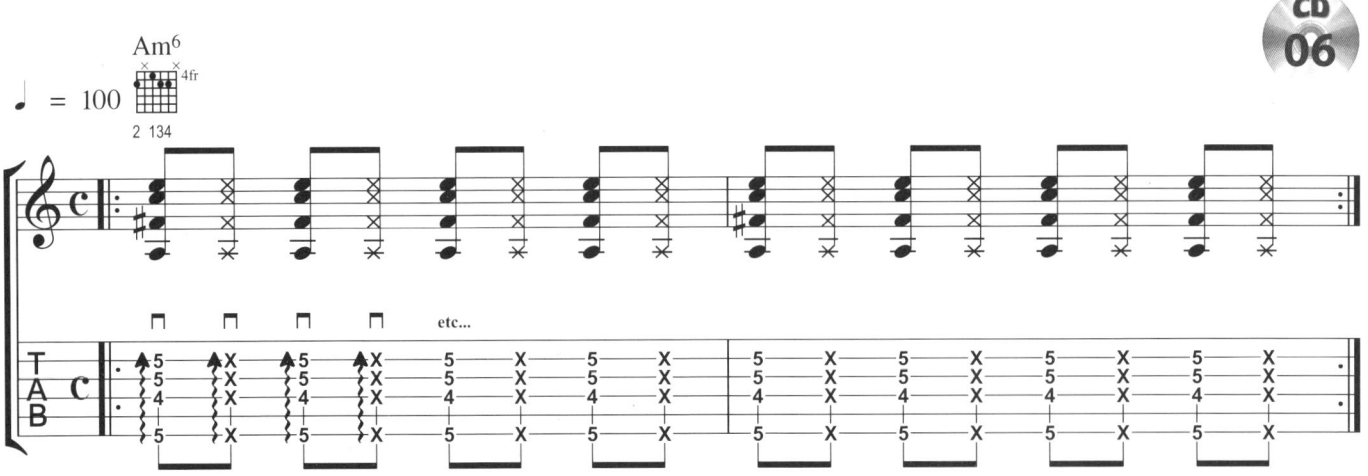

Remember, that up to this point, these are not real accompanying rhythms, just exercises!

Rhythm Excercise 1/1 – Comping *'La Pompe'*

The following exercise is a preview to the real *'La Pompe'* rhythm that I will show you a little later on. The exercise is designed to show the *'Pompe'* rhythm in its basic form and varies regular quarter-notes with quarter-dead-notes (x).

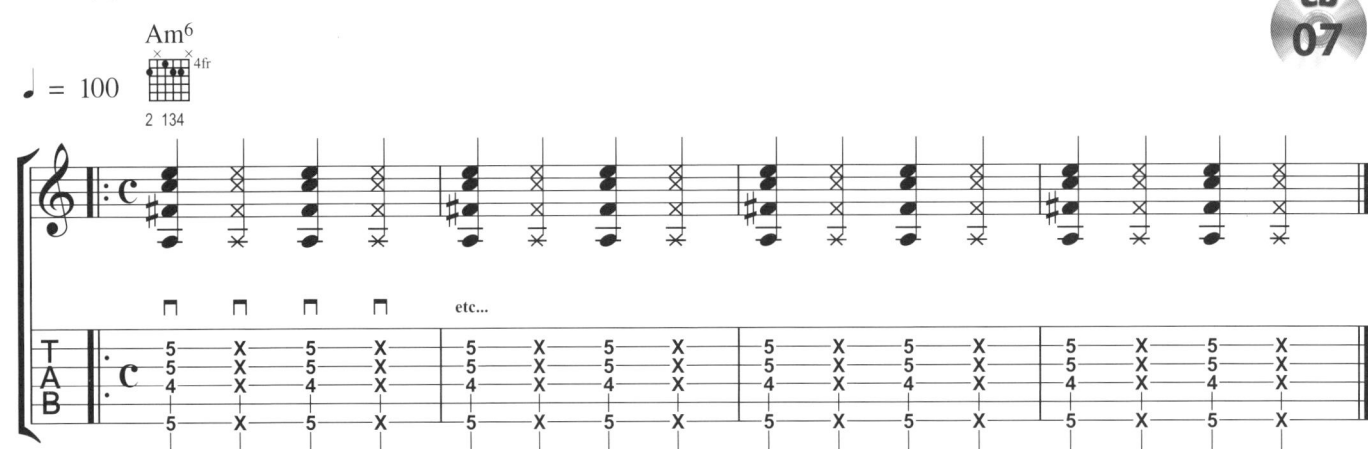

Part 1 – Rhythm Guitar

Rhythm Excercise 1/2 – Comping Valse

From the early days on French Musette or Jazz Waltzes were a very important part of any *Gypsy Jazz* repertoire. The following exercise shows the basic variation of a 3/4 waltz rhythm used in these kind of waltzes.

> *Tip:*
> *Try to learn at least one or two of the regularly played gypsy-waltzes (like 'Swing Valse', 'Montagne St Genevieve (Valse a Django)' or 'La Gitana') for your own repertoire. You can really learn a lot about Gypsy Jazz from these waltzes!*

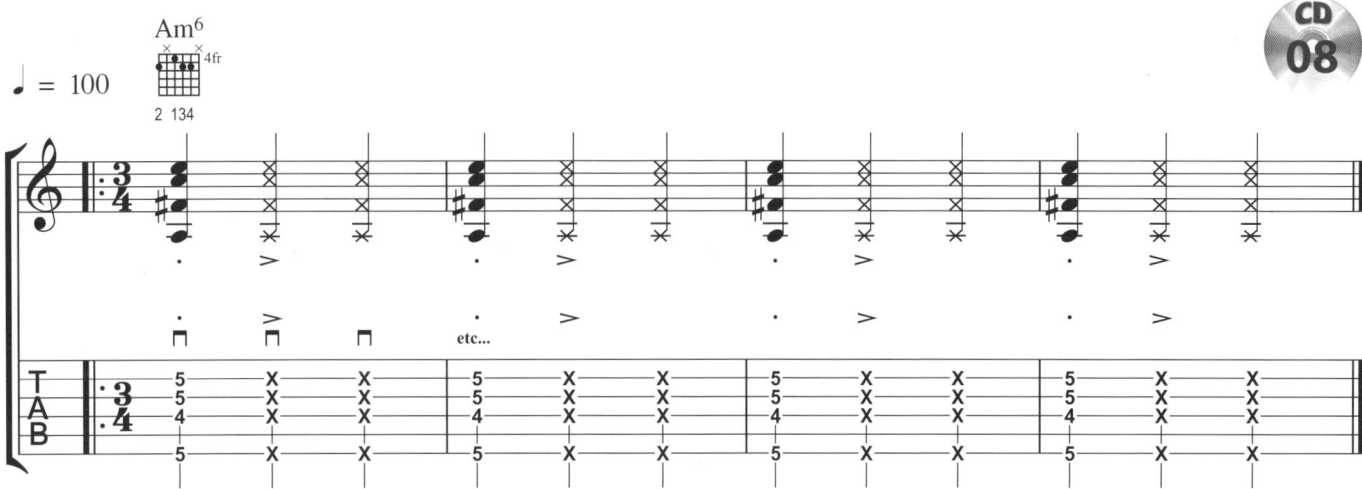

Rhythm Excercise 1/3 – 'La Pompe' (Csárdás)

The rhythm presented here is a mix of a regular 4/4 swing rhythm and the czárdás rhythm normally played by Hungarian Gypsy musicians. The first eighth-notes are hit only on the bass string after the rest of the chord is accented (*staccato*) on the other strings. **Django Reinhardt** used to play this kind of accompaniment in many fast tunes such as 'Hungaria' or 'Les Yeux Noir'.

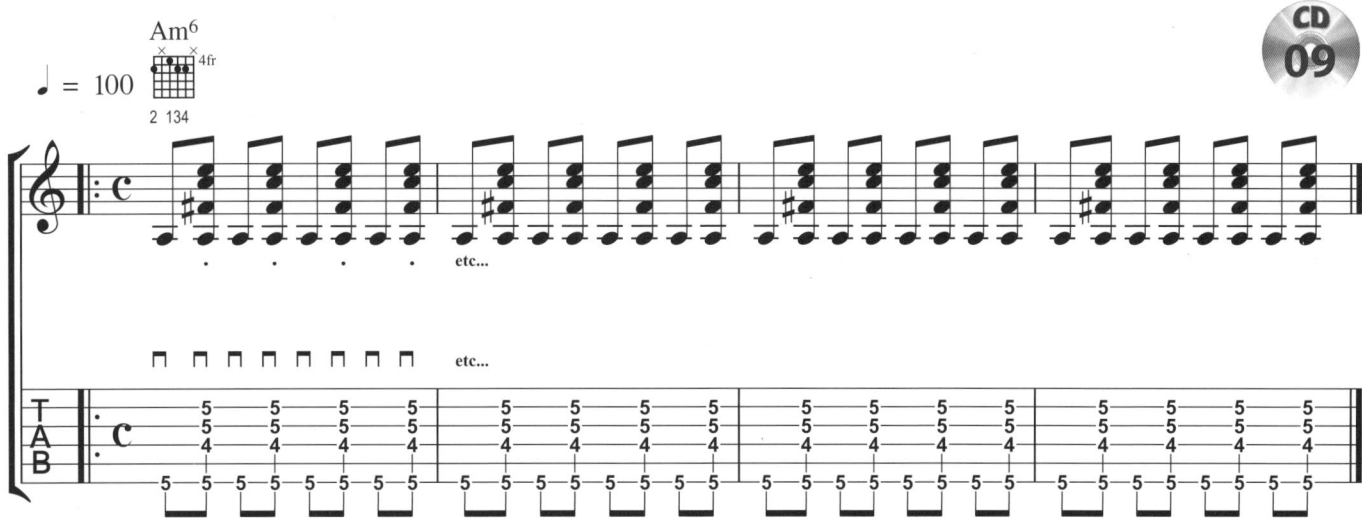

Rhythm Excercise 1/4 – Extended Comping 'La Pompe'

The next exercise extends the '***easy Pompe***' introduced in Rhythm Exercise 1/1 with more added eighths beats. The first eighths are played shortened (*staccato*), then the eighths-notes after the eighths-break are only played as *dead-notes* (*dead-note* = no sound = **chack**). Take care to play all the hits only as down-strokes! We will use this rhythm in the next examples as it is easier to play than Rhythm Exercise 1/1 or the following Rhythm Exercise 1/5.

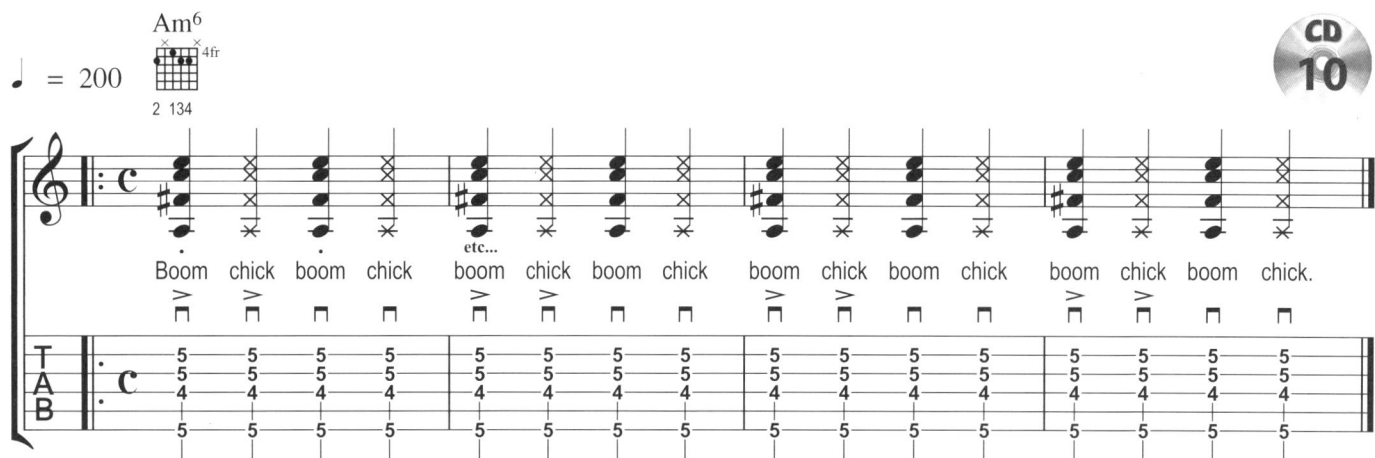

Rhythm Excercise 1/5 – Comping Extended '*Swing-Pompe*'

This example shows the extended 'Swing Pompe' as it would often be played by rhythm players such as **Nous'che Rosenberg, Hono Winterstein** or **Matthieu Chatelein**.
Here, we play the first note as a staccato-quarter-note, the second note as a straight eighth and the following eighth-note is played as a dead-note with an upstroke. Take care to remember that all the other beats should be hit as downstrokes!
This style of playing gives a very light and swingy rhythm but it is harder to play with precise rhythm.

*Tip: Remember to take care of the playing direction at certain beats of the rhythm as well as the triplet character of the eighth-notes.
It is very important to play the first hit short (staccato), because if you don't, your playing will sound something like 'ohwim-ohweh, ohwim-ohweh' which will take all the real 'swing' out of the rhythm.
Very important: when playing a real 'La Pompe', the accents are always on 2 and 4, not 1 and 3!*

Rhythm Excercise 1/6 – Comping 'Staccato Eighths' with added Dead-Notes

This exercise is a variation on Rhythm Exercise 3. By playing the eighth-notes of the swing rhythm only in staccato it makes the rhythm much more sharp and powerful. Be careful of the swing way of playing here! (See the Tip above right)

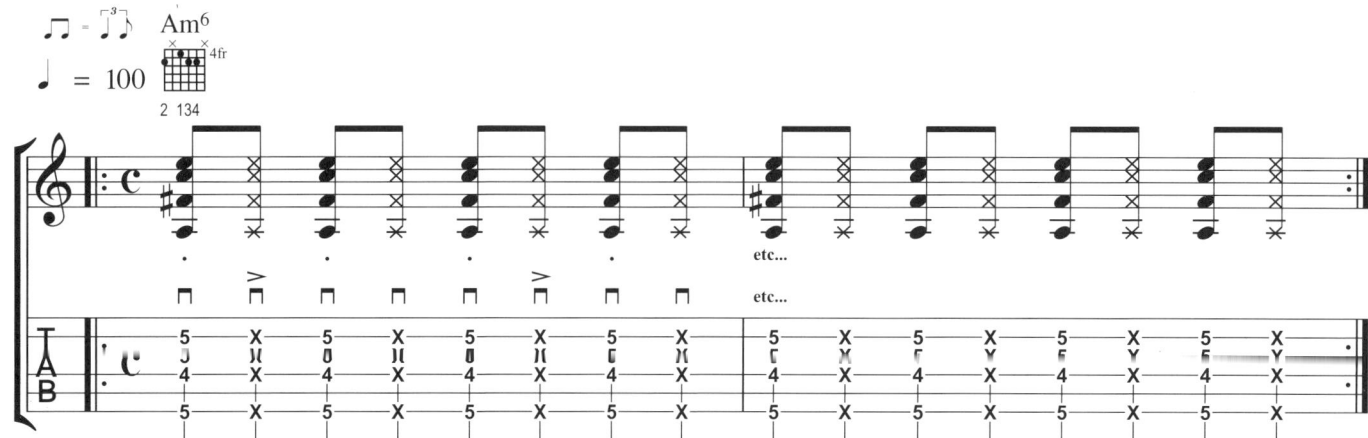

Rhythm Excercises – Lesson 2

Now we have finished the first part of our *Gypsy Jazz* rhythm exercises, we can move on to the practical section of rhythm playing.

Minor Swing
To gain a better understanding of the rhythm examples from the last chapter, and to gain more practical experience with them, we will now switch over to start using what we have just learned.

We are going to use some of these rhythm examples by playing the famous song '*Minor Swing*', composed by **Django Reinhardt** and Stephane Grapelli.
I have chosen the song for this book on purpose due to its direct relation to the blues, because I would guess that nearly every guitarist has come across the blues at least once in their guitar career.
So, to me, this style of music seems best suited for you to successfully take your first steps into *Gypsy Jazz*.
I believe this will give the beginning *Gypsy Jazz* guitarist the best chance to further develop their musical knowledge of the new style and to gain a deeper understanding of *Gypsy Jazz* without having to alter their listening habits too much in the beginning.

The structure of the song '*Minor Swing*', which was written in 1928, can be looked at as a kind of 'standard minor blues'.

The Blues Cadence
The chord sequences used in blues are normally built up from the scale's first chord (step 1 = the root-note), then secondly the sub-dominant-chord (step 4) and the dominant-chord (step 5). They are regularly played or represented by minor-7th and/or dominant-7th-chords.

Unlike in 'traditional Jazz', in *Gypsy Jazz* usually you won't see any regular minor-7th-chords being used as 'main substitutions' but rather, most of the time, being 'substituted' as minor-6th-chords (also see the next chapter on '*Chord Substitution*', page 30).

In blues, dominant-7th-chords very often get 're-harmonized' by another major-6th or major-7th-add9-chords, which is also very common in Jazz.

Django Reinhardt (1951)

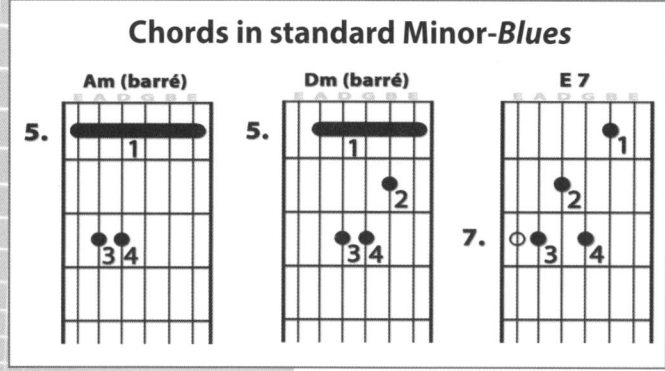

In the following example of '*Minor Swing*' the chords will be played as follows:

Am6, Dm6 and E7 (or E7add9)

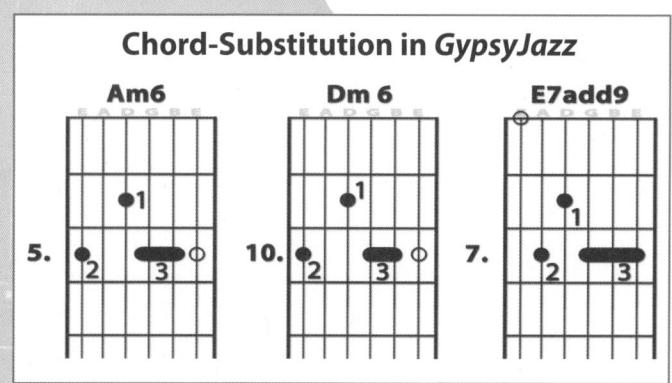

Excercise 2/1 – *'Minor Swing'*

Our first practical rhythm exercise of *'Minor Swing'* is using the rhythm example of Lesson 1, Rhythm Exercise 1/1 (see page 24).

Note: While playing the new chord-voicings, pay special attention to the finger-positions!

The Chord Voicings:

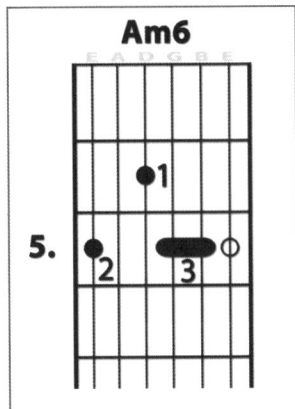
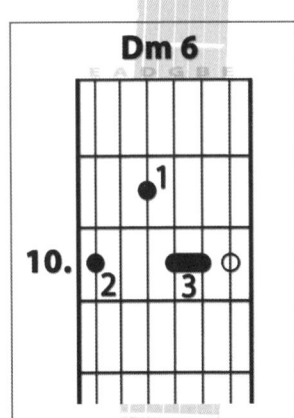
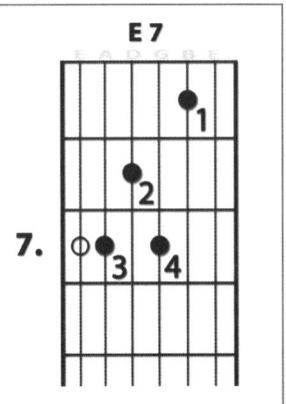

"It Don't Mean a Thing - If It Ain't Got That Swing"

(Duke Ellington 1932)

Minor Swing

Music: Django Reinhardt / Stephane Grapelli

Chord Substitution

In this chapter, we will take a look at what is generally called 'Chord Substitution'. Like in traditional Jazz, this is a very important element in the style of *Gypsy Jazz*.

In Jazz harmony, chord substitution basically means to exchange (to *substitute*) chord voicings from any chord to another, mainly using the direct or non-direct tonalities of that certain chord (see '*chords*' and '*chord substitution*' in the *glossary*).

Right now in this book I don't use the term *chord substitution* in the same functional sense with which it is used in Jazz harmony, but rather just for its own definition 'to exchange one chord voicing with another'. For example: playing an A-minor-6th-chord voicing instead of a regular A-minor-3-tone-voicing (for instance an Am-barré-chord).

Background

Because of his stronly injured left hand, which was damaged by a fire (that totally burnt down his caravan in 1928), *Django Reinhardt* was not able to bend his pinkie finger, it would just stay stiff (see image above right). It would appear that he was able to move his ring finger a little more.
Because of this, he was just about able to play chords with these two fingers as he could slightly move them, but hardly at all for playing scales and licks.
There is more information on *Django's* story on my website *www.Jazzmanouche.de* (go to 'Django & Guitars' then 'Django – the Guitar Maestro').

It also seems that *Django* was unable to play regular dominant barré chords with his two 'nearly crippled' fingers. That said it is pretty clear that regularly played dominant barré chords are not very common in *Gypsy Jazz*.
Thanks to the injury, *Django* was forced to develop a completely new way of fingering regular chord voicings and had to discover a new way of playing any solo-licks and scales with his two remaining movable fingers. Many of his famous eight-note-licks were often played with only these two (!) fingers (pointer and middle finger).

In *Jazz-Manouche*, the style so strongly influenced by *Django Reinhardt*, these unique chord voicings reduced to basic three note chords made up of triads (see *Glossary*) are used because of him.

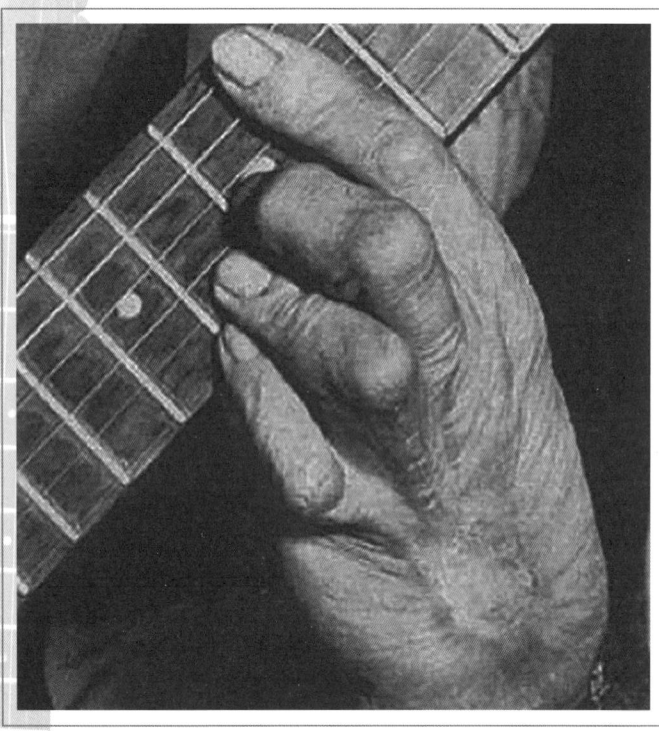

Django´s Left Hand

These newly developed chord voicings invented by *Django* were later on copied by many of the following Jazz guitarists which, in turn influenced the chord playing of many other Jazz musicians.

Generally, in Gypsy Jazz, standard major-chords will always get substituted by major-6th-chords (also often mixed 6th/9th-chords), dominant-7th-chords will mostly get substituted with additions like major-7th-add9 or major-add11-chords, major-7th-add13-chords etc. Standard minor chords will get substituted by minor-6th- or minor-7th-chords.
Depending on the need and the song structure, the corresponding harmonic relations of these chords will be used, for example, a Bm7b5-chord instead of a Dm6th-chord etc.
This is what is sometimes called 're-harmonisation'.

Like other players of 'traditional Jazz', *Django Reinhardt* still used regular substituted Jazz chord voicings. This combination resulted in a very unique playing technique that left a *Django* mark on *Gypsy Jazz* playing which continues to this day.

Let's now take a look at these differently played, but in *Gypsy Jazz*, generally used chord voicings on the next page.

Part 1 – Rhythm Guitar 31

For a chord substitution example, we will take a look at the chord sequence of the song 'Minor Swing'. The root chords of this song would, according to what has been explained previously, be substituted with other chord voicings as follows:

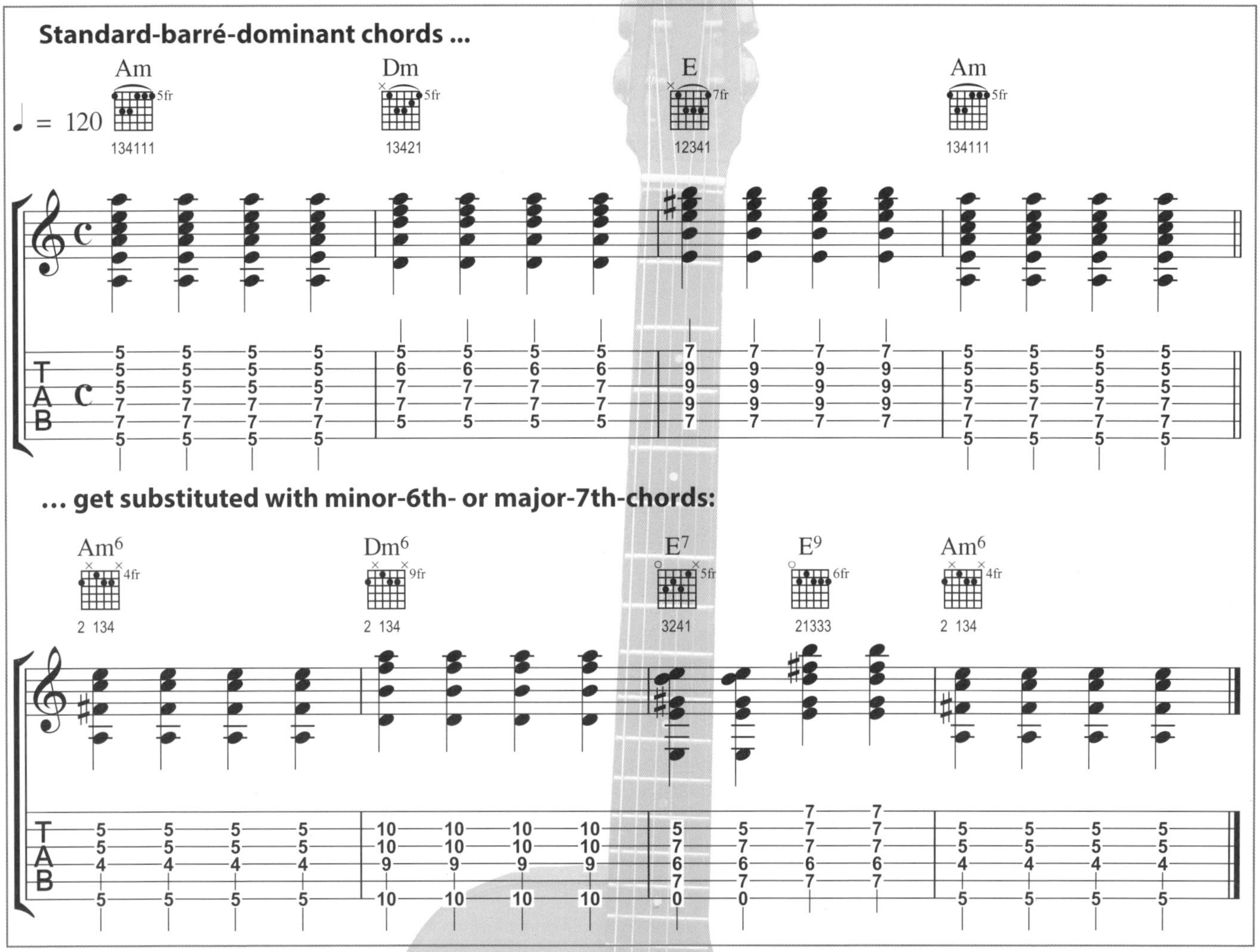

Standard-barré-dominant chords ...

Am — Dm — E — Am

... get substituted with minor-6th- or major-7th-chords:

Am⁶ — Dm⁶ — E⁷ — E⁹ — Am⁶

Instead of regular, dominant-barré three-note-voicings the *Sinti* guitarists usually play a corresponding major-6th or major-6th/9th-chord voicing.

Important note: Very often in *Gypsy Jazz* the deep bass notes of many chords are played with the thumb. Sometimes two bass notes are played with only one finger (C6/9)!

This is the same with basic minor chords. There you would utilize any corresponding minor-6th or minor-7th voicings.

In *Gypsy Jazz* you can always substitute any of the Jazz chords shown below for any C-major chords (be careful of the finger positions, T = thumb, x = two notes with same finger).

(Hint: all the examples of the chords shown below can be played in other keys by just moving them to the appropriate position on the fretboard).

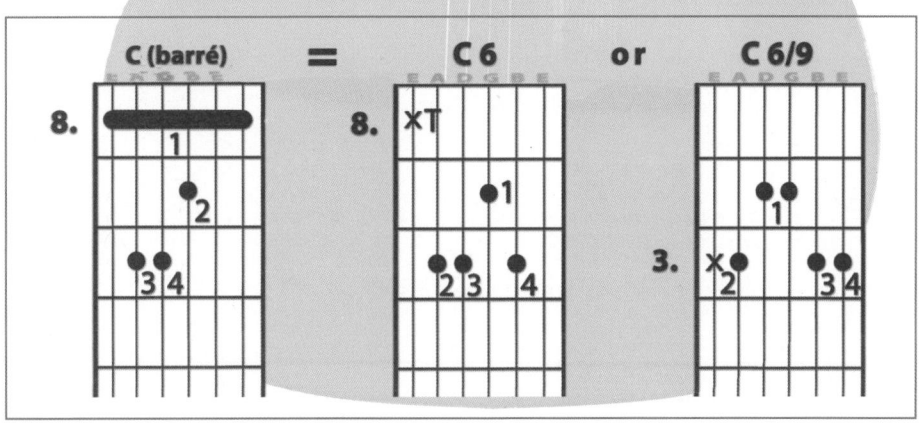

Excercise 2/2 – 'Minor Swing'

As we've had a closer look at the subject of chord substitution, we will now use this knowledge practically on our next exercise with the song 'Minor Swing'.

In the following exercise of 'Minor Swing' we will add more chords in the manner explained before.

The rhythm is played the same as in Rhythm Exercise 1/1 from Lesson 1 (see page 24).

The following overview shows the chords as they get used in *Gypsy Jazz* and how we are going to use them in our following rhythm exercise:

The Chord Voicings:

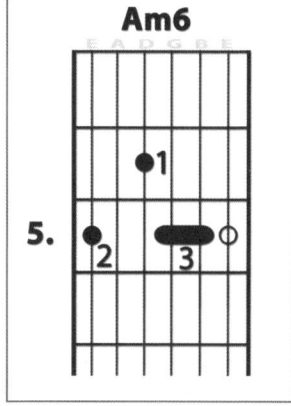
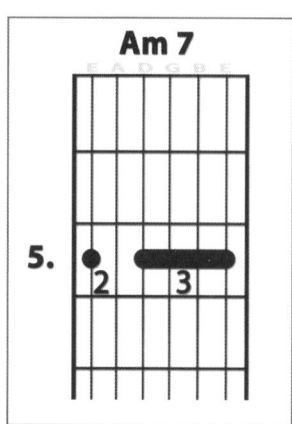
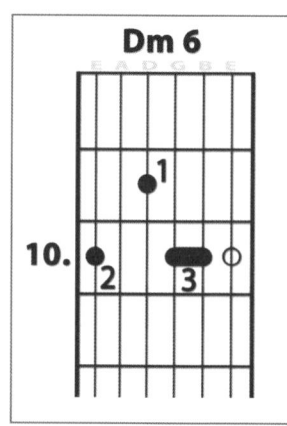
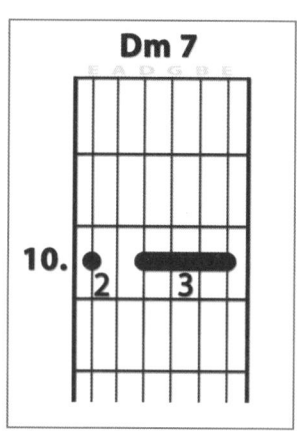

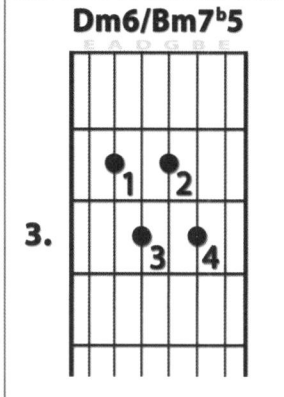
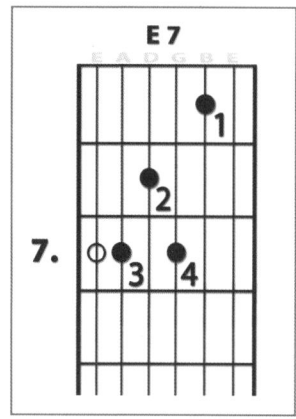
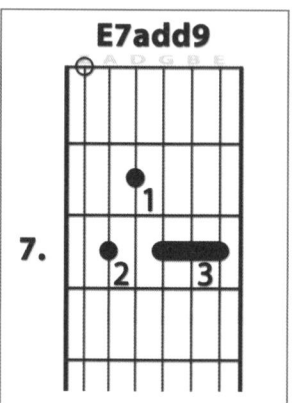

"There is no wrong music, just good and bad ..."

(Leonard Bernstein)

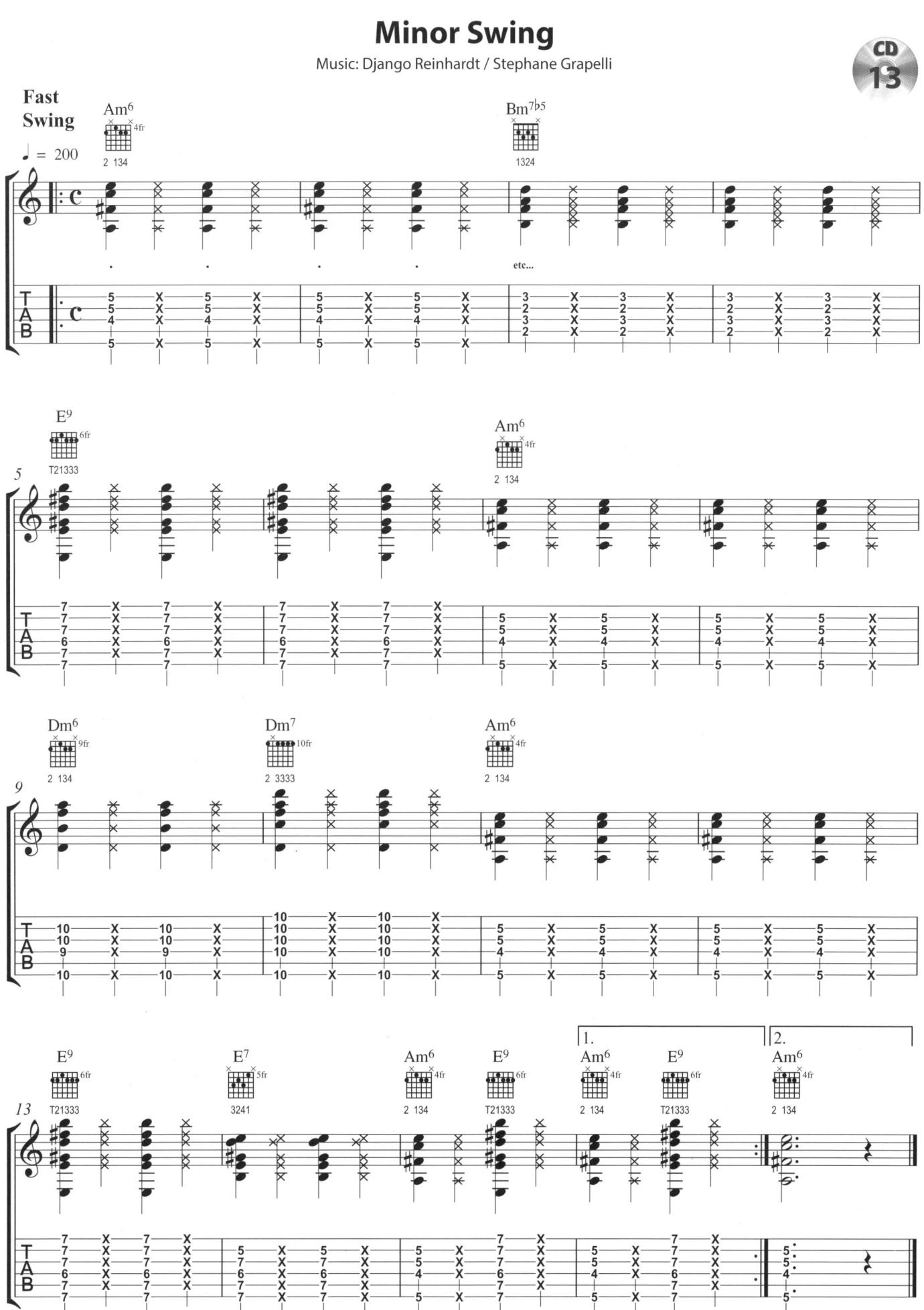

Gypsy Chords

According to the chord substitutions that have been explained previously, in the following table I will show you how some *Gypsy Jazz* chords are often played by *Sinti* guitarists today (watch out for the special finger positions!) Utilized ('substituted') *Gypsy Jazz* chord voicings for standard C-major chords are:

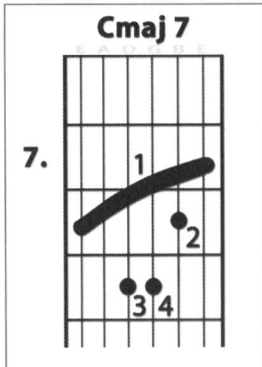 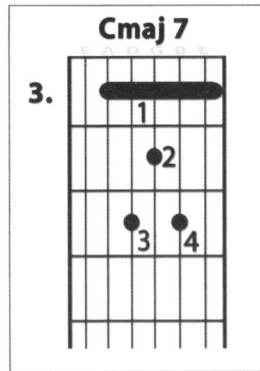 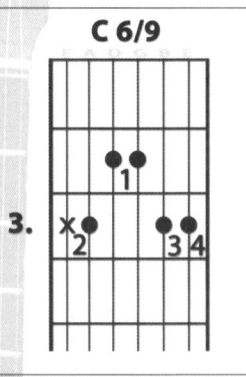 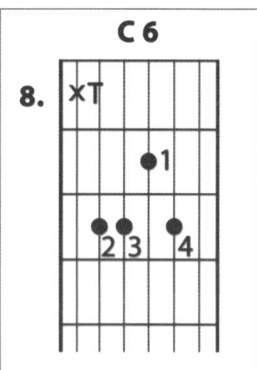

Chord voicing for minor chords in *Gypsy Jazz* (examples in C- and D-minor) are:

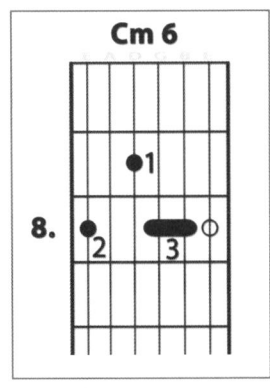 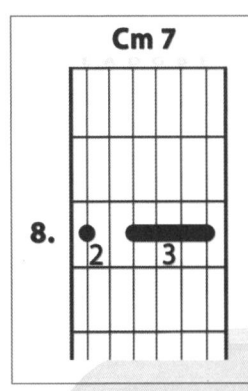 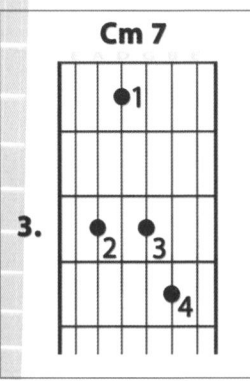 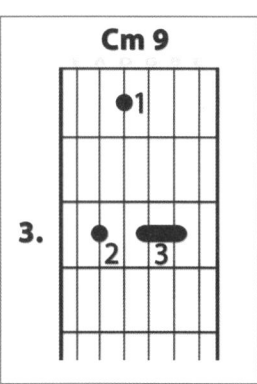

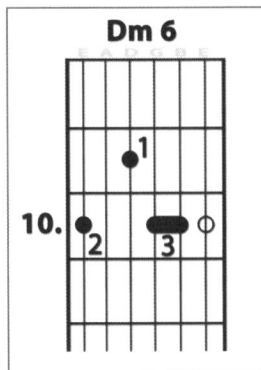 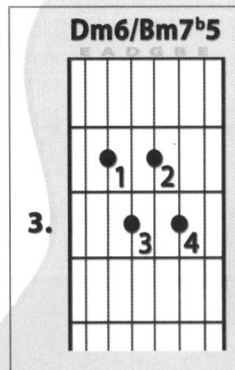 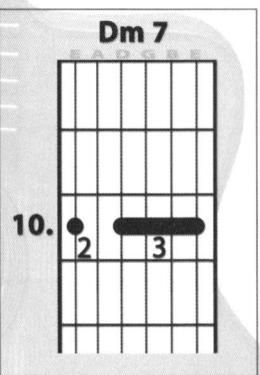 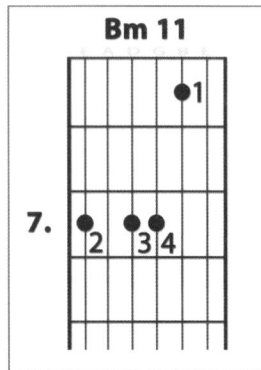

Hint: For some of these voicings the bass notes are played with the thumb (*T = thumb).

These examples are just a glimpse into the subject of chord voicings in Jazz or *Gypsy Jazz*. All the examples of substituted chord voicings that I have shown here are just a small selection of how they might be played by today's Gypsy musicians. Of course there are many, many more possible variations of chord voicings in use.

In my **LIVE 'Masterclass for Gypsy Guitar'**, I go into more depth on this subject.

Part 1 – Rhythm Guitar

Lesson 2/3

In the third exercise of '*Minor Swing*' we will now use the already known Am6 chord instead of a common Am chord. We will then substitute a Bm7b5 chord instead of the regular D-minor chord and we will use a major-E7add9 chord instead of E-major (e.g major-E7 chord).

Furthermore, we will add more variations of the root-chords of this song with the same principle as explained in the chapter before:

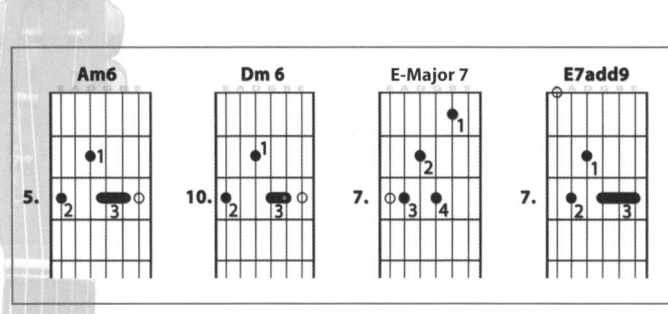

Am6 | Am7 | A7 and Dm6 | Dm7 | Dm7/B (or Bm7♭5) | E7 | E9/B | E7#9

So now, in the next example, you can see the chord voicings that could be played this way by any Gypsy guitarist today in '*Minor Swing*'. The rhythm will be played as in the last exercise of Lesson 1/1 (*extended Pompe*, page 26).

The Chord Voicings

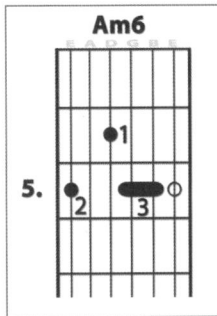 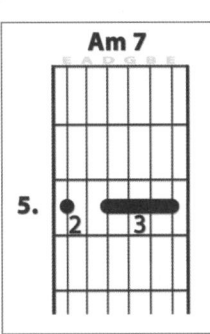 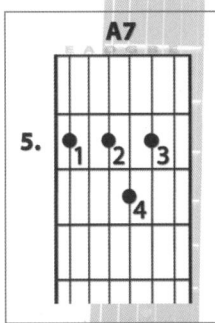 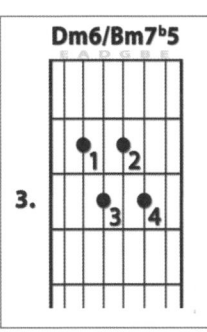 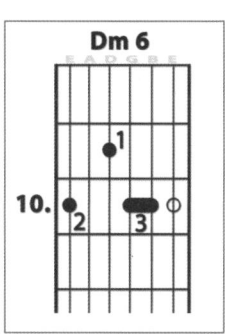

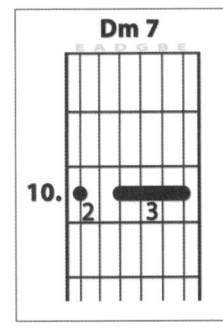 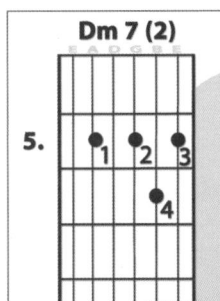 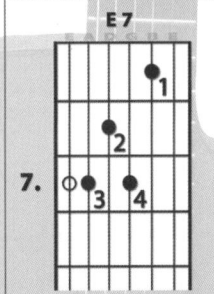 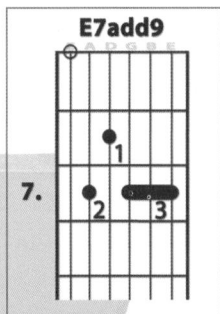 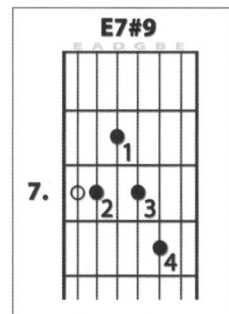

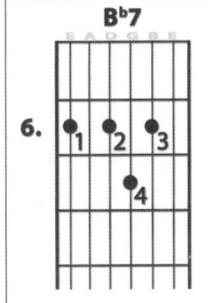

> *As the Manouches (Gypsies) are always on the move in real life, so it is the same with their chord playing in Gypsy Jazz: rarely will they rest on one chord for longer than two bars.*
>
> *Example: even if in a song there is a major-E7th chord notated to last for four bars, a Gypsy would play another substituted chord voicing on each of these four bars!*
>
> that means instead of playing   E7 | E7 | E7 | E7   on 4 complete bars they would
> instead play something like   E7 | E9 | E7#9 | E7   to give more color.

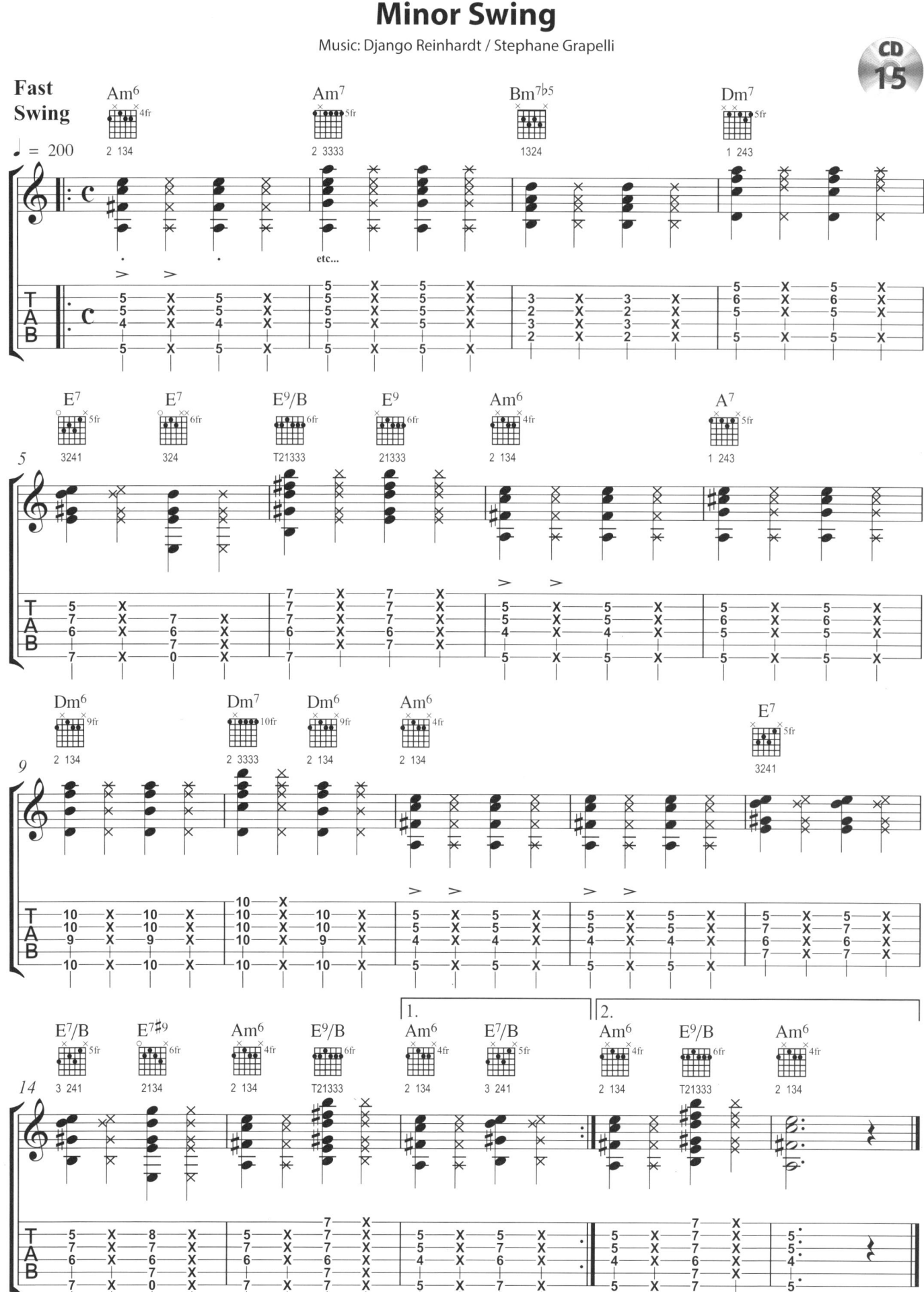

Part 1 – Rhythm Guitar

Lesson 2/4

This following exercise of the song *'Minor Swing'* intensifies the use of chord substitutions. We will now exchange a new chord at almost every bar to bring even more passion and color into our chord playing.

In this exercise we will use the rhythm exercise 1/5 from Lesson 1 (page 26). As chord substitutions we will use the following chord voicings:

Am6 | Am7 | A7 | Dm6 | Dm7 |

Bm7♭5 | E7 | E9/B | E7#9 | B♭7

This is the last lesson on the subject of rhythm thus it is also the end of part one of this book.

There is much more to discover on chord playing and rhythmic tricks in my *LIVE 'Masterclass for Gypsy Jazz Guitar'*. More information about these masterclasses can be found at **www.gypsyJazzworkshop.net**.

The Chord Voicings

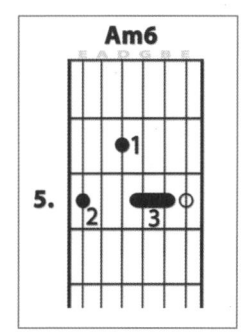

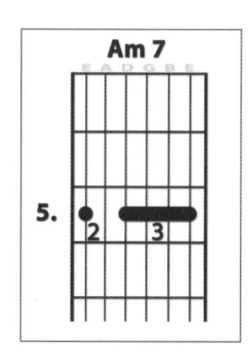

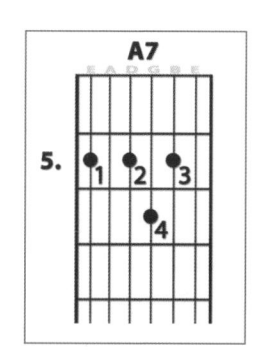

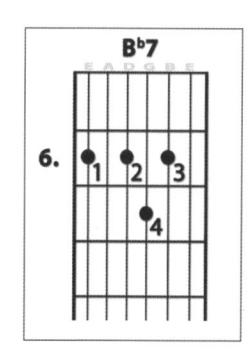

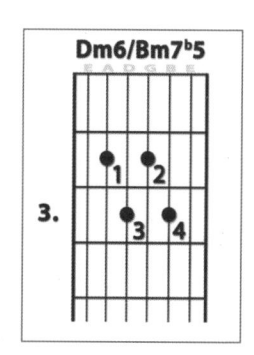

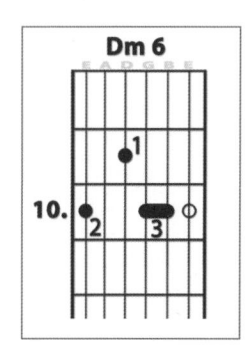

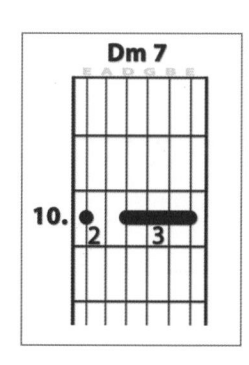

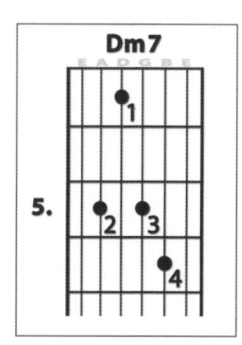

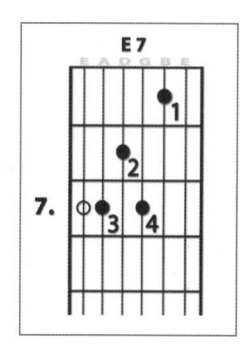

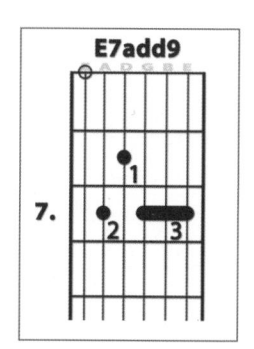

Minor Swing

Music: Django Reinhardt / Stephane Grapelli

Fast Swing

♩ = 200

Part 1 – Rhythm Guitar 39

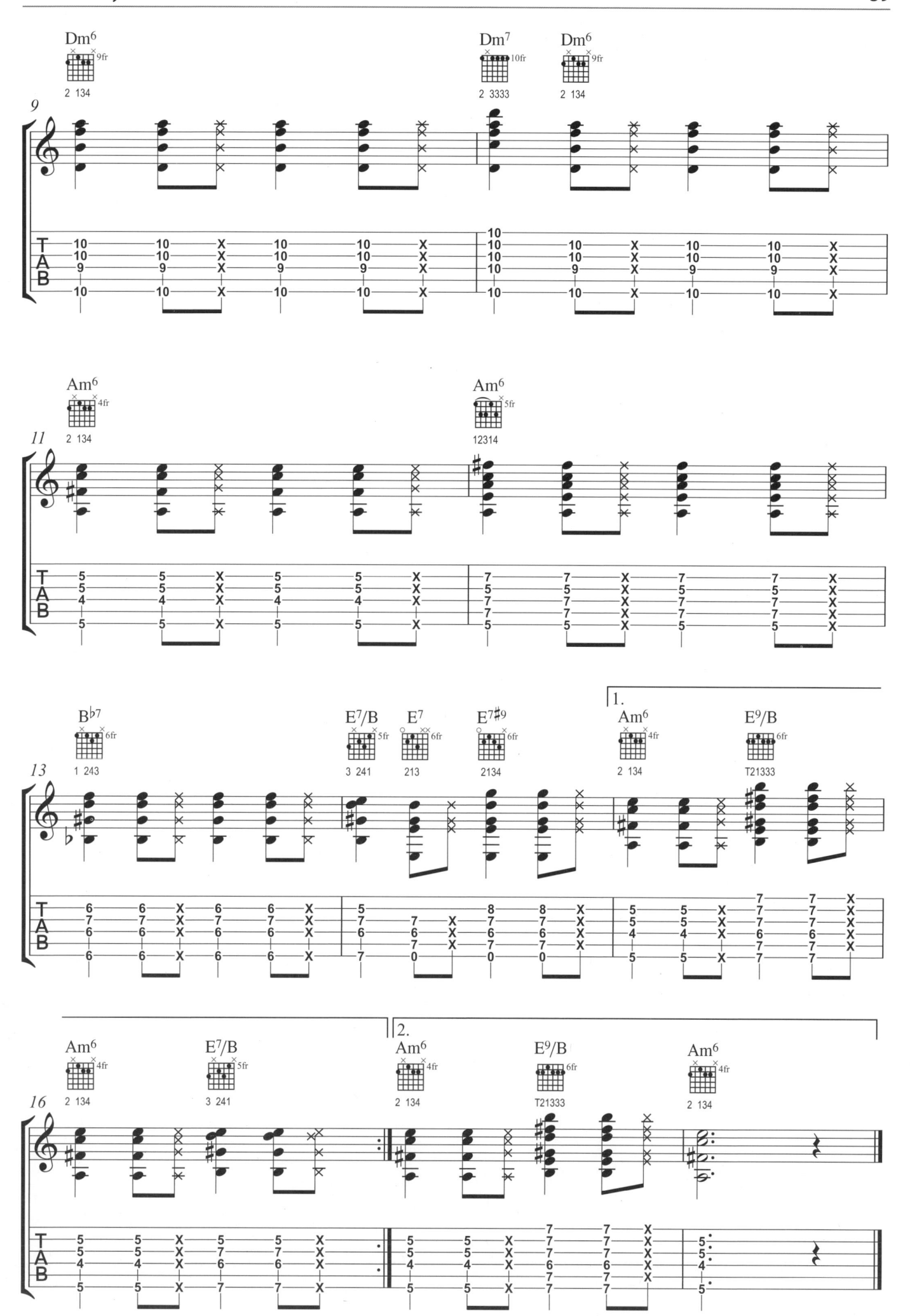

Lesson 3/1

Well, this book isn't aiming to be a 'songbook', there are plenty of those already available on the market.

Nevertheless, you can use the following song notations as useful exercises for practising playing rhythm and perfecting the playing techniques mentioned in the previous chapters.

The *Play-Aong Tracks* (on the CD) are intended for you to play along with so that you are able to practice all the rhythm exercises and, later on, the solo techniques.

At the end of the chapter named '*Introducing Solo Guitar*' (in the second part of this book), you will find all the solo notations of these songs for practicing the solo techniques.

CD 17 Play-along — **Excercise 3/1:** *Minor Swing* (Reinhardt/Grapelli) - Key: G minor, *minor Blues* variation

CD 18 Play-along — **Excercise 3/2:** *Douce Ambiance* (Reinhardt/Grapelli) – Key: G minor, *minor Blues* variation

CD 19 Play-along — **Excercise 3/3:** *Good times – schucka ziro* (Bertino Rodmann) – Key: G major, ‚Anatol' (II-V-I)

CD 20 Play-along — **Excercise 3/4:** *Blues en mineur* (Reinhardt/Grapelli) – Key: G Minor, *minor Blues* variation

CD 21 Play-along — **Excercise 3/5:** *Valse à Bertino – 'Le grand escalier'* (Bertino Rodmann) – Key: G minor, 3/4 waltz

CD 22 Play-along — **Excercise 3/6:** *Blues Clair* (Reinhardt) - Key: C major, *major Blues*, II-V-I-variation

CD 23 Play-along — **Excercise 3/7:** *Swing 48* (Reinhardt) - Key: G minor, *minor Blues* variation

Modèle Bertino, No. 001, built in 2006, Leo Eimers Guitars

When practicing with the *Play-Along Tracks* on the CD, first practice in the written notation and then try to play the songs with all the rhythms from the Rhythm Exercises 1/1, 1/4, 1/5 and 1/6 from Lesson 1.

Tip: when learning a song, first always (!) learn the chords and rhythm and then (once you really know how to play that) learn to play the theme or melody and improvisation, always trying to memorize so that you don't need to use notation. Do this with as many songs as possible.

To take your first step towards learning new songs, you can download many 'Grilles' (chordtables), TABs and transcriptions of Jazz and Gypsy Jazz songs at my site www.Jazzmanouche.de for free. Check it out!

Part 1 – Rhythm Guitar 41

The Chord Voicings to Lesson 3/1 *'Minor Swing'*

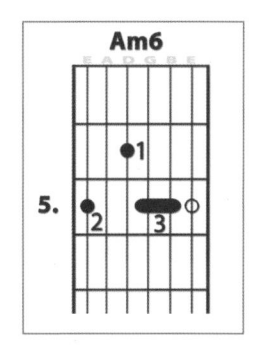

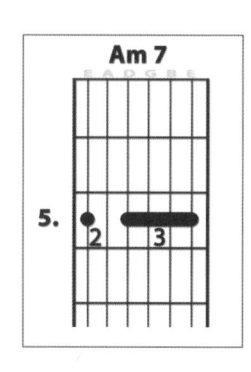

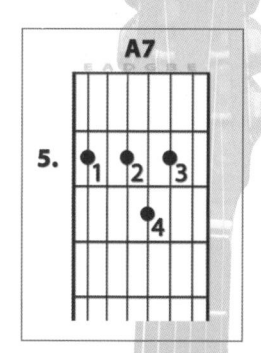

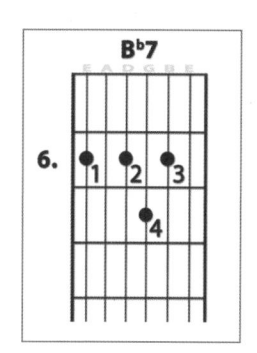

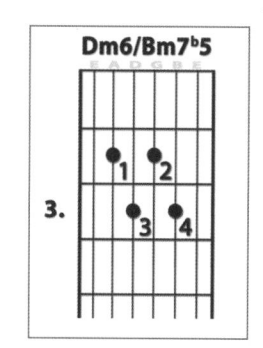

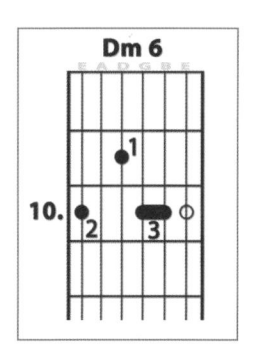

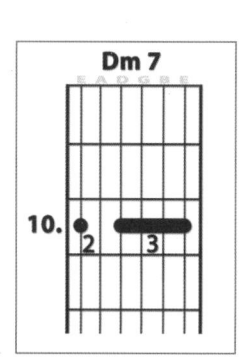

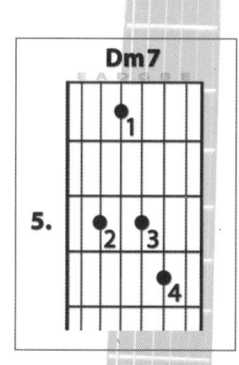

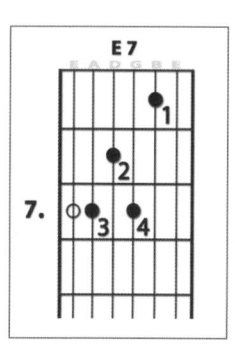

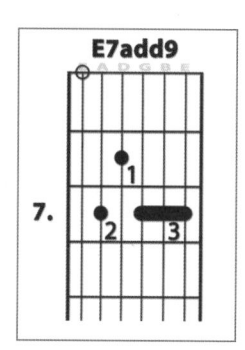

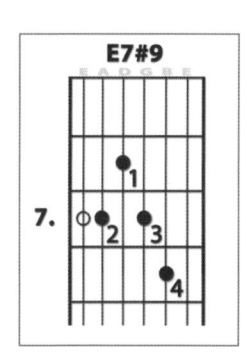

Minor Swing

Music: Django Reinhardt / Stephane Grapelli

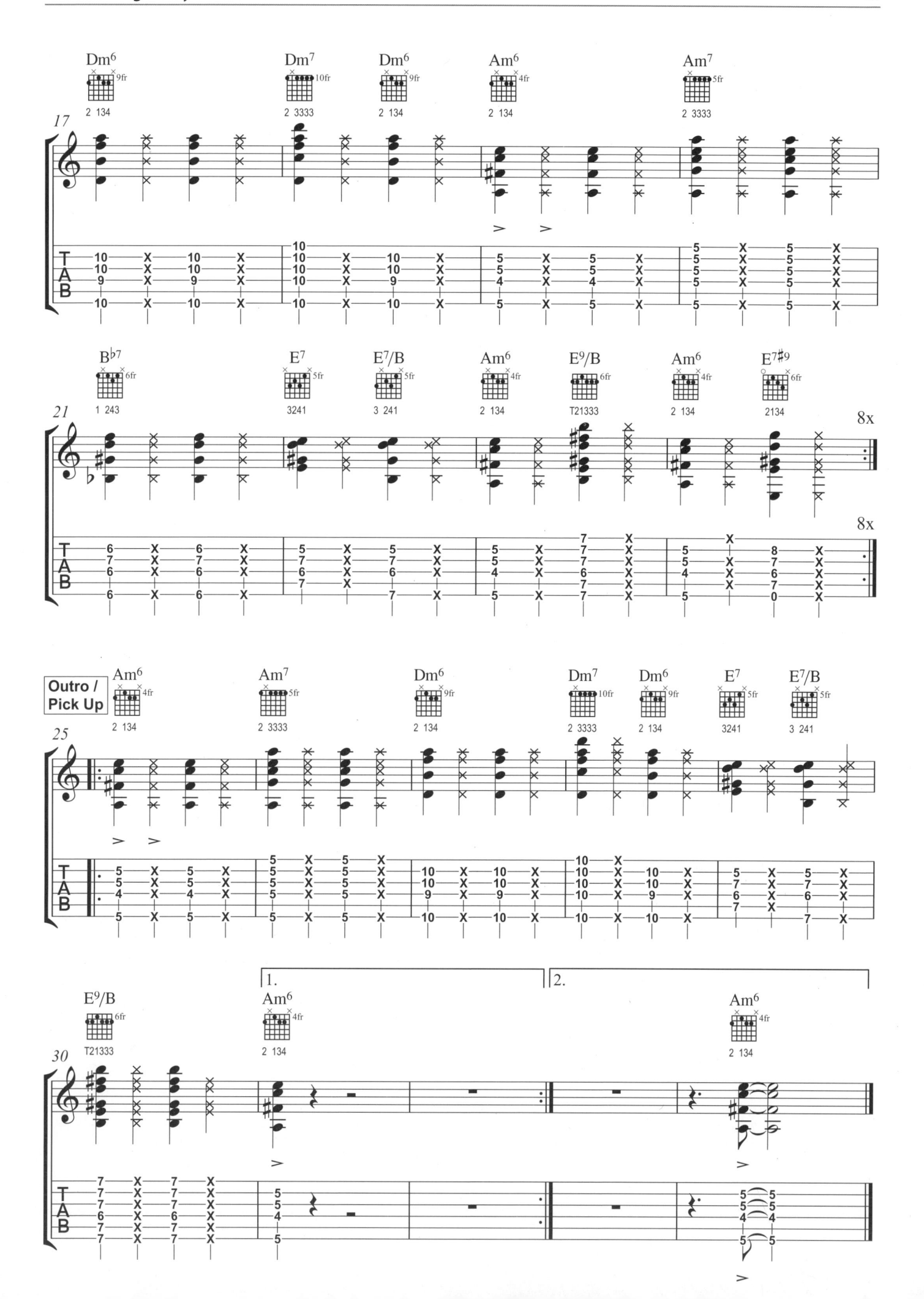

Minor Swing – Rhythm Guitar

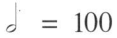

The Chord Voicings to Lesson 3/2 *'Douce Ambiance'*

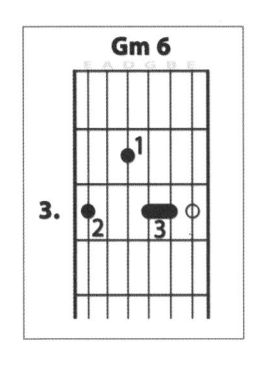

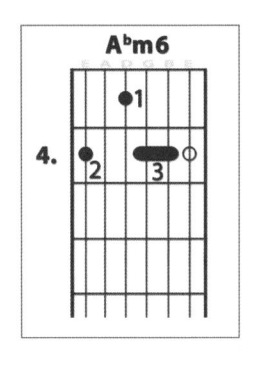

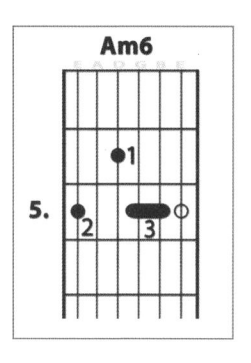

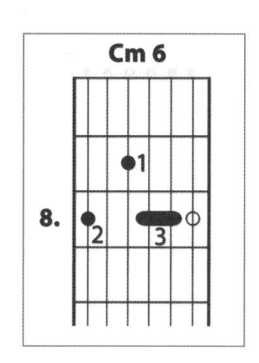

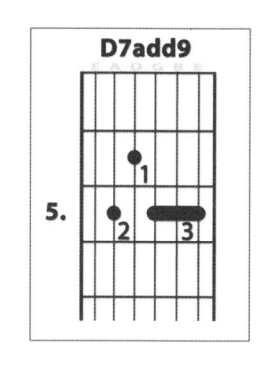

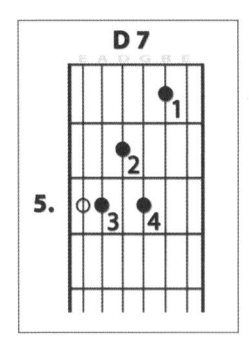

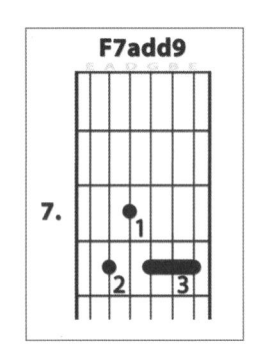

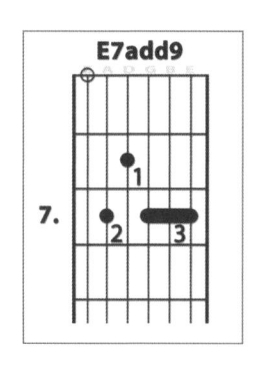

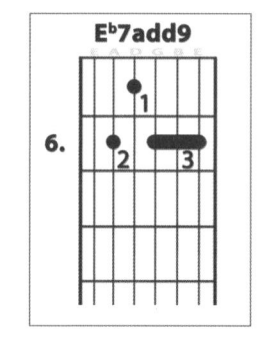

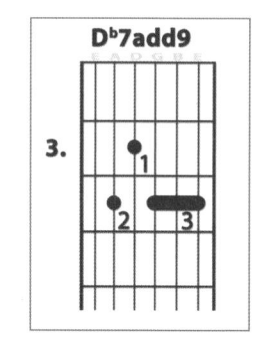

Douce Ambiance

Music: Django Reinhardt

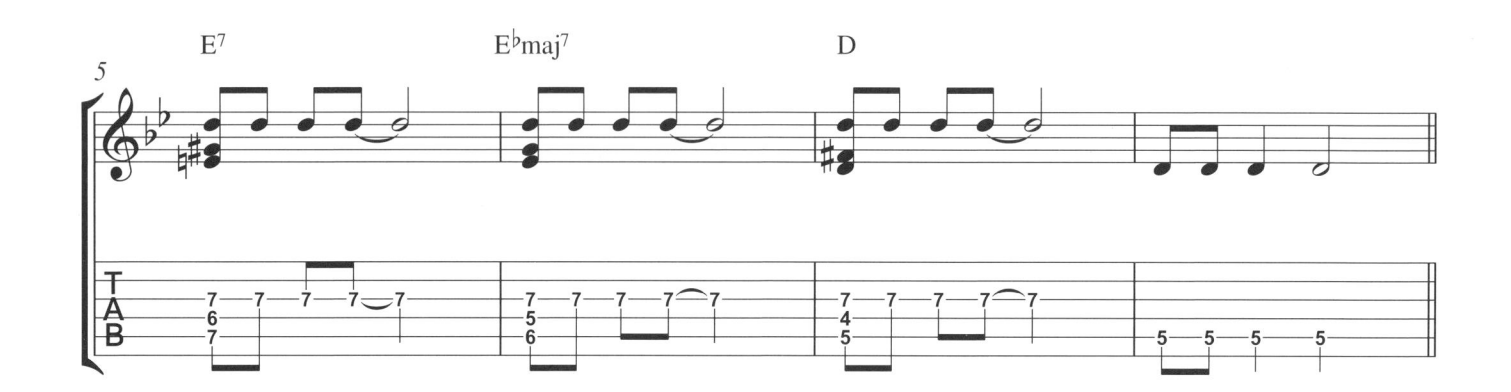

Fast Swing
♩ = 100

© 1944 EMI Music Publishing France
Exclusive Worldwide Print Right Property of FMI Music Publishing France. All Rights Reserved. Used by Permission

Douce Ambiance – Rhythm Guitar

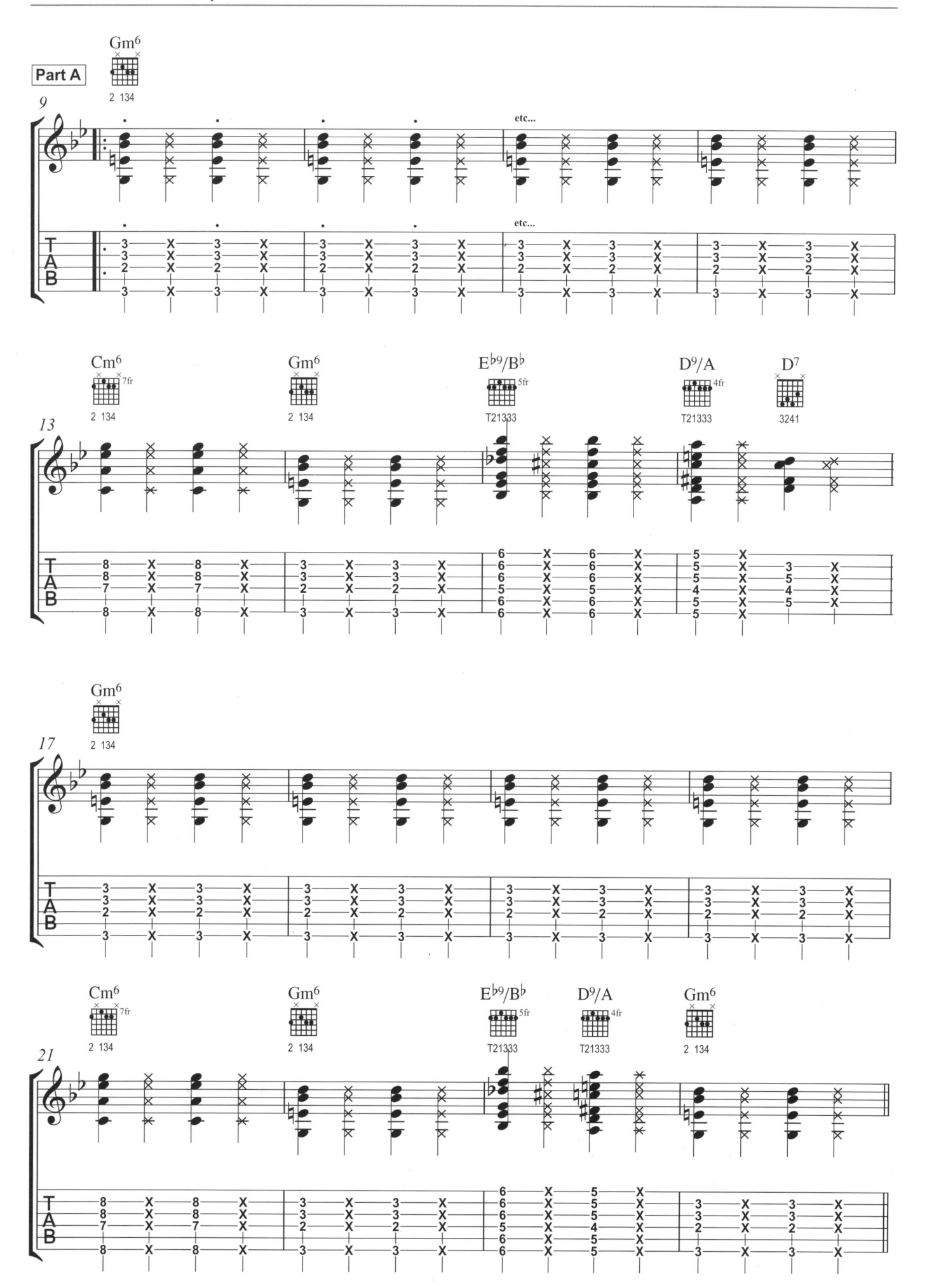

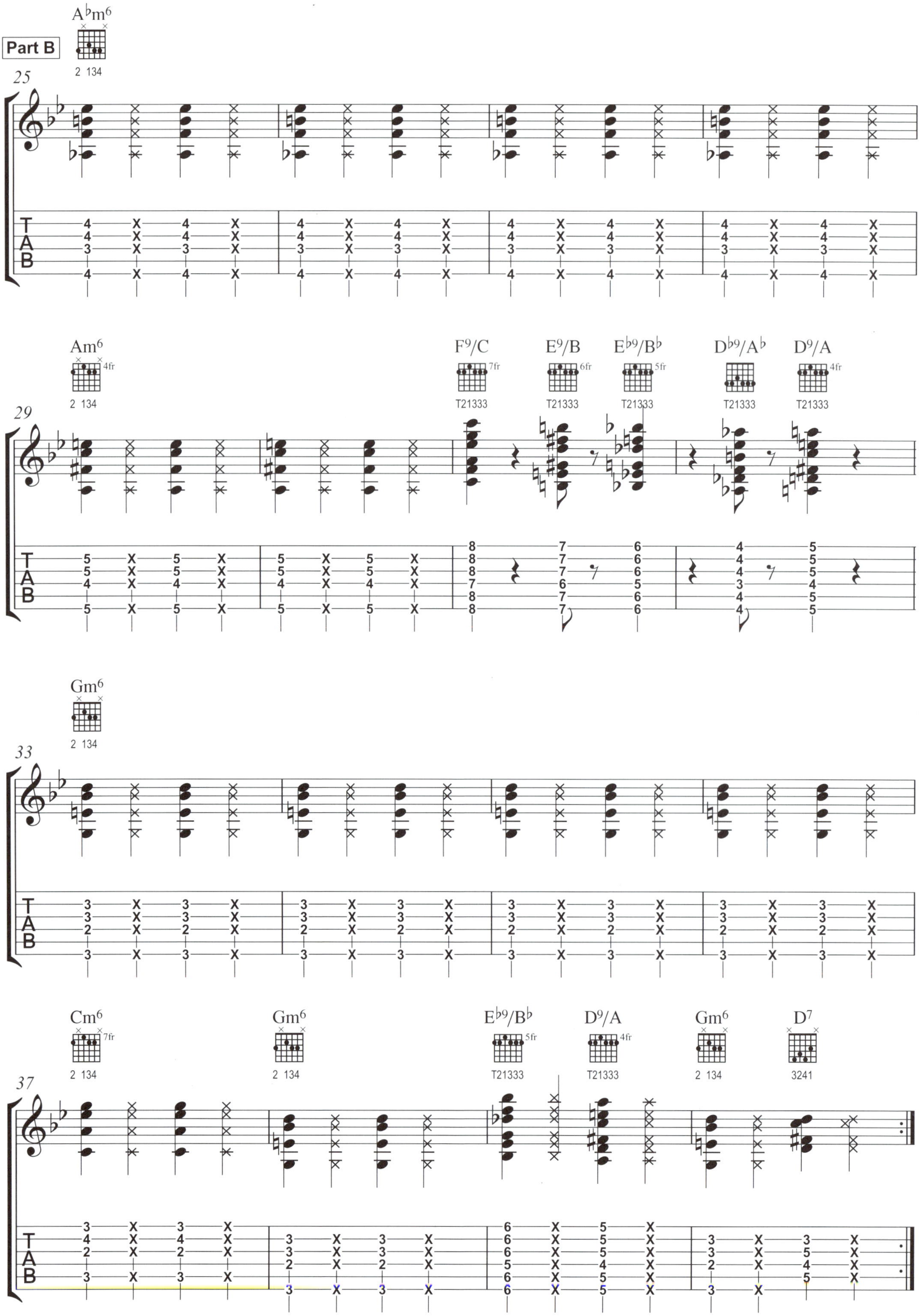
Part B
A♭m6
2 134
25
Am6
2 134
F9/C
T21333
E9/B
T21333
E♭9/B♭
T21333
D♭9/A♭
T21333
D9/A
T21333
29
Gm6
2 134
33
Cm6
2 134
Gm6
2 134
E♭9/B♭
T21333
D9/A
T21333
Gm6
2 134
D7
3241
37

The Chord Voicings to Lesson 3/2 *'Douce Ambiance'* (Variation)

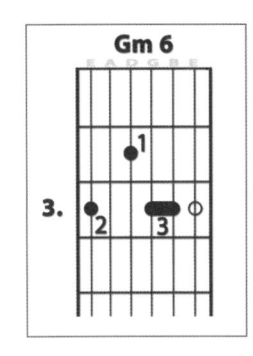

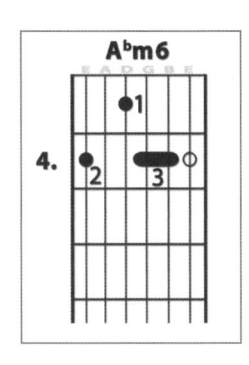

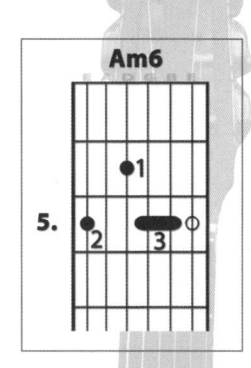

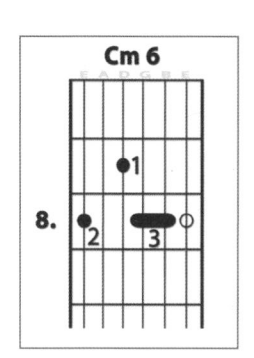

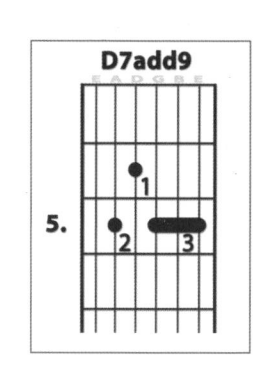

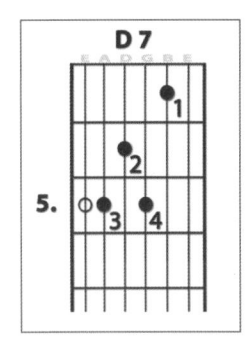

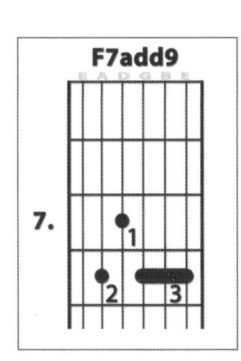

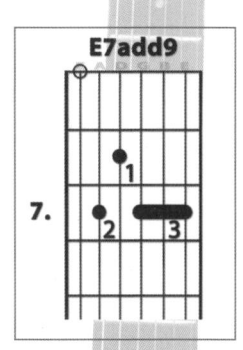

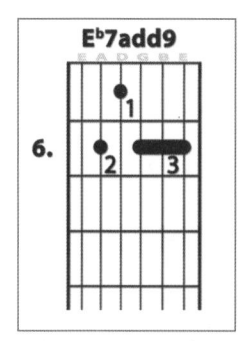

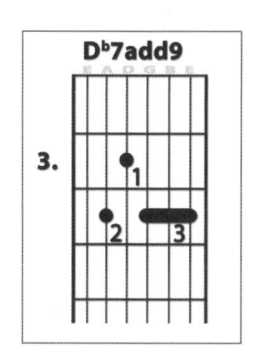

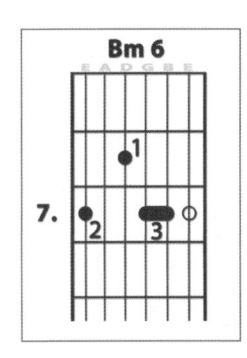

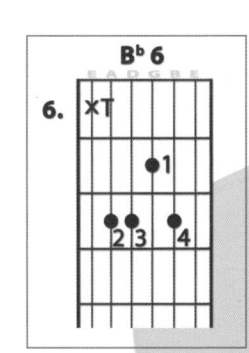

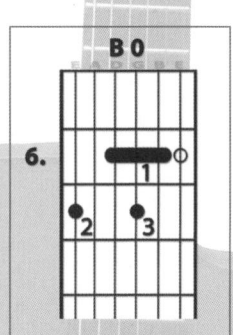

| Gm6 (3.) | A♭m6 (4.) | Am6 (5.) | Cm6 (8.) | D7add9 (5.) |
| F7add9 (7.) | E7add9 (7.) | E♭7add9 (6.) | D♭7add9 (3.) |
| D7 (5.) |
| Bm6 (7.) | B♭6 (6.) | B0 (6.) |

"Don't fear any mistakes ... there are none"!

(Miles Davis)

Douce Ambiance

Music: Django Reinhardt

Fast Swing
𝅗𝅥 = 100

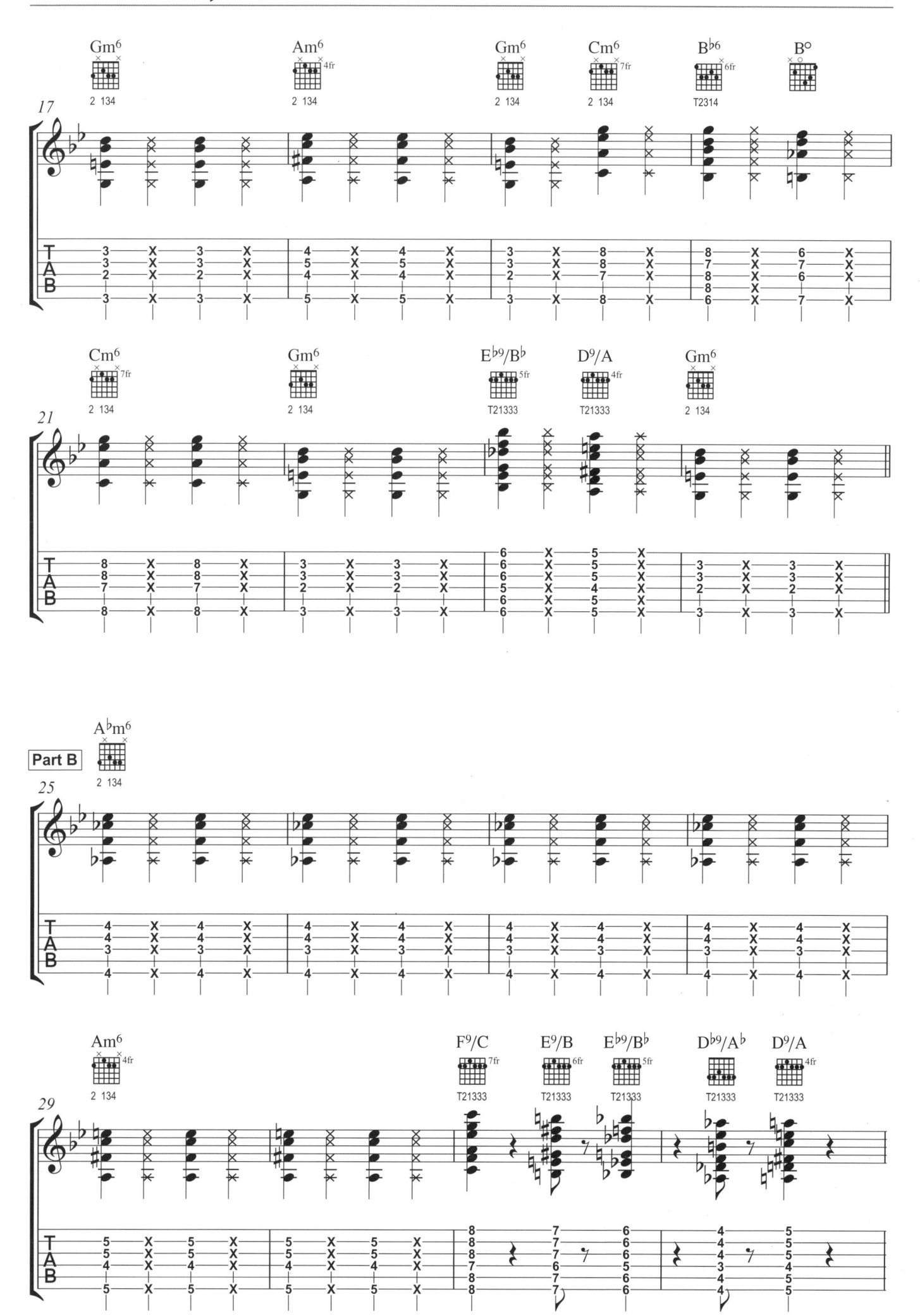

Douce Ambiance – Rhythm Guitar

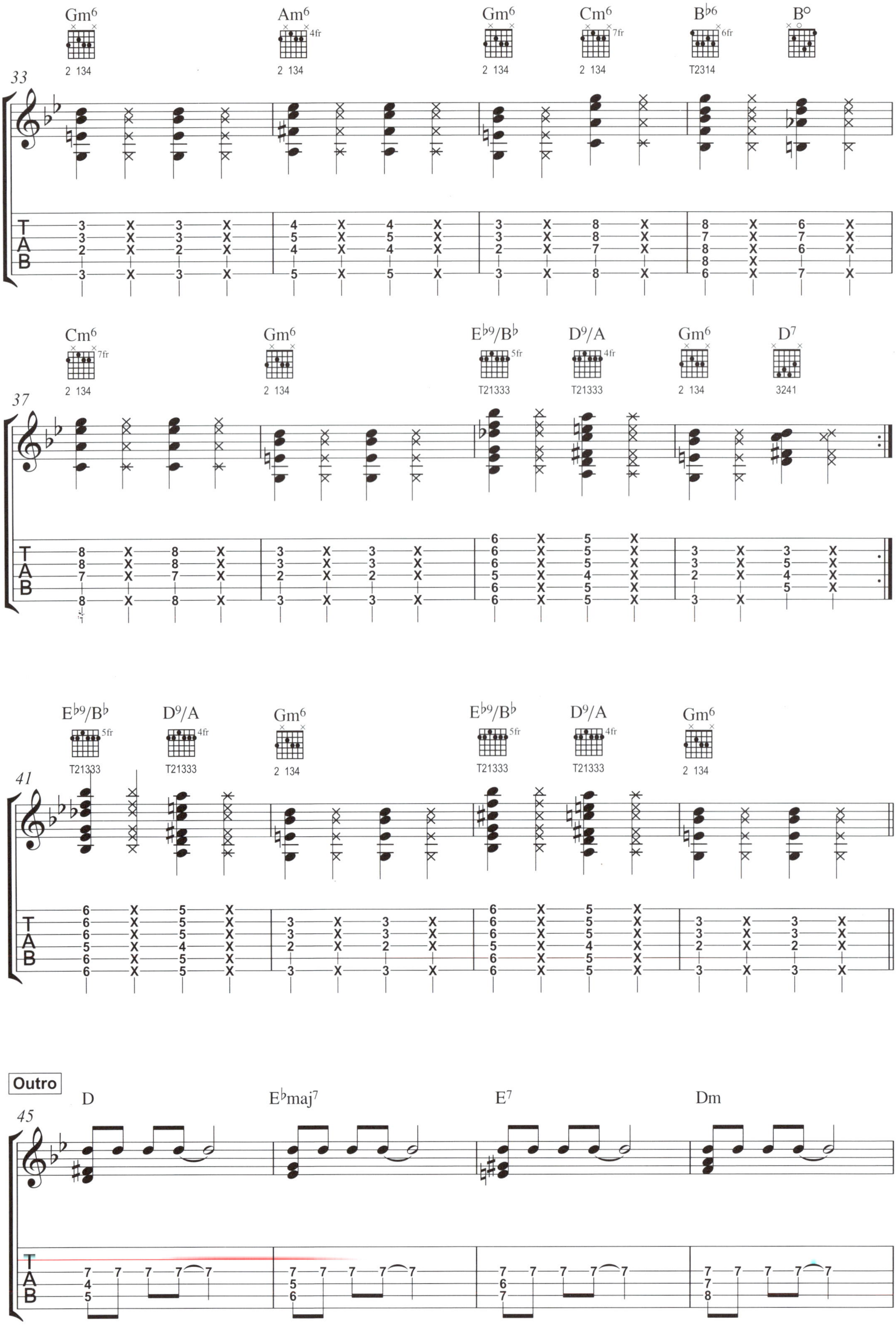
Gm6
2 134
Am6
4fr
2 134
Gm6
2 134
Cm6
7fr
2 134
B♭6
6fr
T2314
B°
33
Cm6
7fr
2 134
Gm6
2 134
E♭9/B♭
5fr
T21333
D9/A
4fr
T21333
Gm6
2 134
D7
3241
37
E♭9/B♭
5fr
T21333
D9/A
4fr
T21333
Gm6
2 134
E♭9/B♭
5fr
T21333
D9/A
4fr
T21333
Gm6
2 134
41
Outro
D
E♭maj7
E7
Dm
45

Douce Ambiance – Rhythm Guitar

The Chord Voicings to Lesson 3/3 *'Good Times (Schuckar ziro)'*

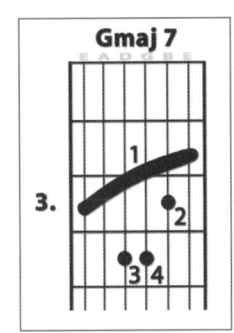

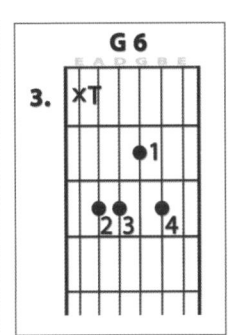

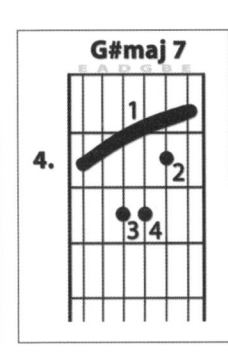

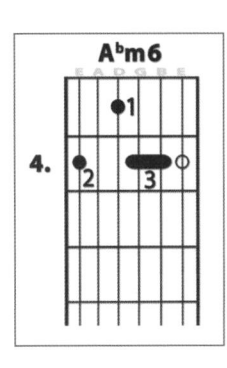

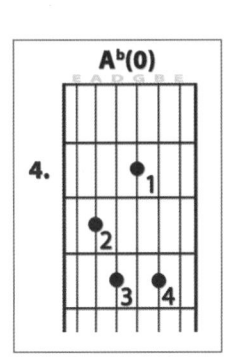

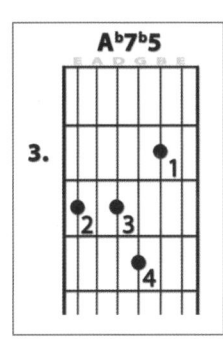

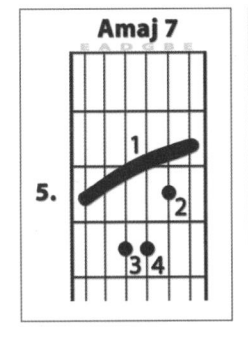

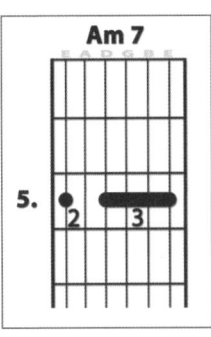

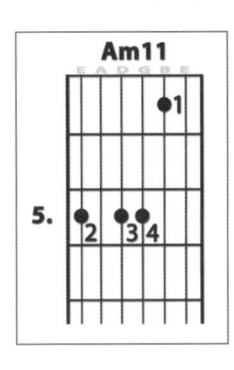

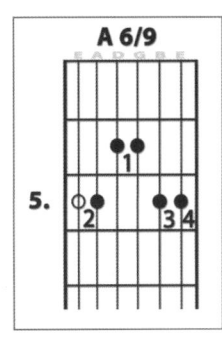

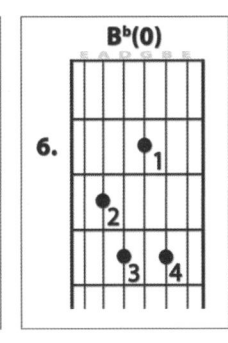

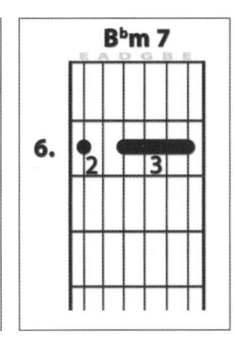

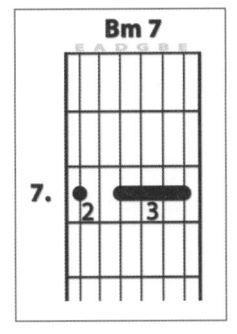

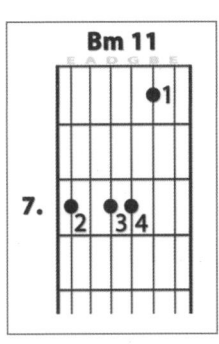

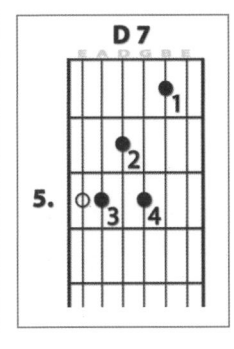

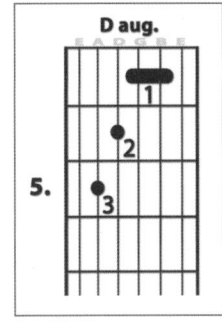

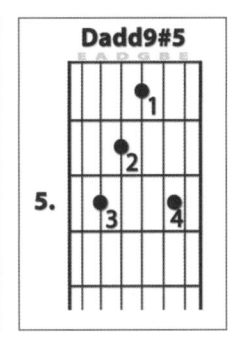

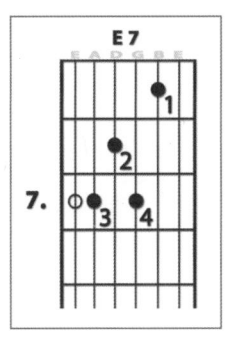

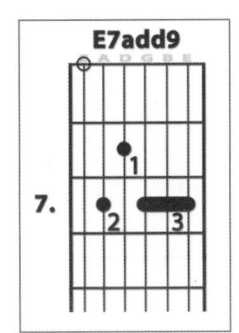

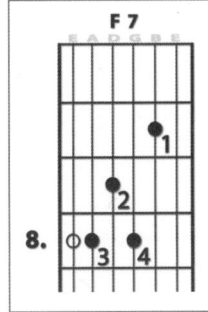

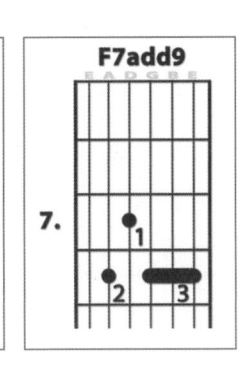

Good Times (Schuckar ziro)

Music: Bertino Rodmann

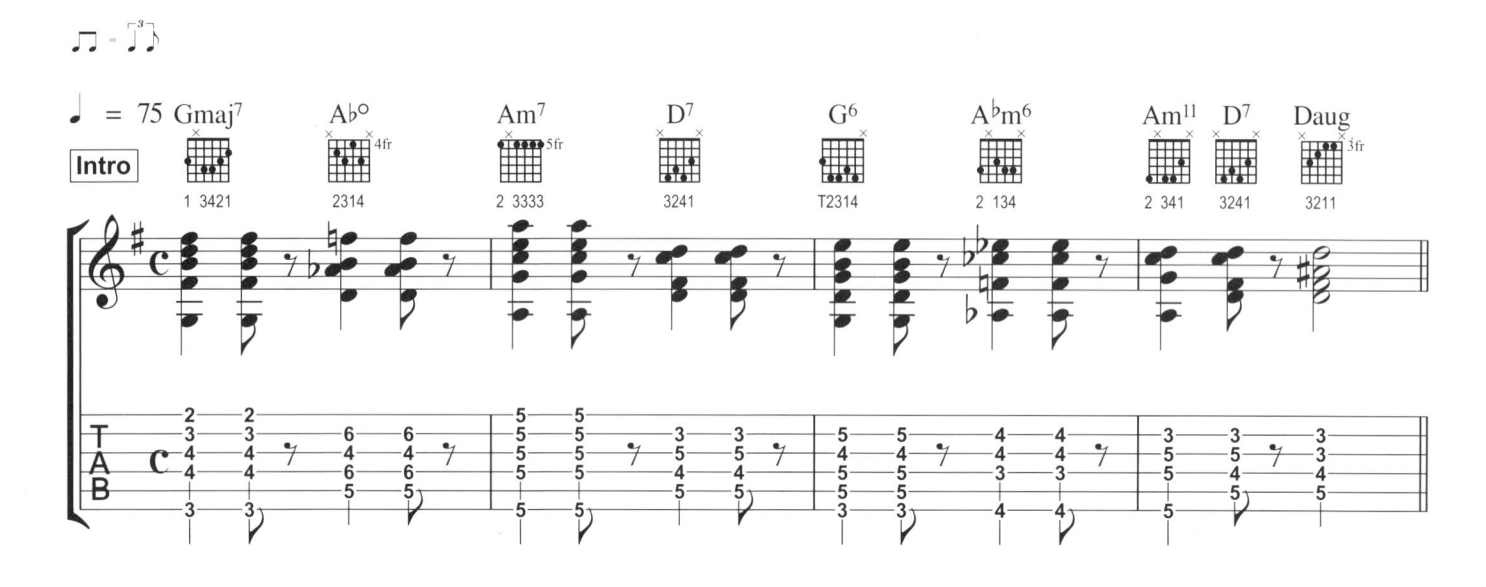

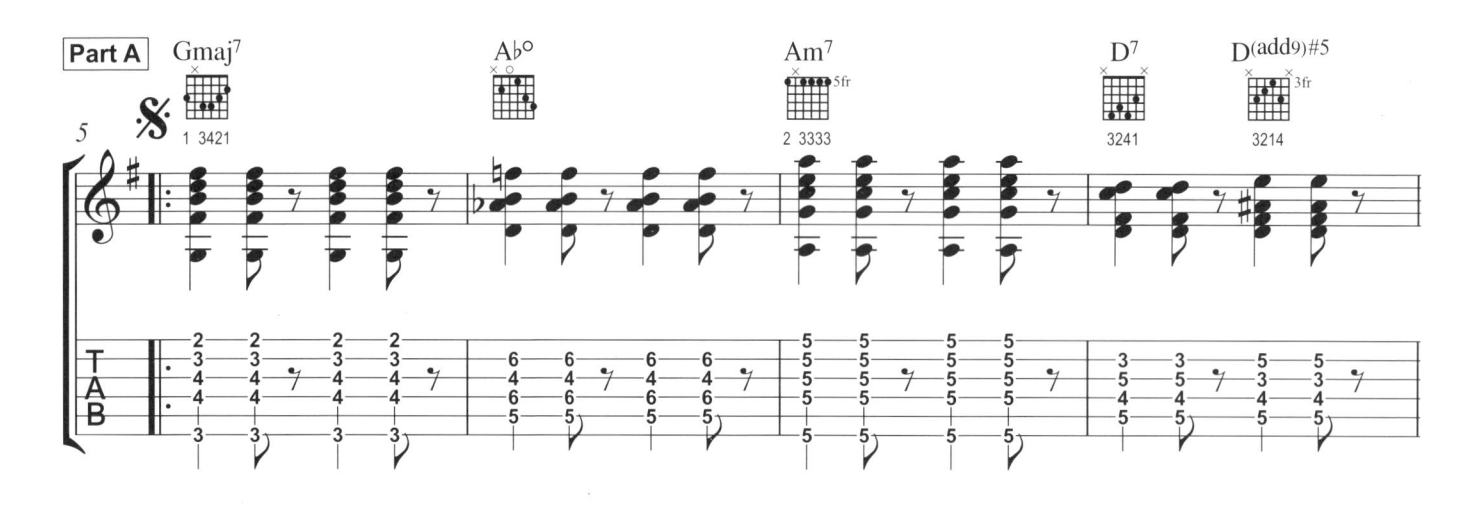

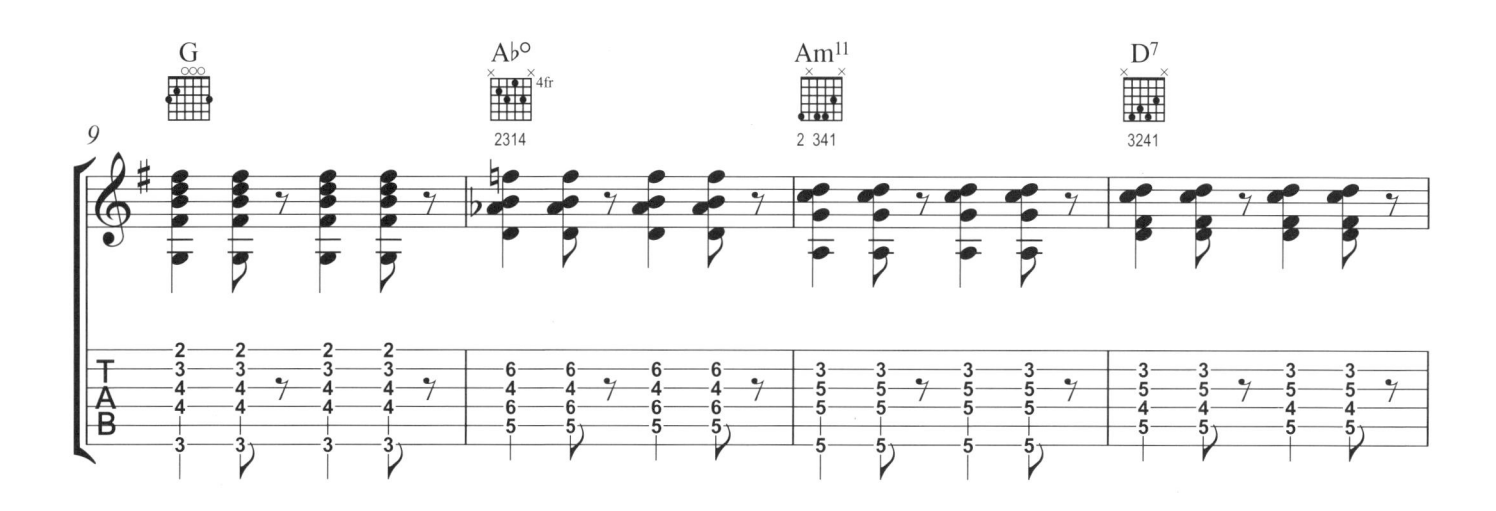

Good times (schukar ziro) – Rhythm Guitar

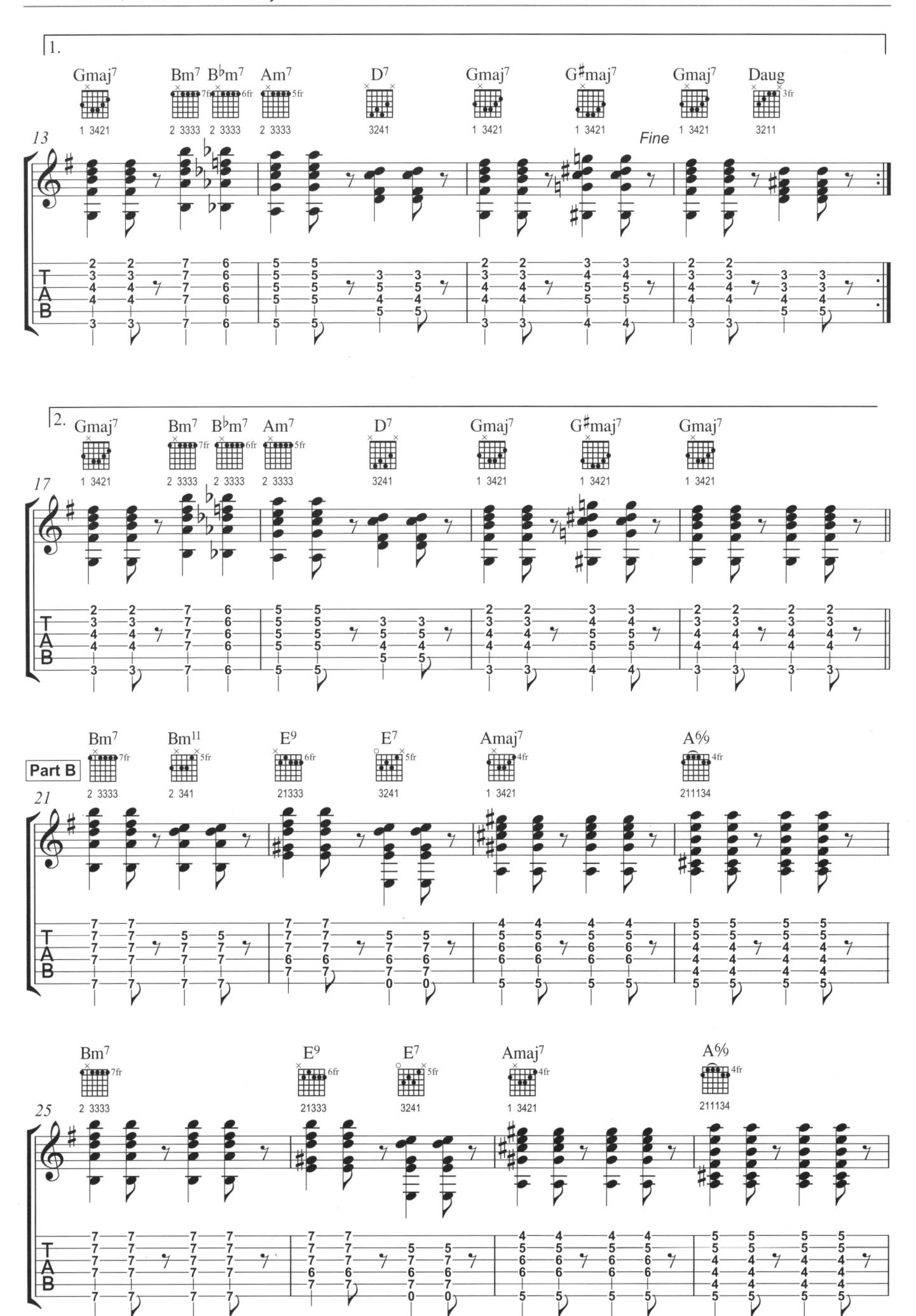

Cm11 F9 F7 Bm7 B♭m7 Am11 A♭7♭5 Daug
Part A
Gmaj7 A♭○ Am7 D7 Daug
Gmaj7 A♭○ Am7 D7
Gmaj7 Bm7 B♭m7 Am7 D7 Gmaj7 G♯maj7 Gmaj7 Daug
D.S. al Fine

Blues en mineur – Rhythm Guitar

The Chord Voicings to Lesson 3/4 *'Blues en mineur'*

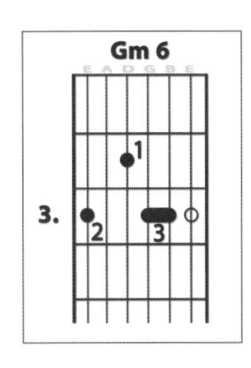

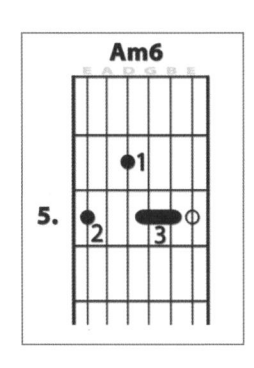

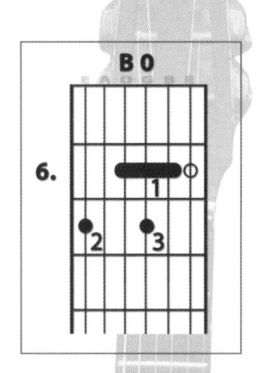

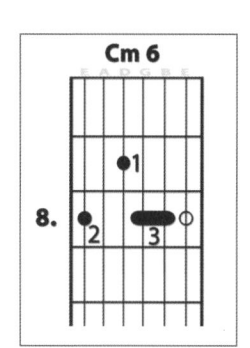

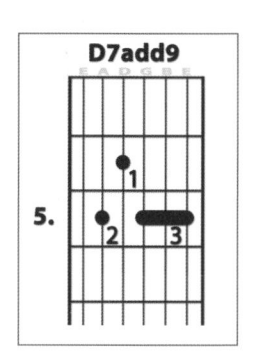

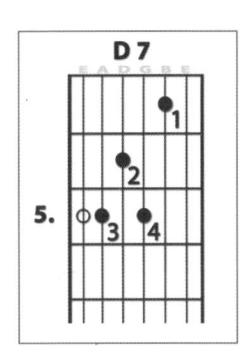

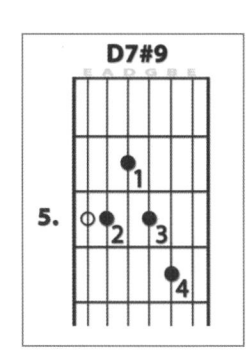

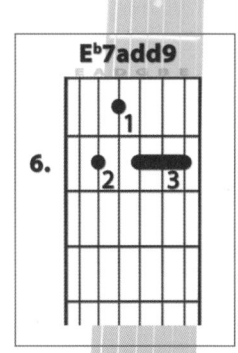

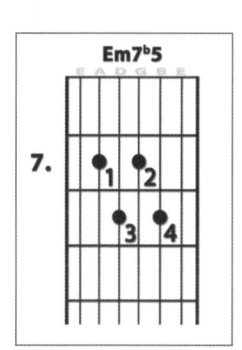

Blues en mineur

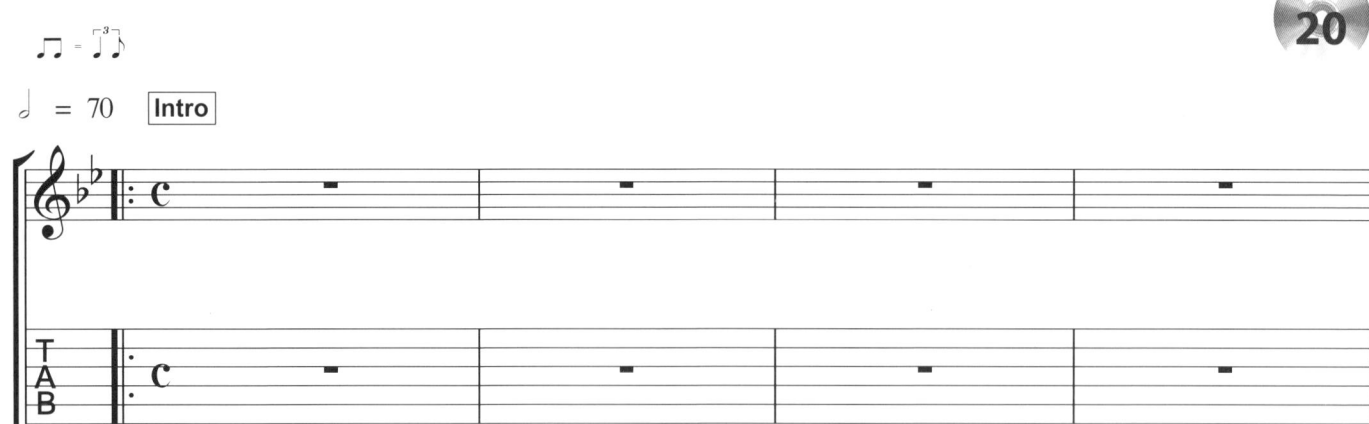

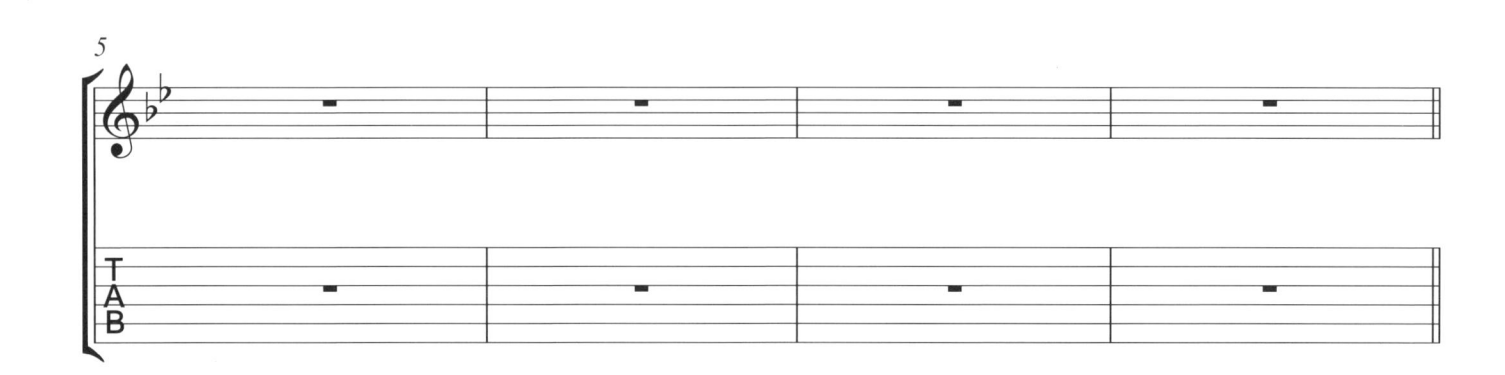

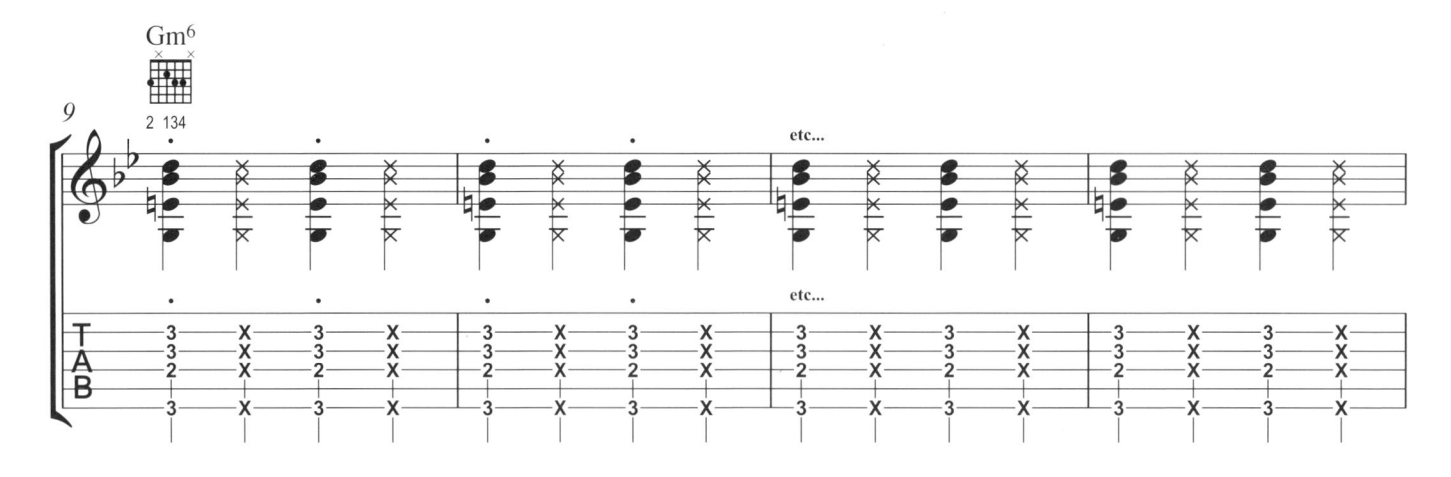

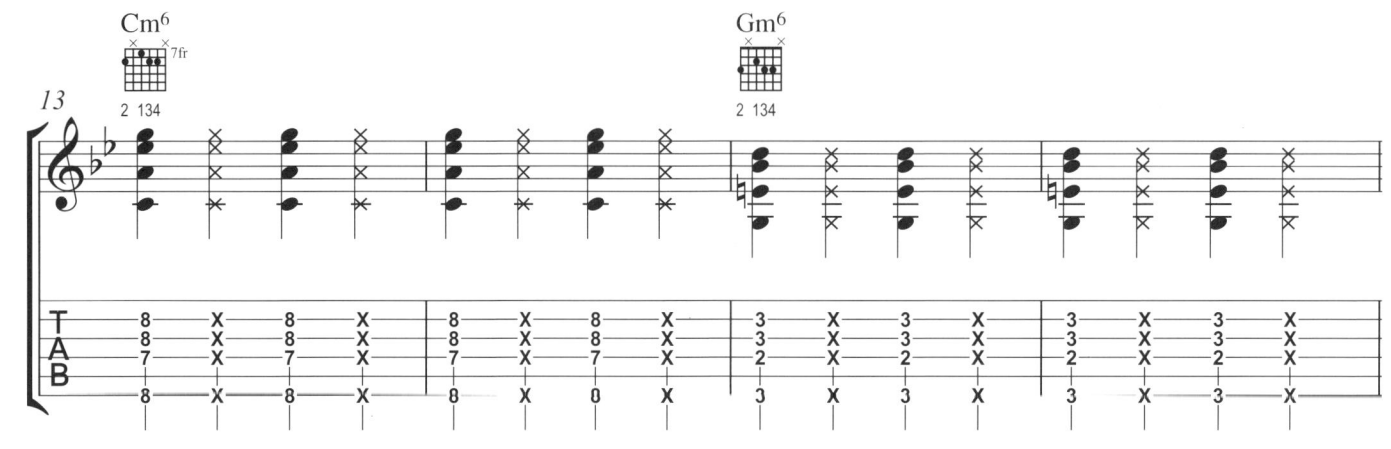

Music: Django Reinhardt / Stephane Grapelli

Blues en mineur – Rhythm Guitar

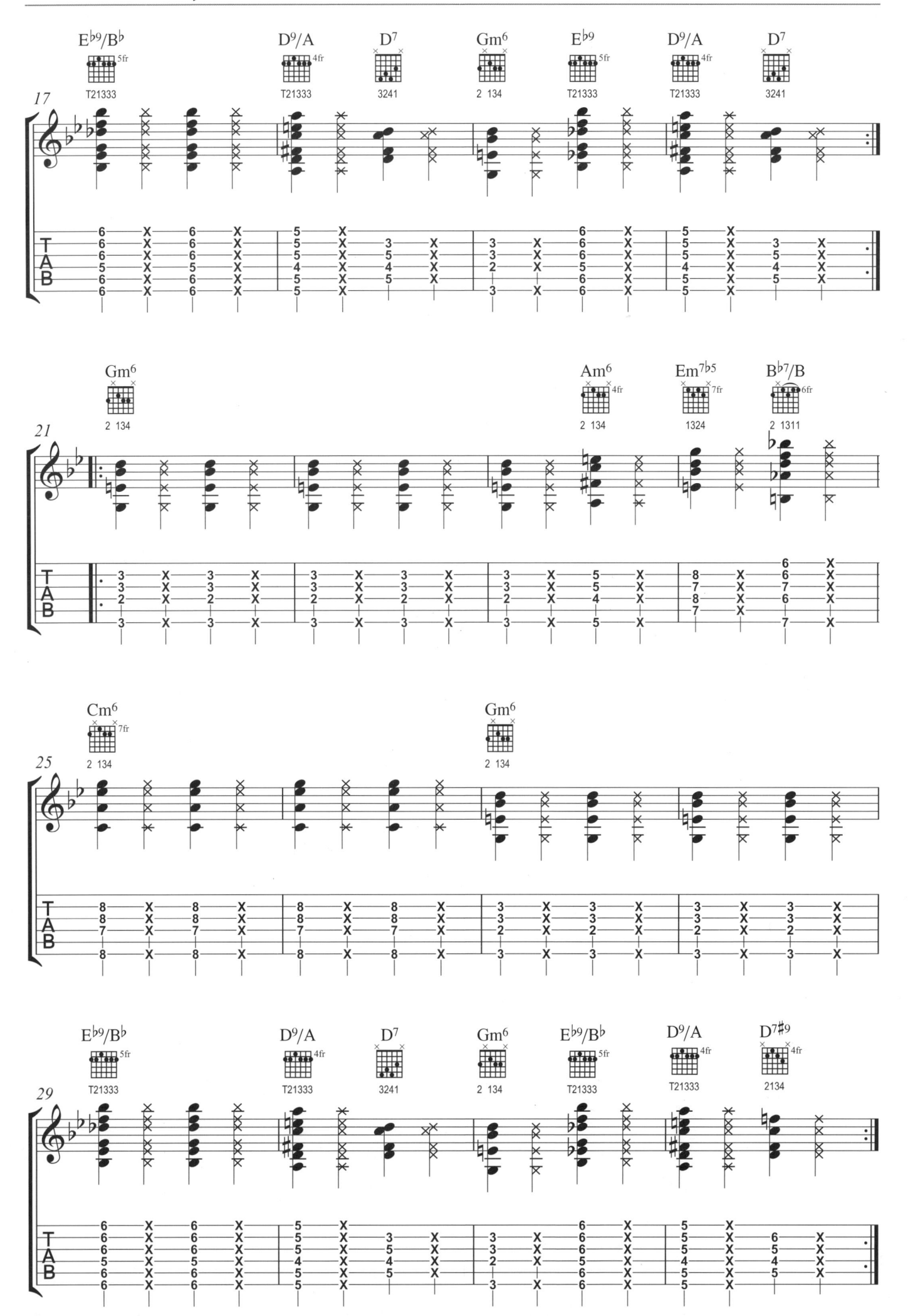

"Without music, life would be an error..."

(Friedrich Nietzsche)

The Chord Voicings to Lesson 3/5 *Valse à Bertino (Le grand escalier)*

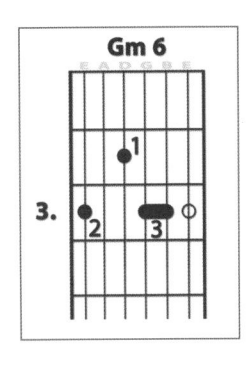

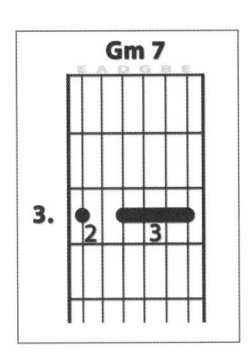

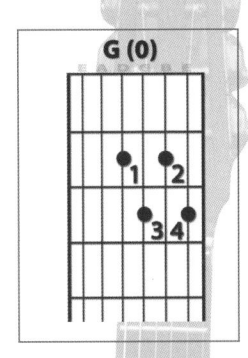

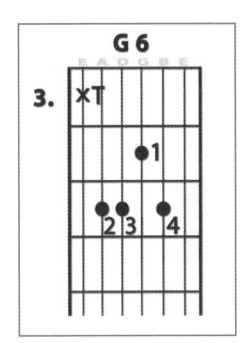

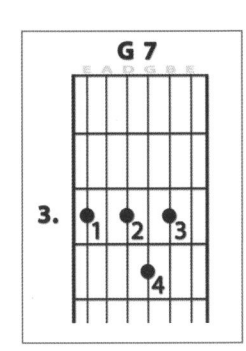

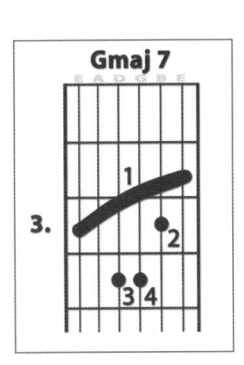

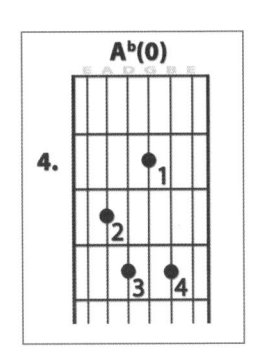

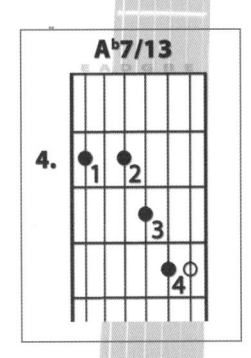

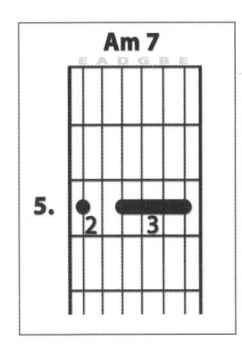

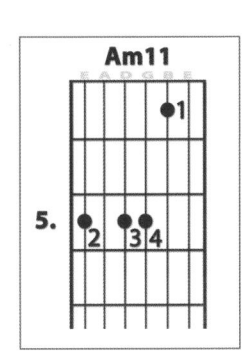

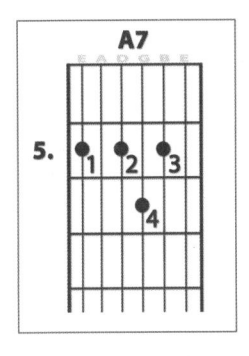

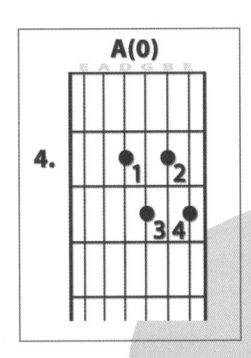

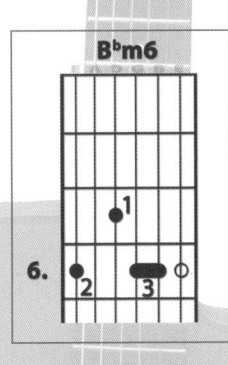

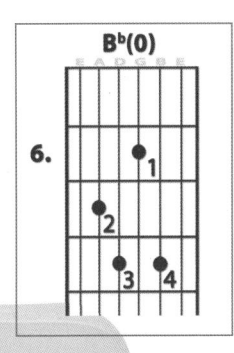

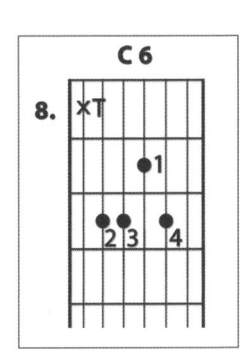

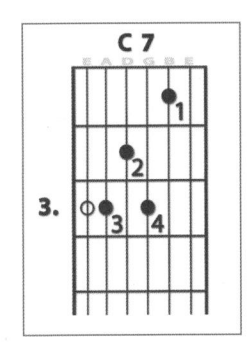

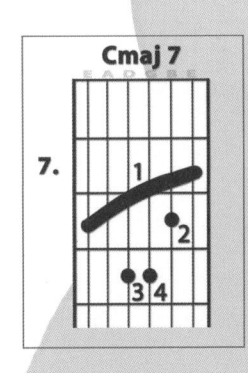

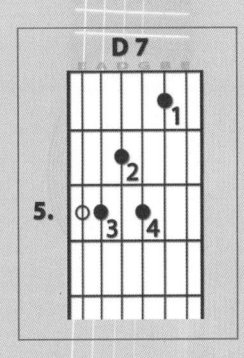

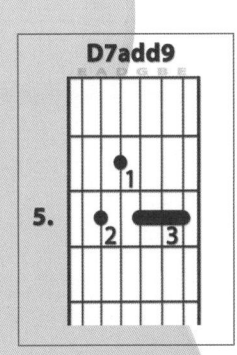

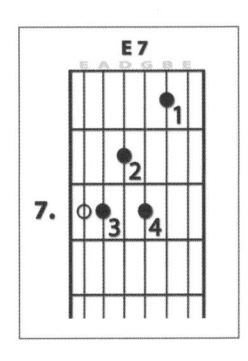

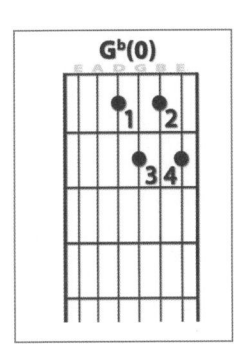

Valse à Bertino (Le grand escalier)

Music: Bertino Rodmann

Valse à Bertino (Le grand escalier) – Rhythm Guitar

B♭°
G°
D9
D7/A
33
Gm6
B♭m6
Am7
D7
Gm6
37
Part B
A7
D7
Gm7
Gm6
41
A7
D7
Gm7
Gm6
45
TAB

Valse à Bertino (Le grand escalier) – Rhythm Guitar

A° 1324
G♭° 1324
D9 21333
D7/A 33241
65
Am7 2 3333
A♭13 1 234
Gmaj7 1 342
D7 3241
69
Gmaj7 1 342
C9 21333
Gmaj7 1 342
G6 2314
73
G7 131241
C6 T2314
Cmaj7 1 3421
77
T
A
B

Valse à Bertino (Le grand escalier) – Rhythm Guitar

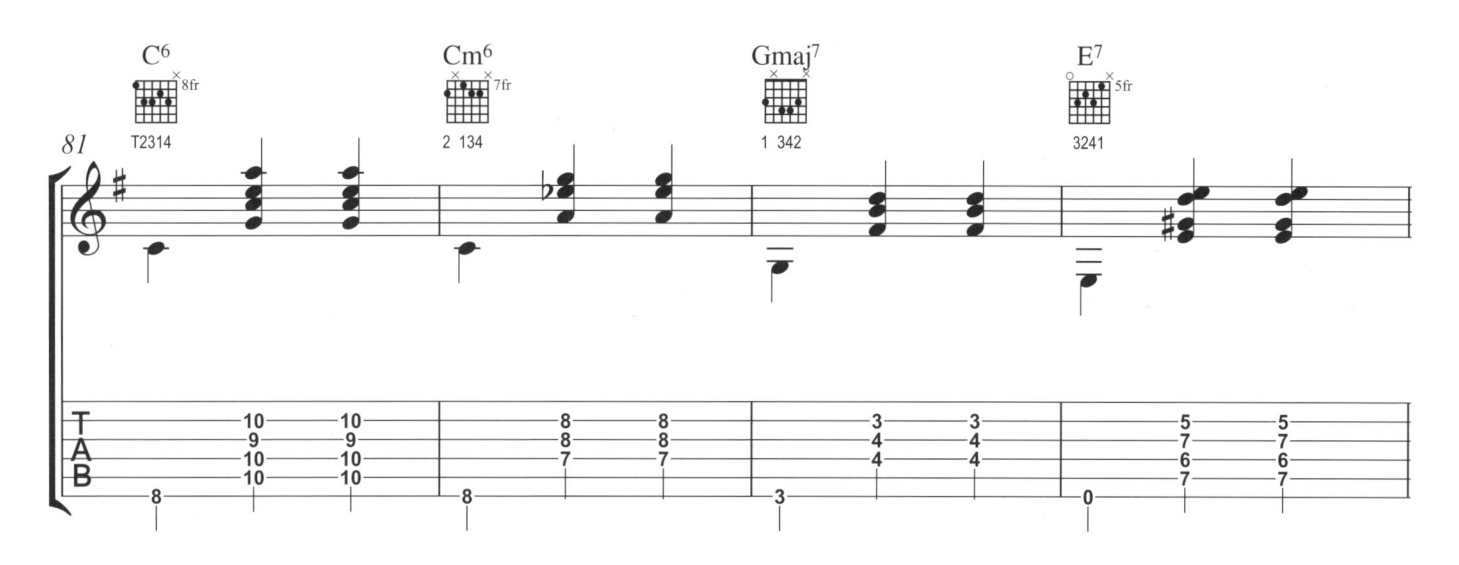

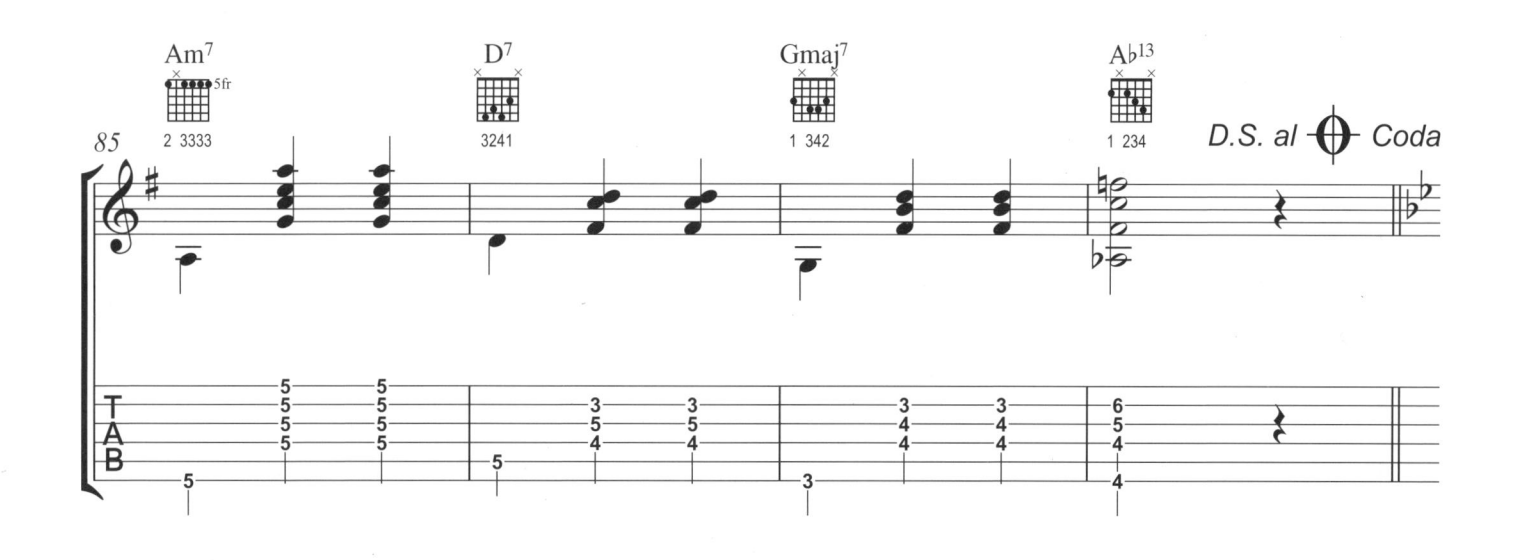

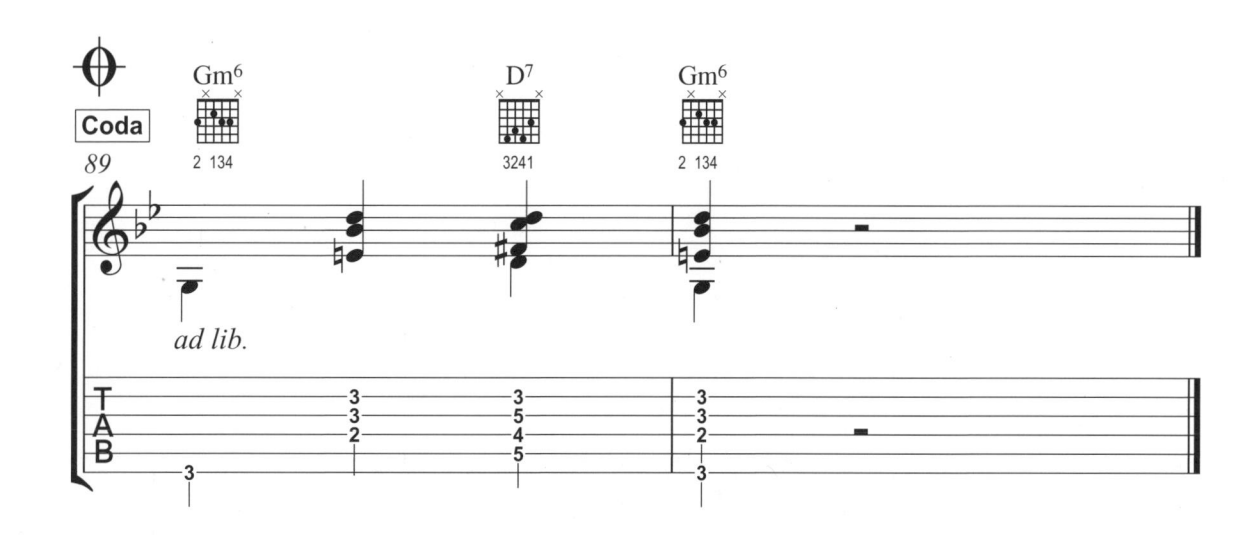

"The biggest fault of a musician is to play notes instead of playing music".

(Isaac Stern, 1920 - 2001, American violinist)

Blues Clair – Rhythm Guitar

The Chord Voicings to Lesson 3/6 'Blues Clair'

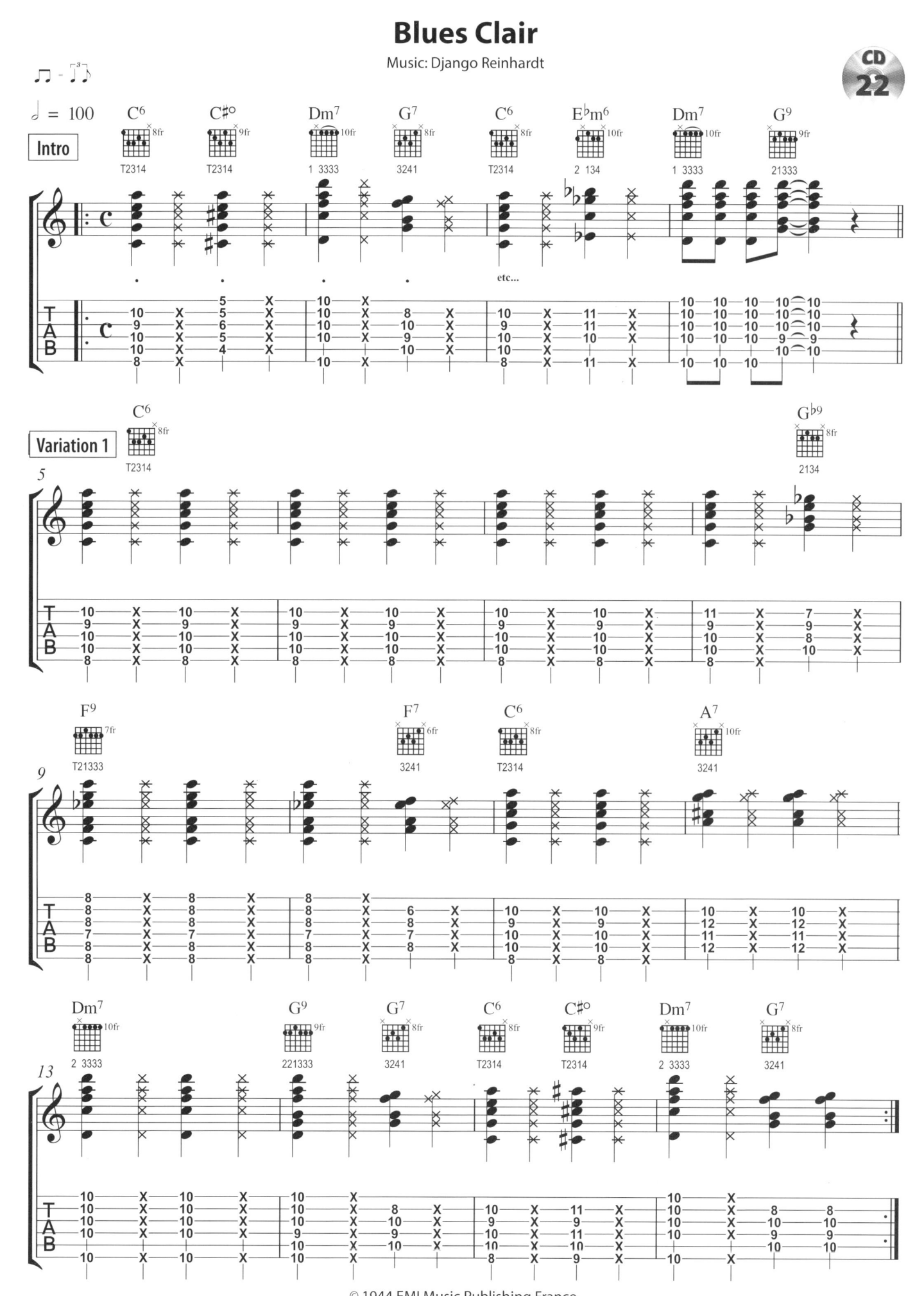

Blues Clair

Music: Django Reinhardt

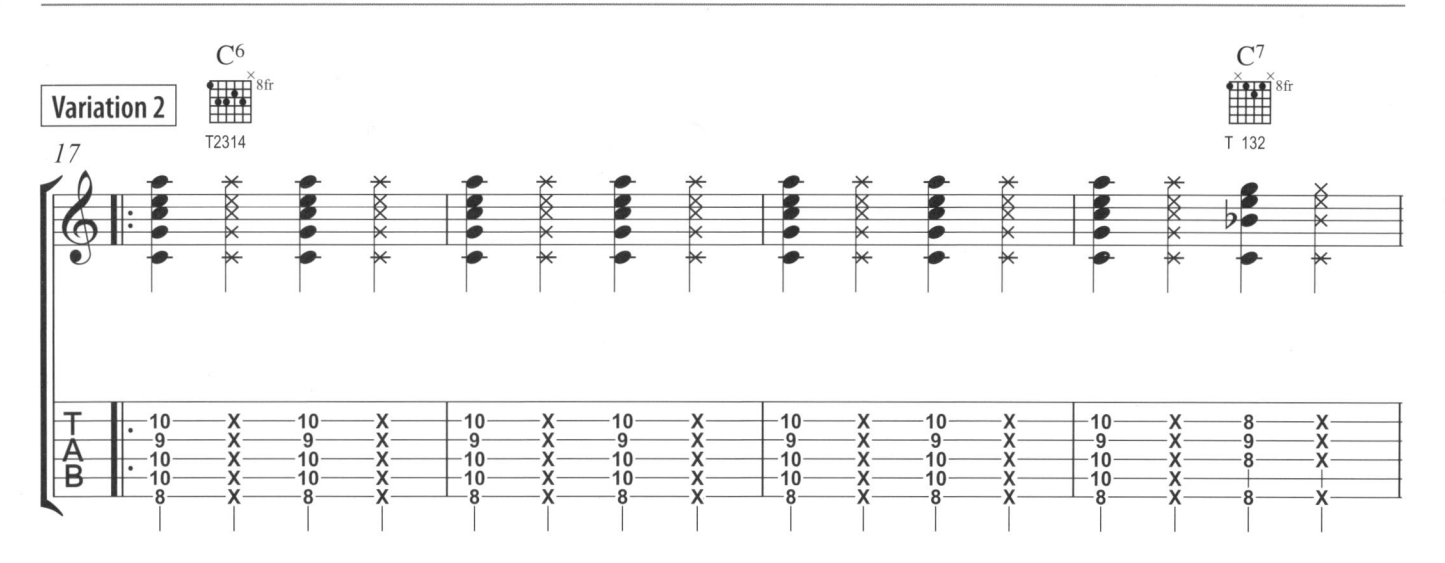

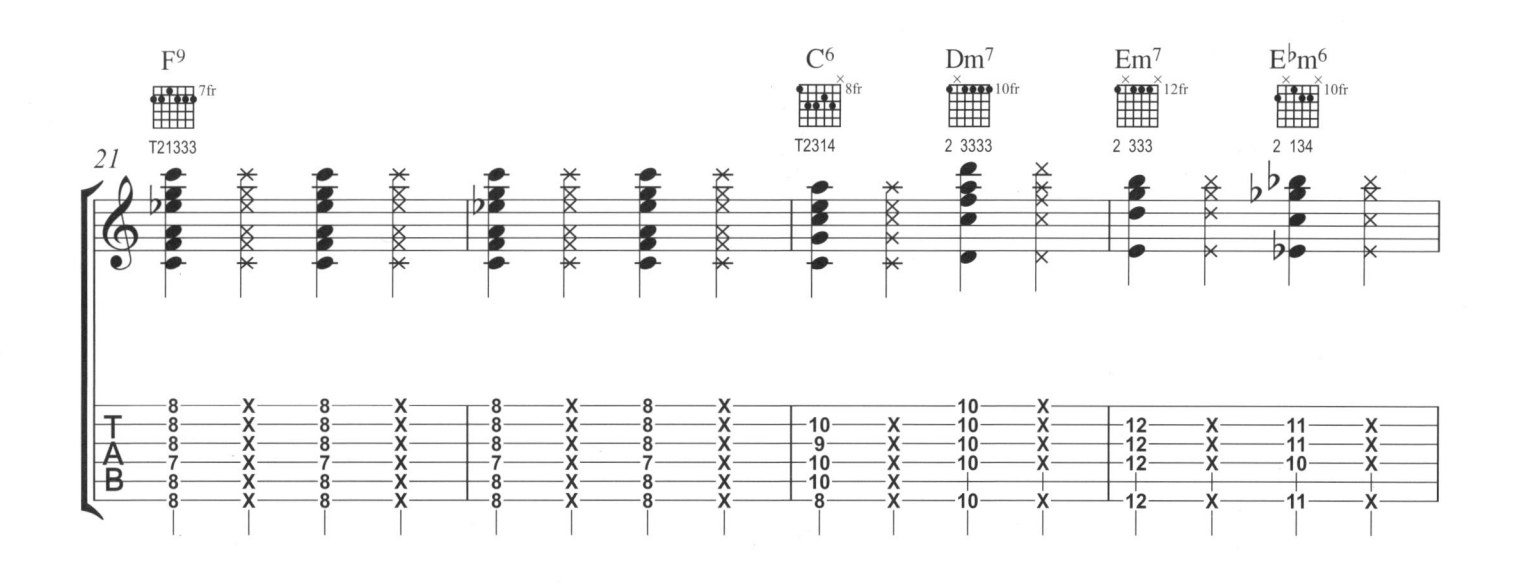

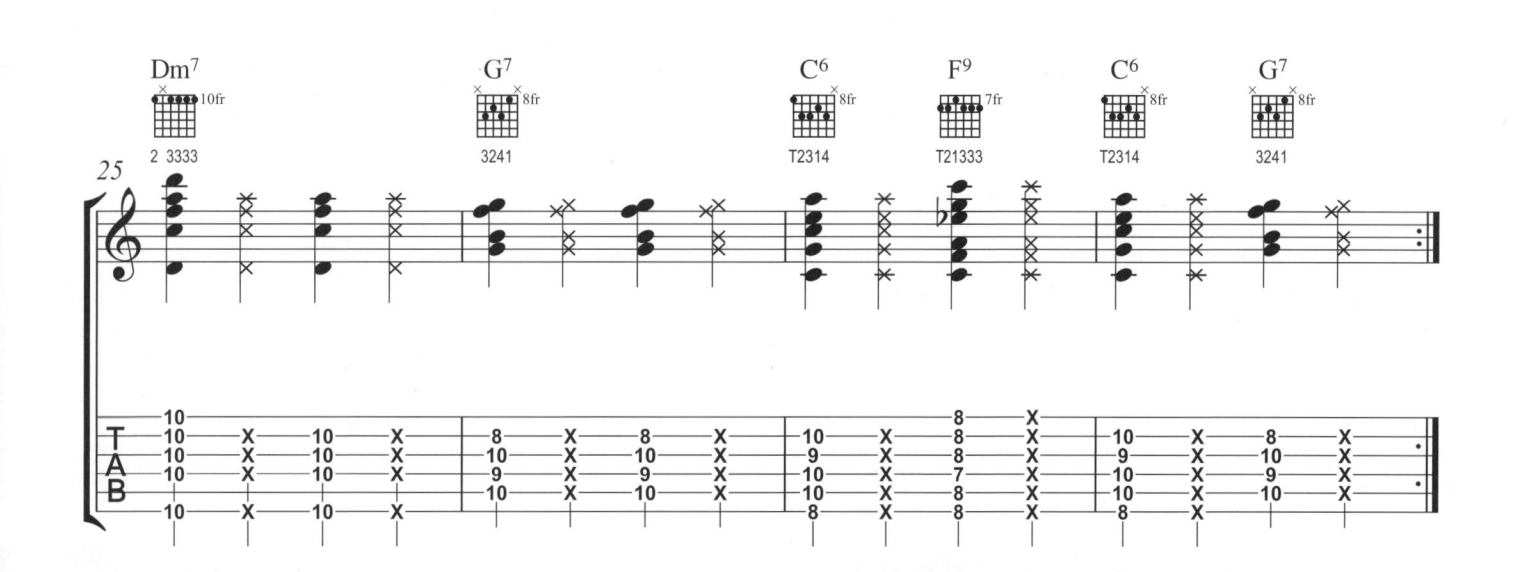

Blues Clair – Rhythm Guitar

The Chord Voicings to Lesson 3/7 'Swing 48'

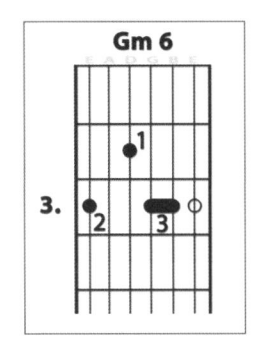

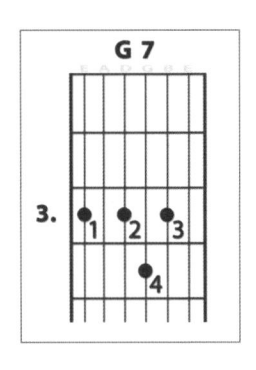

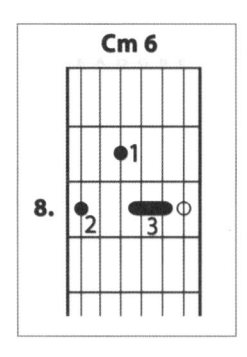

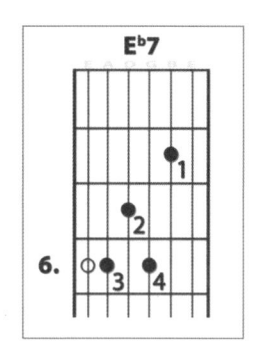

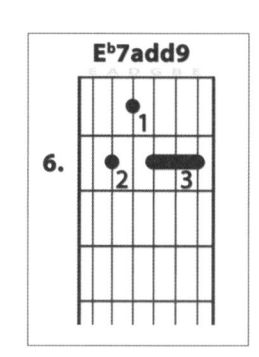

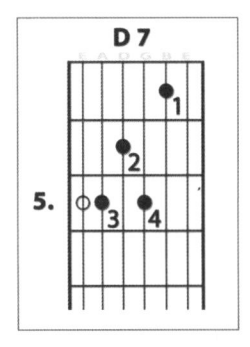

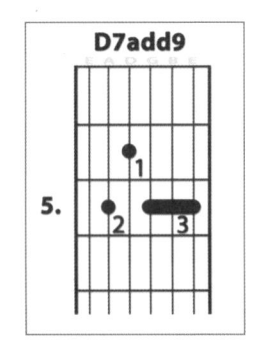

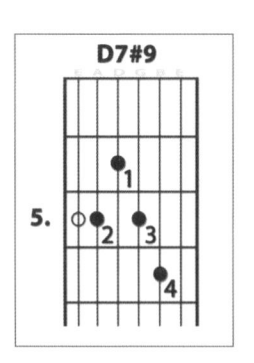

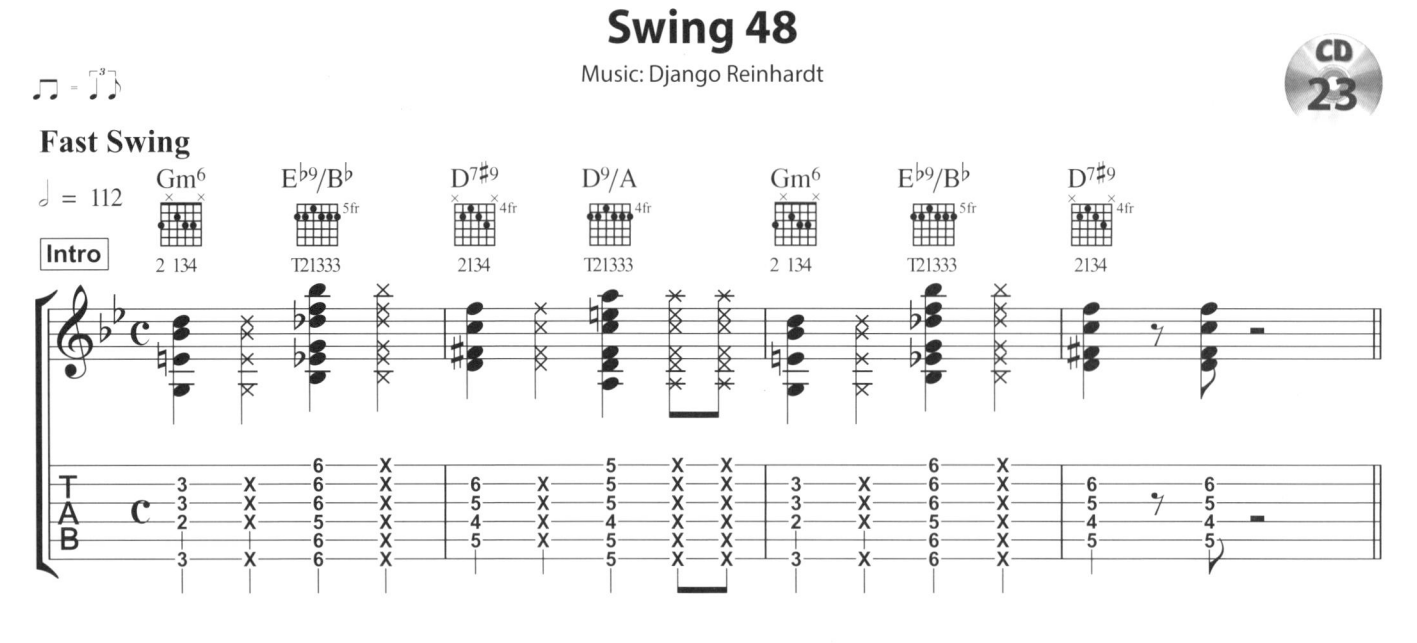

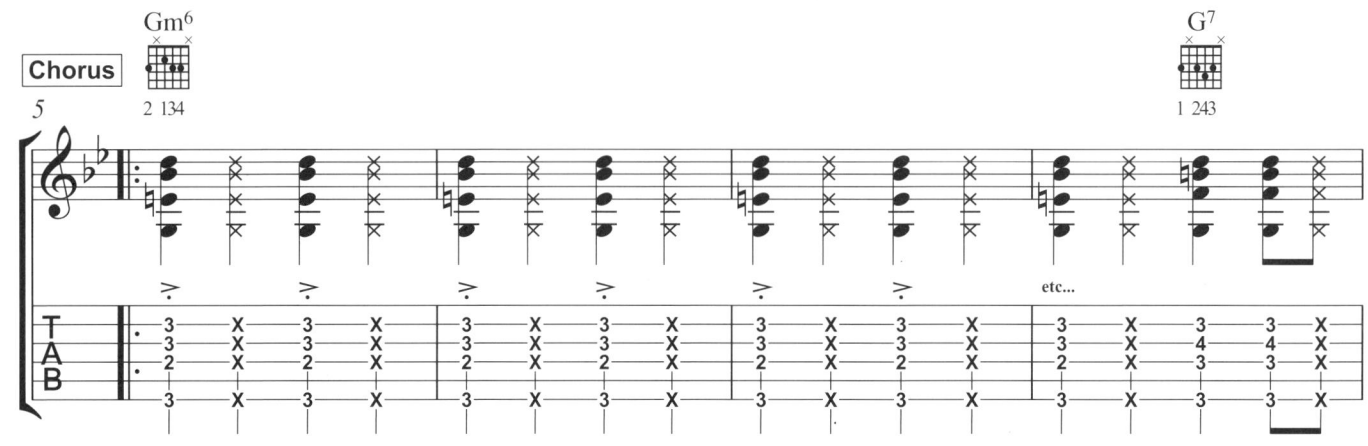

Swing 48

Music: Django Reinhardt

Fast Swing

♩ = 112

Intro

Chorus

© 1947 EMI Music Publishing France
Exclusive Worldwide Print Right Property of EMI Music Publishing France. All Rights Reserved. Used by Permission.

Swing 48 – Rhythm Guitar

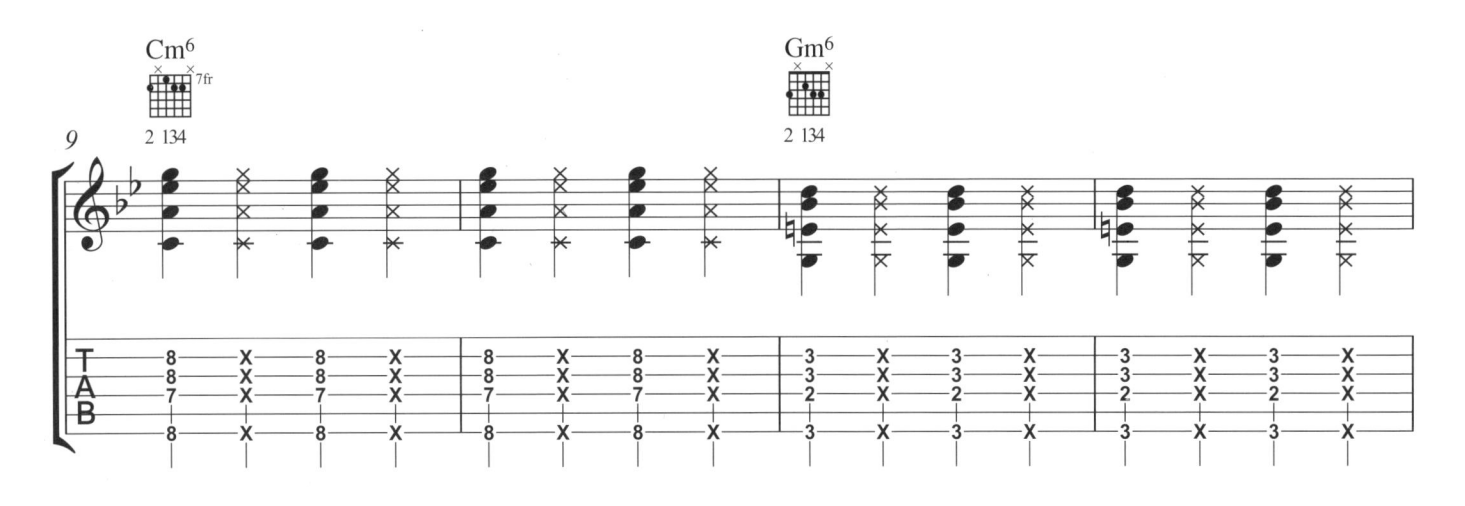

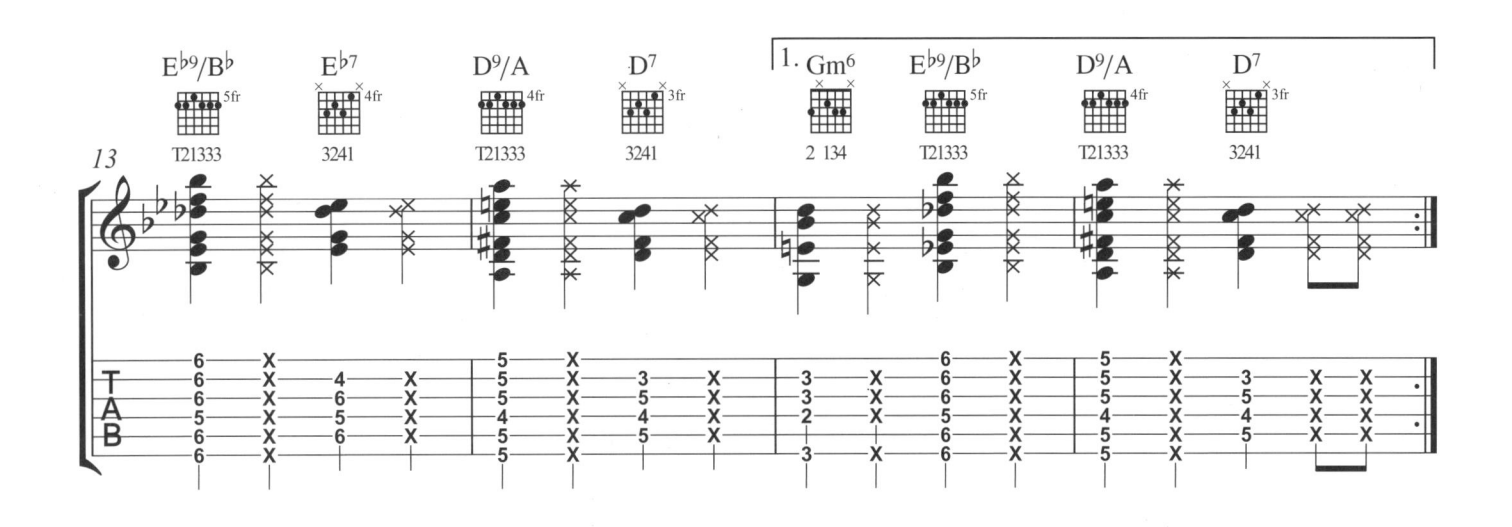

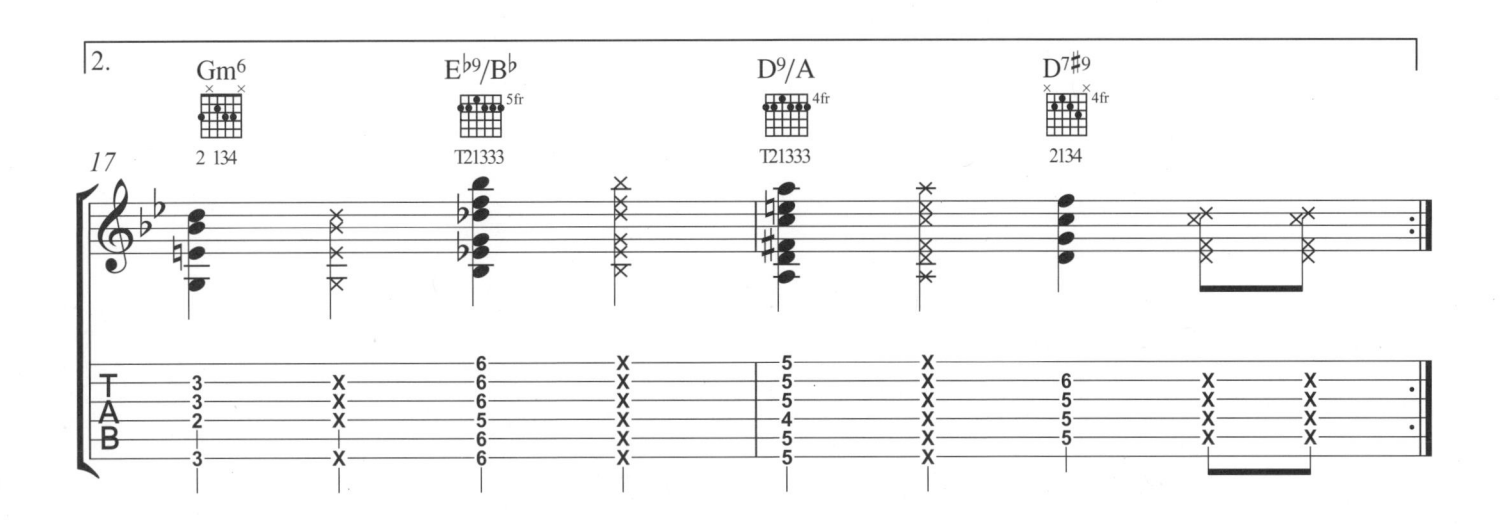

"Music and the music business are two different things.
The music business is motivated by money.
Music is motivated by energy and feelings".

(Erykah Badu)

Gypsy Jazz Guitar

Part 2
Solo Guitar

Introducing Solo Guitar – The Right Hand Placement

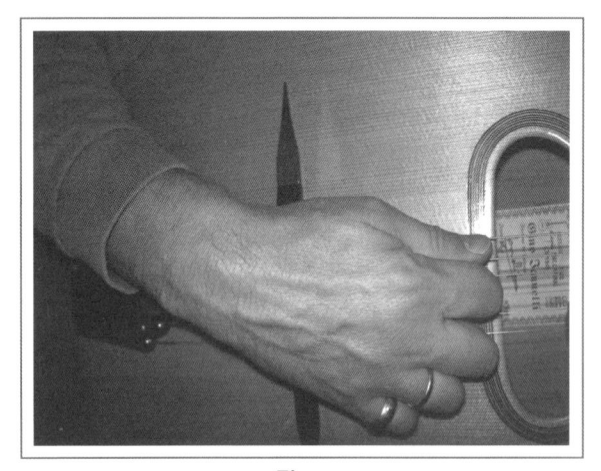

Fig. 1

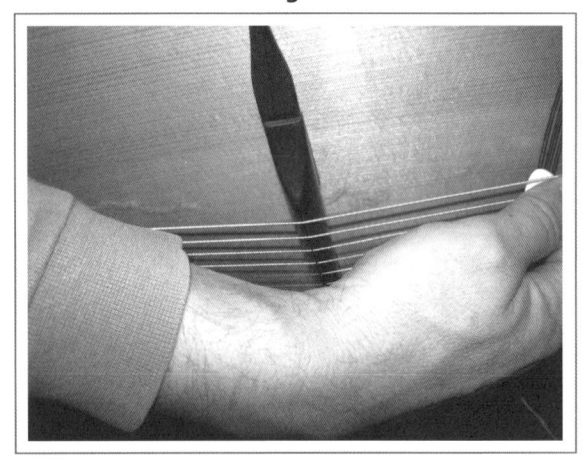

Fig. 2

Fig. 3

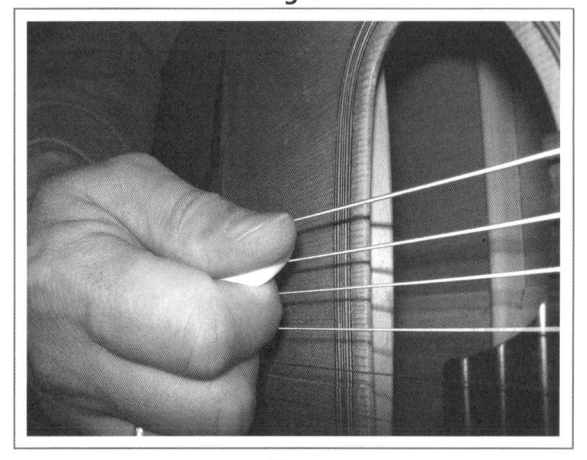

Fig. 4

To really understand the playing techniques of **Django Reinhardt** and many of today's *Sinti* guitarists (such as **Stochelo Rosenberg, Bireli Lagrene** or **Tschawolo Schmitt**) and to play them authentically, there are some important basic points to consider.

Of course, as already discussed (see *Introduction*, page 12-15), choosing the right instrument (e.g. ***Selmer** style guitar*) and choosing the right pick and strings are all important factors when it comes to creating an authentic *Gypsy Jazz* sound.

Among other crucial elements in the style of *Gypsy Jazz mentioned earlier*, the most important things to be pointed out are the 'right hand placement' and the 'picking techniques'.

Here are the important facts on these two subjects:

1. The right hand should ideally be placed parallel to the strings, almost in a right angle to the guitar without touching the bridge of the top of the guitar (see *Figure 1*).

2. The wrist should be held lightly angled to produce the kind of 'pressure' for playing a strong rhythm as well as for solos. Important note: resting your hand on the bridge or the top of the guitar (as is common when playing electric guitar) must be strictly avoided at all times! (See *Figure 2*).

3. Whether you are playing rhythm or solo, the pick should rest on the next following string after playing any string whenever possible (*see Figure 3, 4 and 5*). This generates greater precision in playing and therefore results in a feeling of 'playing security' for the guitarist as you stay in contact with the strings through the pick at all times.

4. By using the 'reststroke'-technique, you can create a much stronger sound while the playing still remains easier and less exhausting.

By 'letting fall' the pick onto the string you don't have to put any additional muscle power into your playing as you are using gravity instead (*see the next chapter 'Picking Technique' on page 75*).

Fig. 5

Part 2 – Solo Guitar

1. Picking Technique

Guitarists that previously used to play blues, pop or rock guitar mostly pick the guitar with what is called 'alternate picking'. In this style, picking every beat on a string is being hit just up-and-down with the pick, regardless of changing a string or which string you might play (see *example 1* taking note of the picking direction!)

Example 1: Alternate Picking

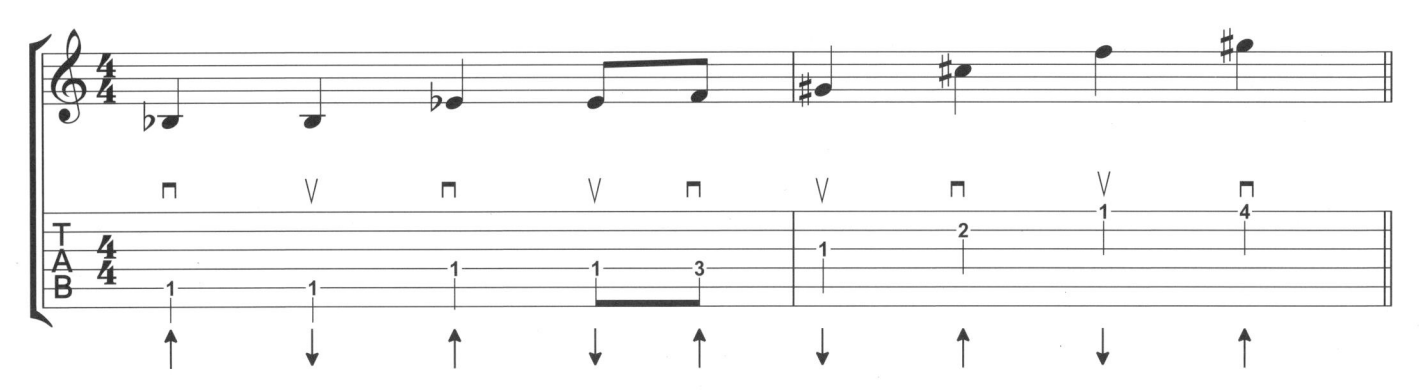

Well, **Django Reinhardt** and all the other *Gypsy Jazz* guitarists that are playing in his tradition use a completely different picking technique which firstly, is much louder, and secondly, much more precise.

This technique is called 'reststroke' picking (also known as 'Apoyando' from playing classical guitar).
By playing with reststroke picking (unlike alternate picking) the pick will be stopped by the following string, hence *rest*stroke (to rest on a string). Additionally, the first beat of a melody will always be played with a 'downstroke', and every change of strings will consequently also be played with DOWNstrokes (see the picking direction in *example 2*). In many cases, even the end (or last) note of a melody is played with a downstroke.

Example 2: Reststroke Picking

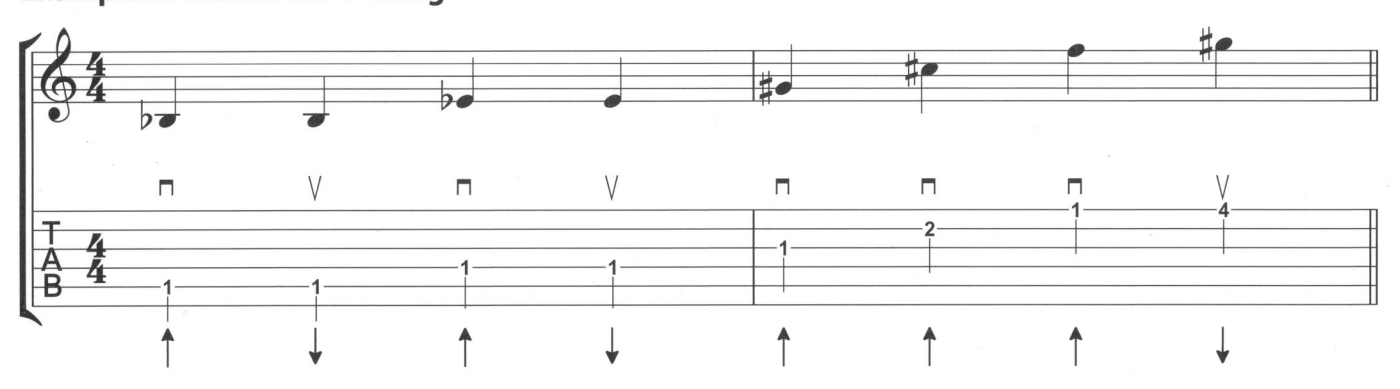

But it is not only the direction of the picking that is important, but also the execution!

When playing with reststroke picking, the pick is allowed to 'fall' on to the string instead of plucking it… to be stopped by the next string (see *Lesson 1/1 'Picking Technique'* on page 77).
So the picking is not done by muscle tension like it is with alternate picking, but is done by pure physical lever action of turning the hand. When using this technique the picking is precise and louder and results in a much stronger tone.

Here is another description of this picking technique from the book *'Gypsy Picking'* by **Michael Horowitz**:

>> In a nutshell, **Django's** right-hand technique is a plectrum version of the commonly used classical guitar finger stroke, known as **Apoyando** or **'Reststroke'**.

The plectrum version of this technique has all the benefits of the fingerstyle stroke:

reduced fret buzz,
a secure feeling of placement,
reduced muscle tension and
a loud, full tone.

In addition, the plectrum rest-stroke takes advantage of basic principles of physics by using the weight of the hand, instead of the muscles, to propel the pick in much the same manner as a hammer falls down on a nail.

Unlike the more commonly used free stroke (e.g. 'alternate Picking'), which activates the string by pushing the pick through the string, the Rest-stroke activates the string by letting the pick hand fall, using gravity rather than your muscles, to provide the necessary force.

A Rest-stroke is completed by letting the pick rest on the next adjacent string; hence the name 'Rest-stroke'. The result is volume, tone, and speed without the discomfort of tense muscles in your wrist and forearm.<<

Excerpt from: 'Gypsy Picking' by Michael Horowitz, Page 12 – 13, available from: DjangoBooks.com

"Never play anything the same way twice".

(Louis Armstrong)

Part 2 – Solo Guitar 77

Now, in the following examples we will practice how this technique can be played. All of these examples are still used in playing *Gypsy Jazz* today.

> *Important note:*
> *When practising these exercises make sure that the pick really stops on the next following string!*
>
> *The picking movement is supposed to be played with a relaxed wrist and without any additional muscle tension but with the use of gravity. The UPstroke is to be played with a little more muscle tension by turning the hand with the pick upwards.*
>
> *It is very important that the strokes are always played with a relaxed turning of the hand, not by using the whole forearm. This way you can produce an easy, swinging kind of playing!*

1/1 Reststroke Picking

This exercise shows the reststroke by using the empty strings E, A, D, G, B and E. All strings are picked only with downstrokes. The pick 'rests' on the next following string (except on the low E-string (6th string)) after picking until the next note is played.

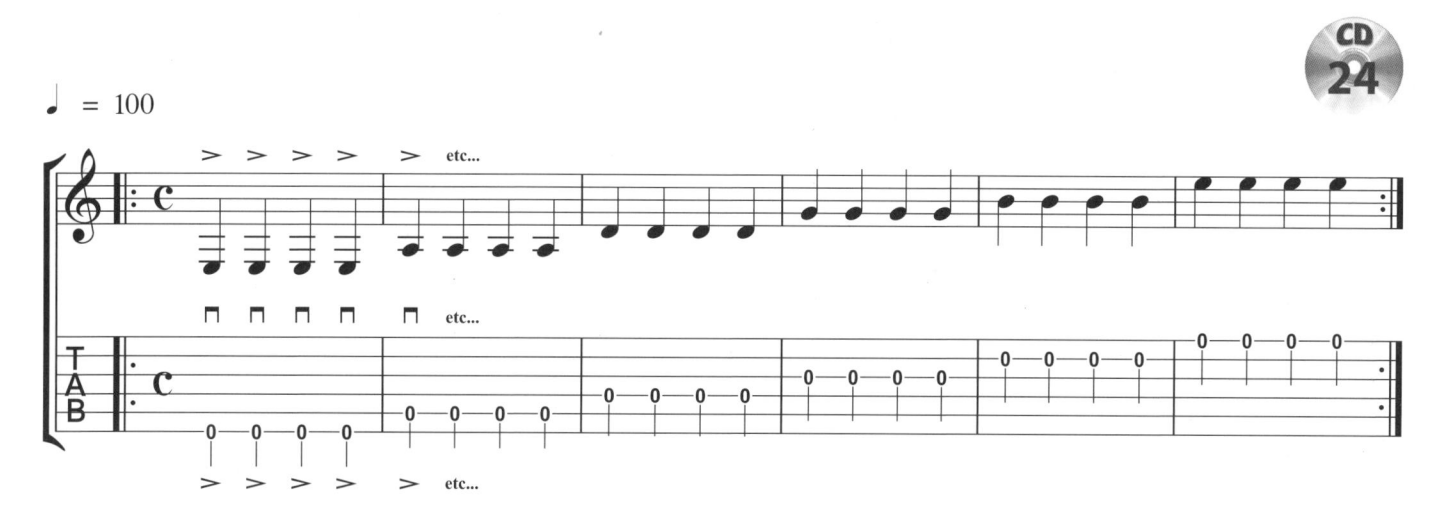

CD 24

♩ = 100

1/2 Up and Down Reststroke Picking

Next, we will hit the E 6th string with a downstroke, rest shortly on the A (5th-)string with the pick and again pick the E (6th-)string with an upstroke after that. We will then practice the same thing with the empty A, D, G, B, E strings.

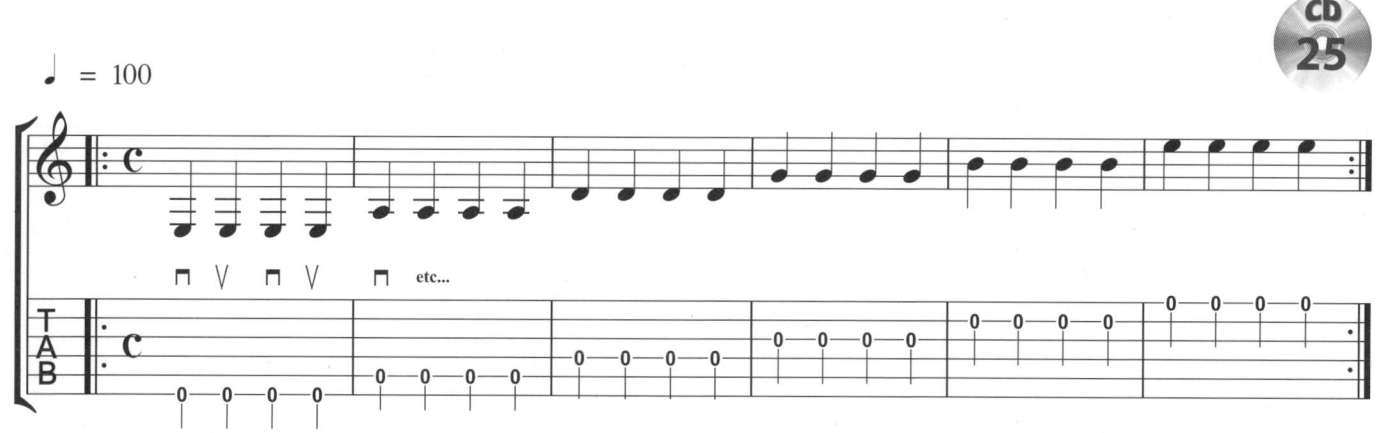

CD 25

♩ = 100

1/3 Sweptstroke Picking

To 'sweep' over strings means that if you want to play more than one string shortly after another, the pick doesn't leave the strings but strikes (i.e. sweeps from one string to another) with a little additional muscle tension to keep the pick on the strings at all times.

This example shows a special playing technique invented by **Django Reinhardt** which he used in many slow ballads as well as fast songs. A good example for this picking technique is one of **Django's** solos played in '*Les Yeux noir*' (Black Eyes). This technique can be used for playing chords as well as chord solos.

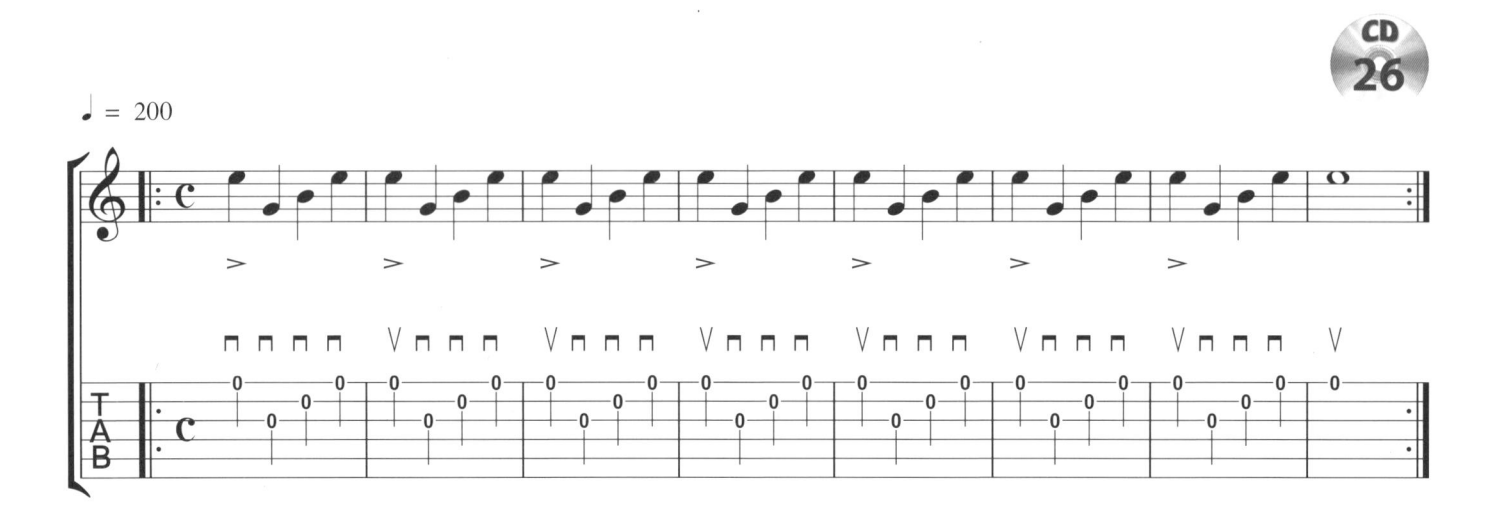

1/4 Arpeggio Picking

In the following chapters, we will talk about the immense importance of Arpeggios (i.e. 'broken chords') in *Gypsy Jazz*. The exercise 1/4 shows the so called '*Arpeggio Picking*' which is used with arpeggios most of the time. It is very similar to the example for sweptstroke.

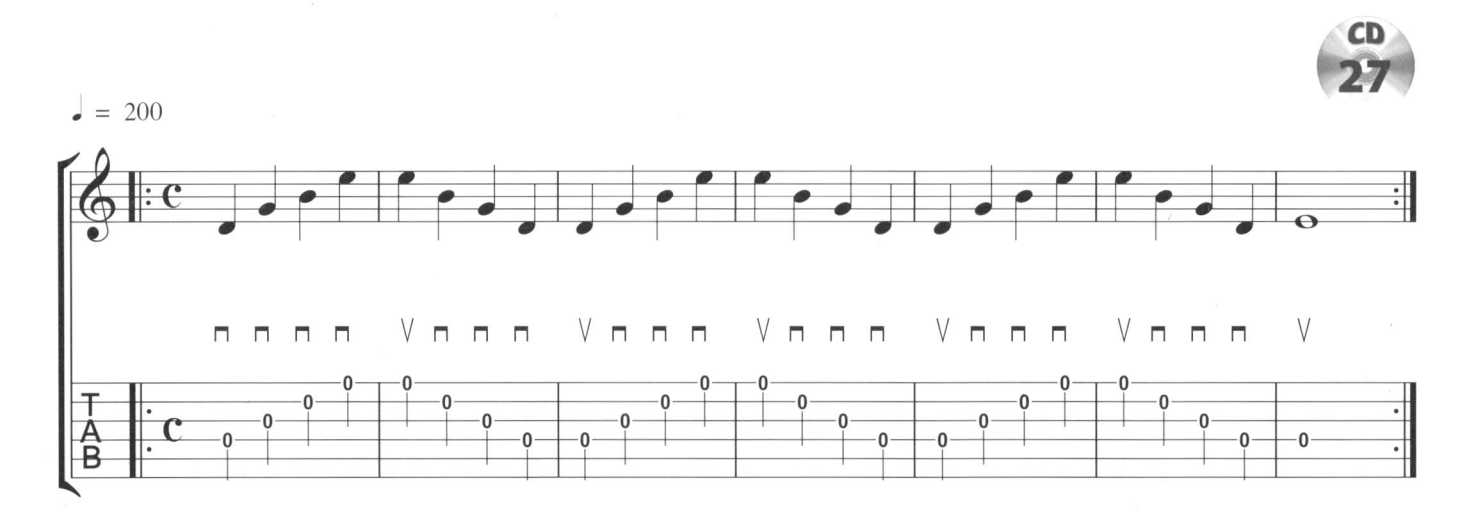

Part 2 – *Solo Guitar*

2. Scales

Every musician (not only guitarists) that has some experience in playing music knows about the importance of scales.

Scales connect the keys to each other through their direct or indirect tonal relations. Moreover, scales are one of the most important stylistic devices for improvising in almost any kind of music.

Besides the pure major or minor, there are many other types of scales. For example, reduced five note versions, known as 'pentatonic' scales, 'diminished' scales or also pure scale versions with added 6th, 7th or 9th notes, whole note scales etc… the list of possible scales is almost endless.

The following examples in this chapter show some of the scales that are commonly used in *Gypsy Jazz*.

For all the examples we will use the previously explained reststroke picking technique (see *Introduction to Solo, Picking Technique* on *page 75*).

> *Tip:*
>
> *All licks and scales should always (!) be practised forwards and backwards and should be played with a metronome. Important: always start practising slowly, never play too fast in the beginning!*
>
> *Only if you are able to play a scale or lick about 10 to 20 times without making any mistakes, can you maybe start to know you are playing right!*
>
> *Much later after a lot of practising and only once the scale (or lick) has been understood and practised slowly in every key, should you then start to turn your attention to the issue of speed (see Epilogue, page 139).*
>
> *Be aware: Speed is something that comes naturally once you have understood and practised something well and slowly for a long time!*

Scale 2/1: Simple Pentatonic in Am

This example shows a simple pentatonic scale in A minor. Five tones without half note steps: A C D E G

CD 28

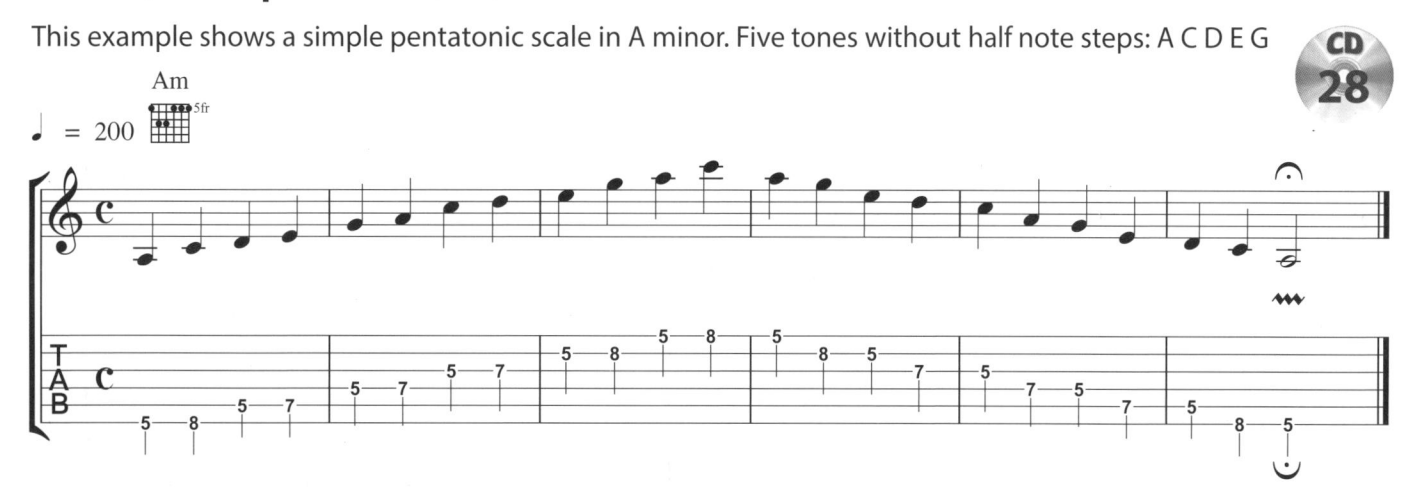

Scale 2/2: Pentatonic in Am with added sixth (Am6)

This example shows a pentatonic scale in A minor with an additional 6th note (F#): A C D E F# G

CD 29

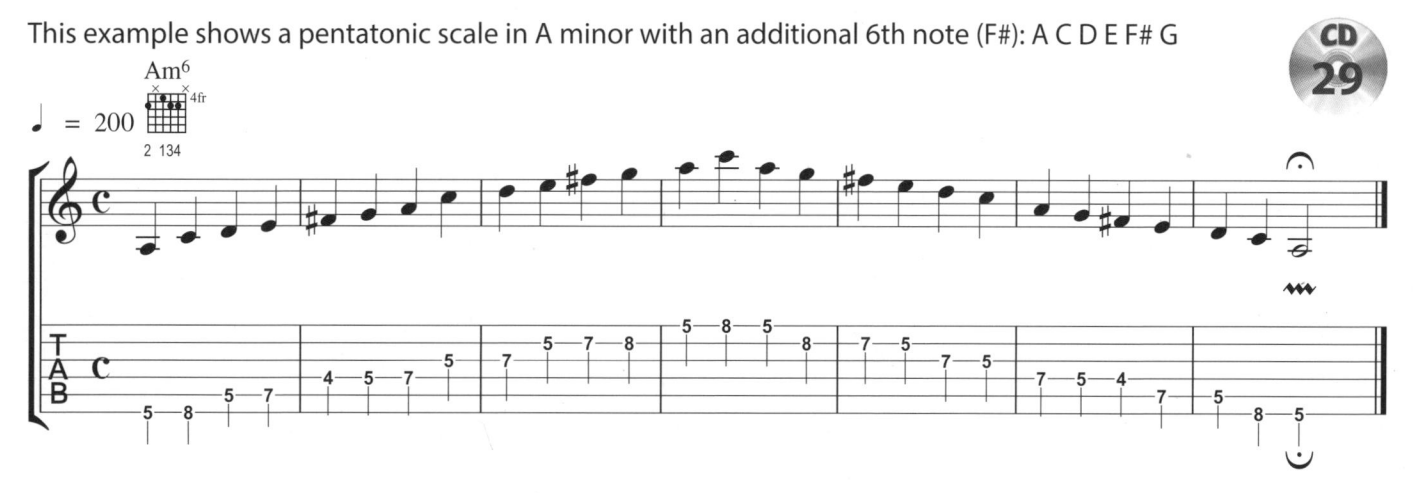

Scale 2/3: Minor scale in Am with additional 6th note

This example shows a regular minor scale in A minor (root notes A C E) with an additional 6th note (F#).

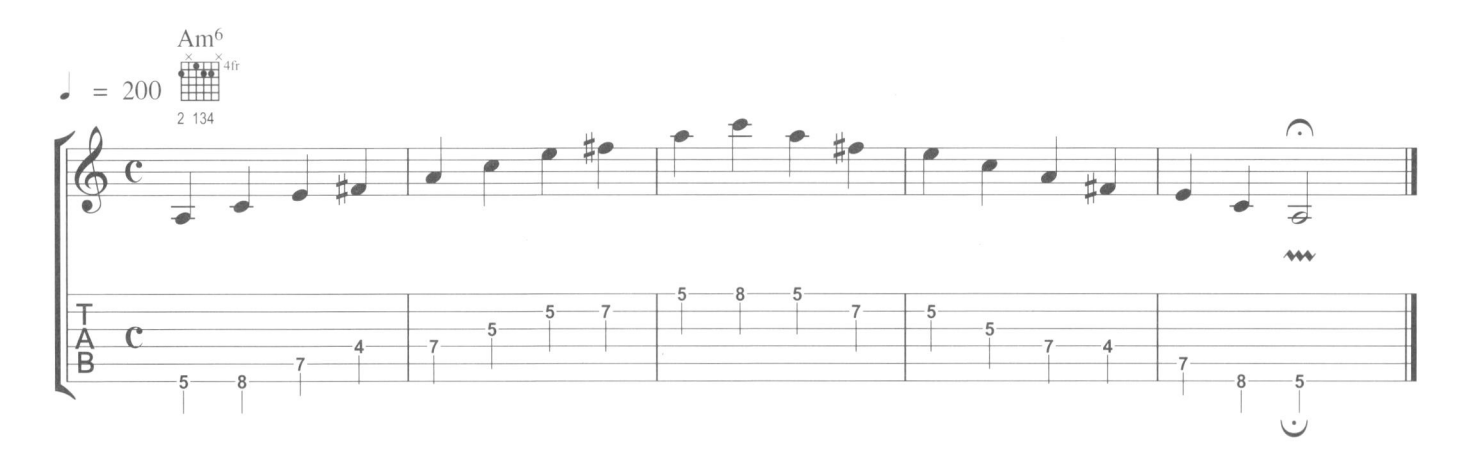

Scale 2/4: Major scale in D

This example shows the seven tone major scale in D, often used in *Gypsy Jazz*: D E F# G A B C# D

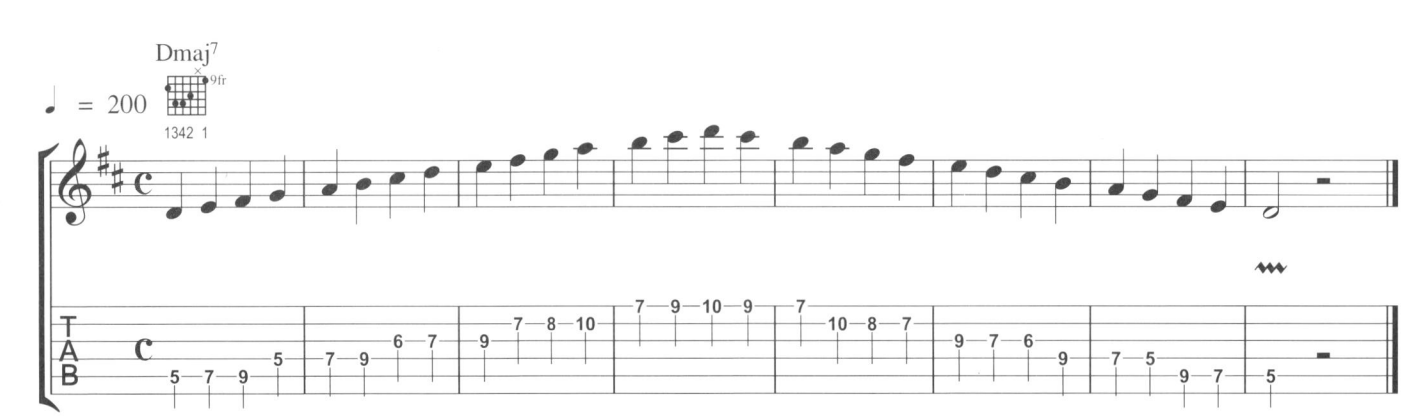

Scale 2/5: Seventh scale over E7th

This example shows a regular major scale in E major (E G# B) with an added minor 7th note (D).

Part 2 – Solo Guitar 81

Scale 2/6: Diminished scale over E7th

Like it is usually done in Jazz, it is also possible in *Gypsy Jazz* to play a corresponding diminished scale over any major 7th chord (example: E7).

In this example we have an A-dim scale (A°) that can be played over an E major 7th chord (or E7add9).
Important: take care of the diagonal direction of playing and the root note of 'E' (start and end point of the scale)!

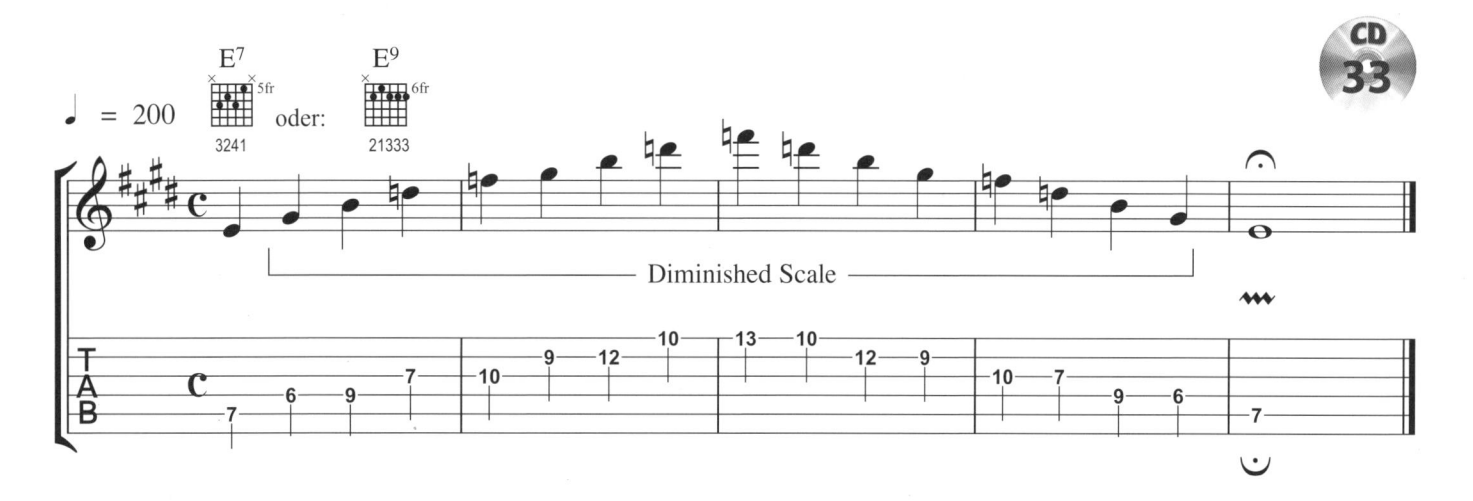

Scale 2/7: A7th scale over A7

This example shows an arpeggio type major scale in A major 7th.

Scale 2/8: Gmaj7 scale (F# locrian)

This is a typical example of a major 7th scale in 'G' beginning on the major 7th note (maj7), the note F#.

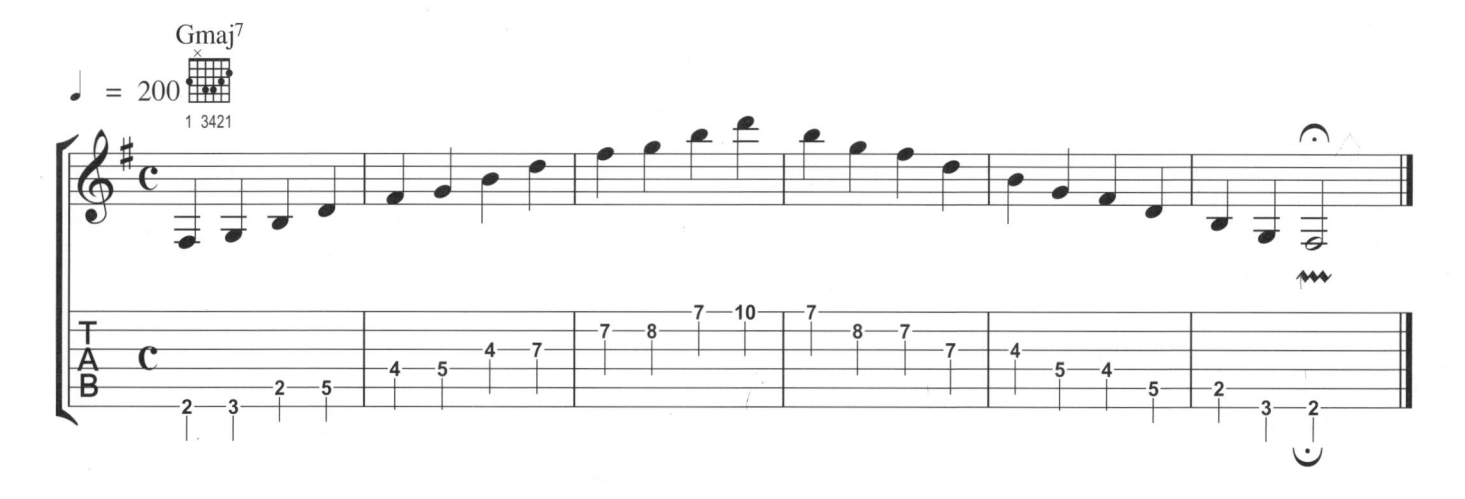

Scale 2/9: G major scale (Django style)

This example shows a regular major scale in 'G' but how it would have typically been played by *Django*.

Tip: these types of scales would most likely have been played by *Django* in a diagonal manner over the fretboard. It seems it would have been easier for him to play it this way with only two fingers. So, give it a try and play it with just your pointer and middle fingers – you'll be amazed at how good this works after a little practice!

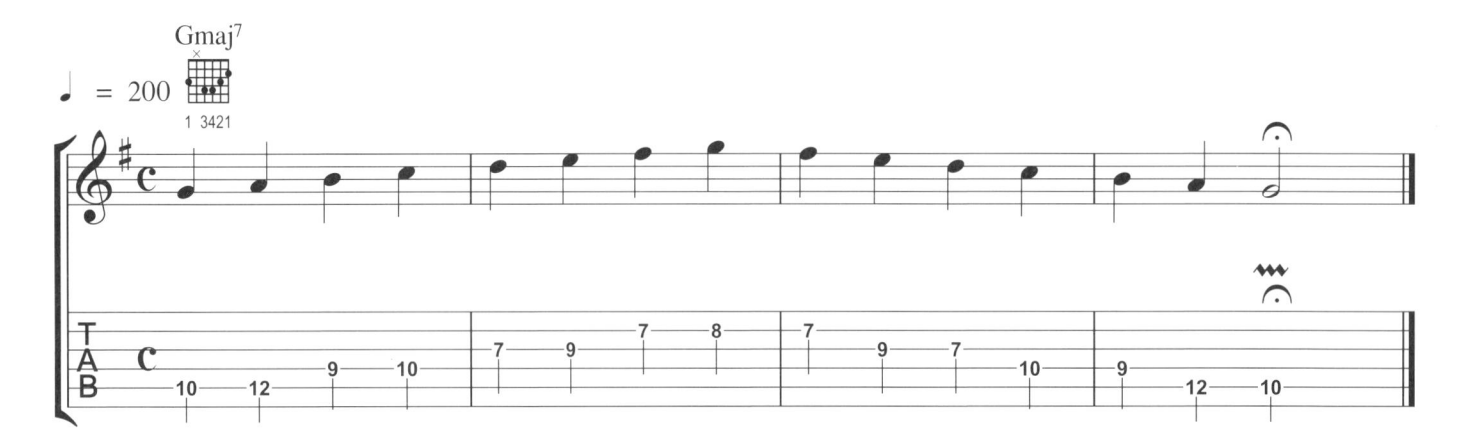

3. Arpeggios

As already discussed in *Part 1 – Rhythm Guitar* in the lesson about chord playing (page 30), *Django Reinhardt* was unable to move all the fingers of his left hand after an accident. This forced him to develop a very unique and special technique for playing not only chords, but also any single notes when soloing.

Django used arpeggios (i.e. 'broken' chords that are played as single notes) very often in his playing and many of his solos are based on long arpeggio chains creating wonderful melody lines (which were often played very fast in eighth notes). Because of this, arpeggios have become a very important part of *Gypsy Jazz* improvisation.

In the following chapter I would like to show you some of these major and minor arpeggios that are played in this way or similarly in *Gypsy Jazz* today.

> **Tip:**
>
> *With the right picking technique it is possible to play arpeggios very fast e.g. with sweeping or arpeggio picking (see Introduction to Solo Guitar, Picking Technique, page 78).*
>
> *Practice all the following arpeggios shown in the key that they are written in first, with the right picking technique.*
>
> *As soon as you can play them fluently (forwards and backwards), then try to transpose and play them in all the other keys that exist too!*

Arpeggio 3/1: Am arpeggio

This example shows a simple A minor arpeggio on the base of a 'common' A minor barré chord.

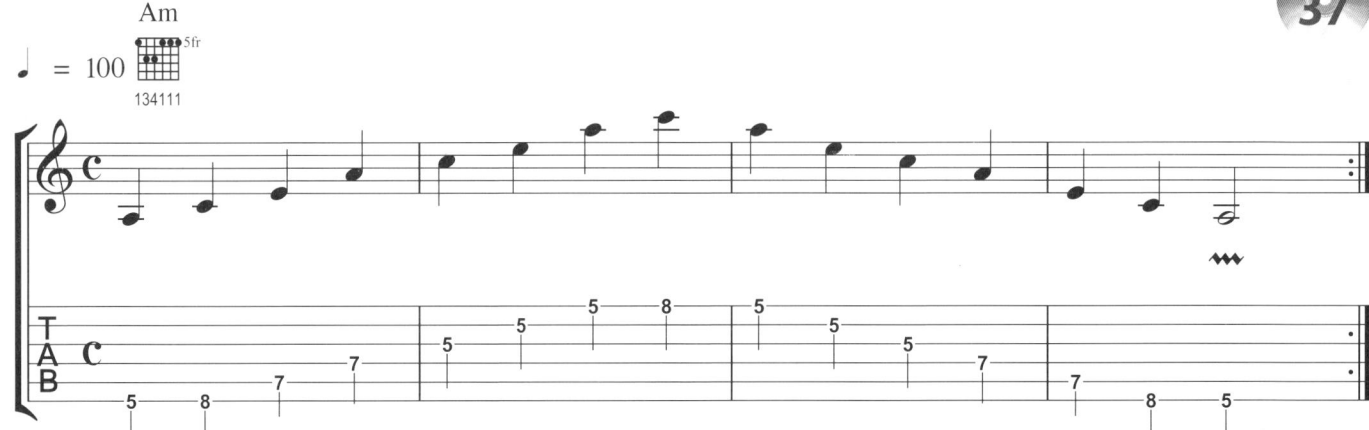

Part 2 – Solo Guitar

Arpeggio 3/2: Am6 arpeggio

This shows an A minor arpeggio on the base of a regular A minor barré chord with an added 6th note.

Arpeggio 3/3: Am6 arpeggio (variation)

This example shows another variation of the Am arpeggio with an added 6th note shown in 3/2.

Arpeggio 3/4: G major arpeggio

This example shows a G major arpeggio on the base of a standard G major barré chord.

Arpeggio 3/5: G major arpeggio (variation)

This example shows a variation of the G major arpeggio explained in example 3/4 but over three octaves.

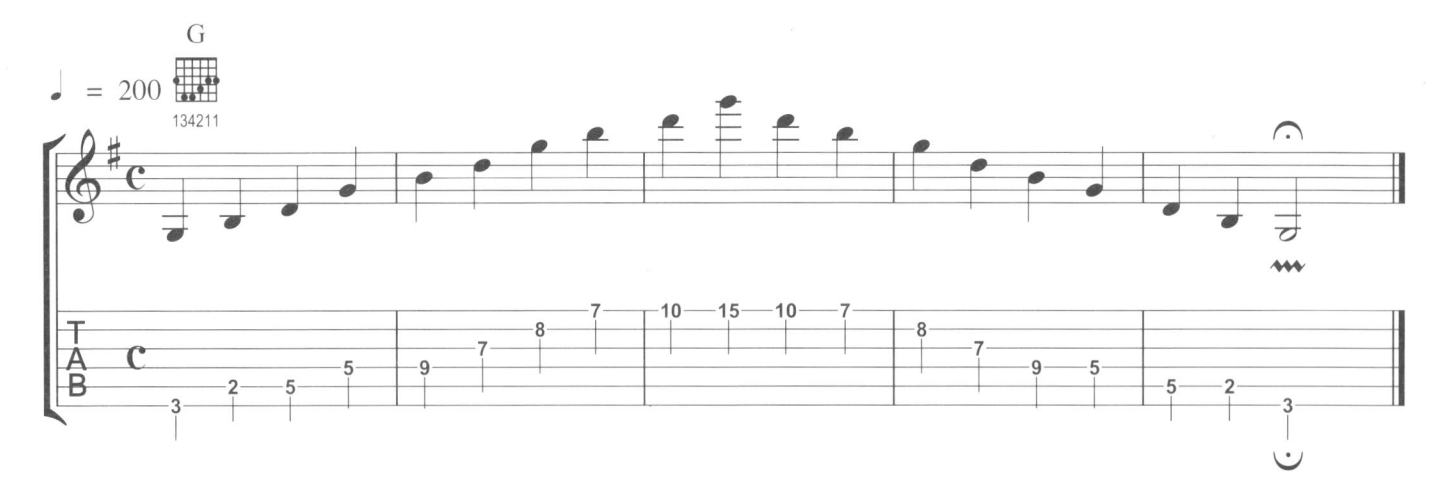

Arpeggio 3/6: G major arpeggio (D shape)

This example shows another G major arpeggio on the base of a 'D shape', thus based on playing a regular D major chord moved to the 7th fret.

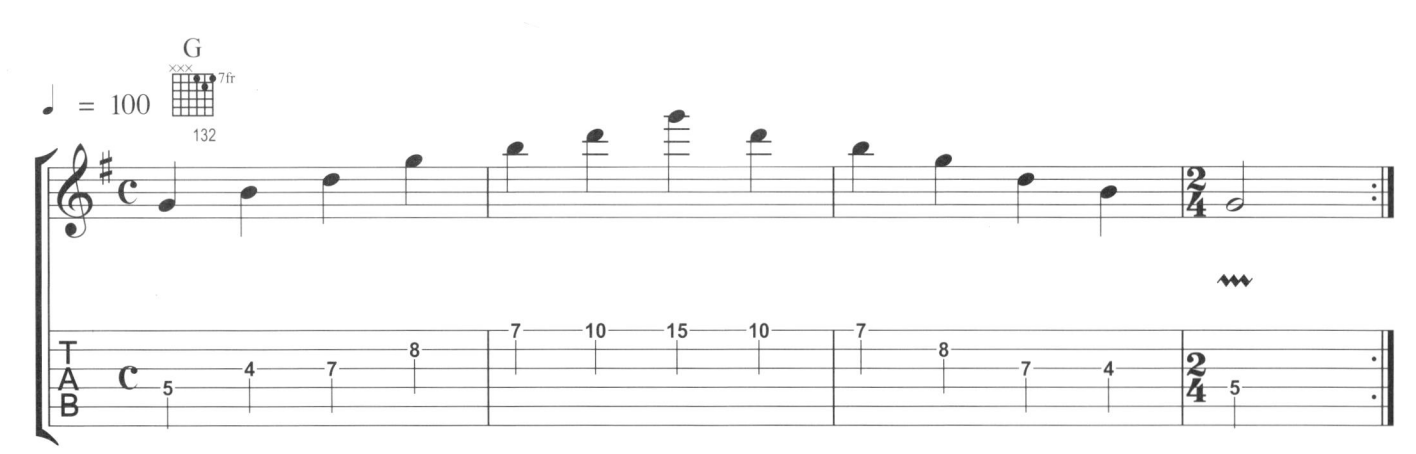

Arpeggio 3/7: C minor arpeggio

This example shows an arpeggio in C minor on the base of a regular C minor barré chord.

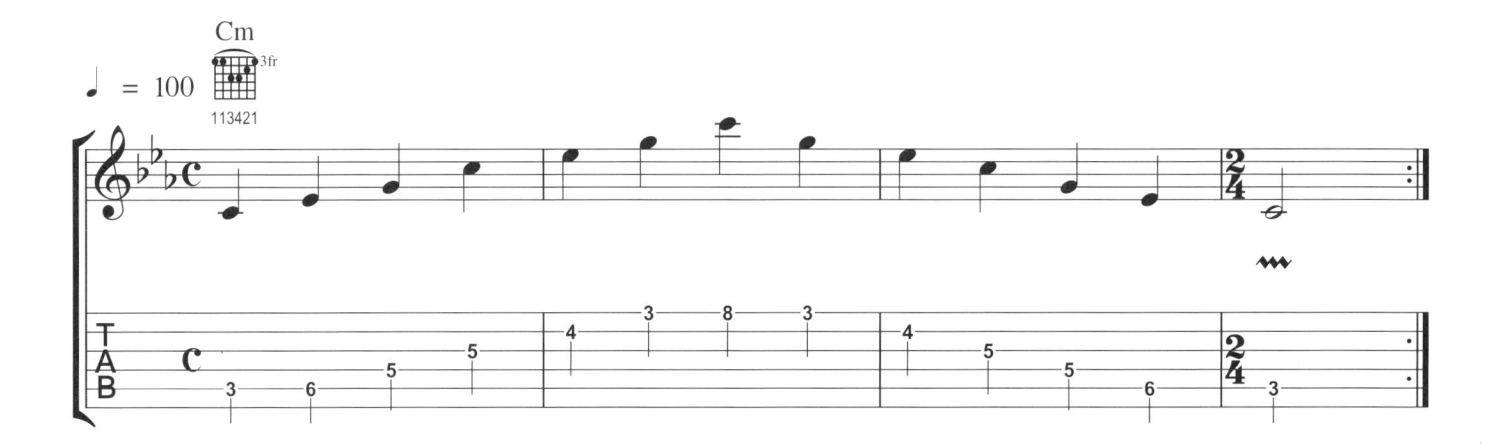

Part 2 – Solo Guitar

4. Solo Licks

Let's practice what we have been talking about, up till now just theoretically. Let me show you eight different licks in the next chapter that *Django Reinhardt* played in his famous solo of '*Minor Swing*' (recorded in 1937).

In conjunction with all the examples of scales and arpeggios shown in the last chapters, these licks can give you a good first glimpse into how *Django* developed his solos: many times as a mixture of licks, scales, tricks and, of course, arpeggios. Whenever you analyse in depth a guitar solo you can get a good impression of the signature licks, tricks and even pitfalls of the style.

> *Tip 1:*
> *the following licks can be transposed and used on other songs or keys very easily by setting them into relation to the played chords. Always practice all licks and tricks, arpeggios and scales in ALL keys on the guitar. This way you will be able to use them in songs or keys other than the ones mentioned in this book.*

This is the reason why I like to use the '*Minor Swing*' solo to demonstrate how single lines, licks and arpeggios can be played together over certain chords to make up the complete solo. Through this, it is possible to see how *Django* and today's *Sinti* guitarists play.

More licks and arpeggios will follow in the chapters *Introducing Solo Guitar – Tips and Tricks*, page 105 and *The Use of Scales and Arpeggios in Gypsy Jazz*, page 110.

Lick 4/1

The first lick shows the first part of *Django's* '*Minor Swing*' solo, starting from Am6 leading to Dm6.

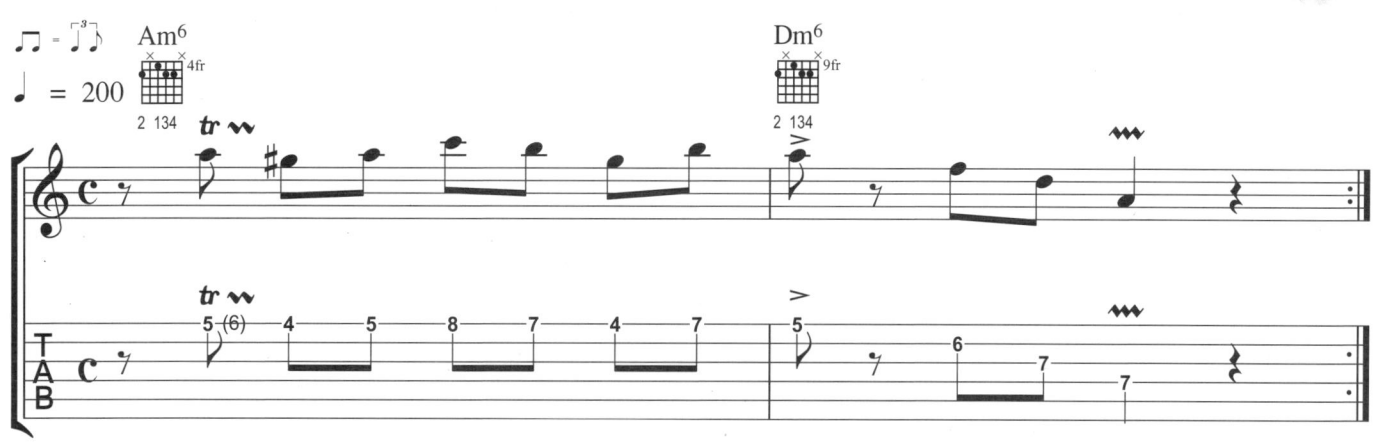

Lick 4/2

The second part shows the transition from the Dm6 chord (subdominant) leading to the E7 chord (dominant).

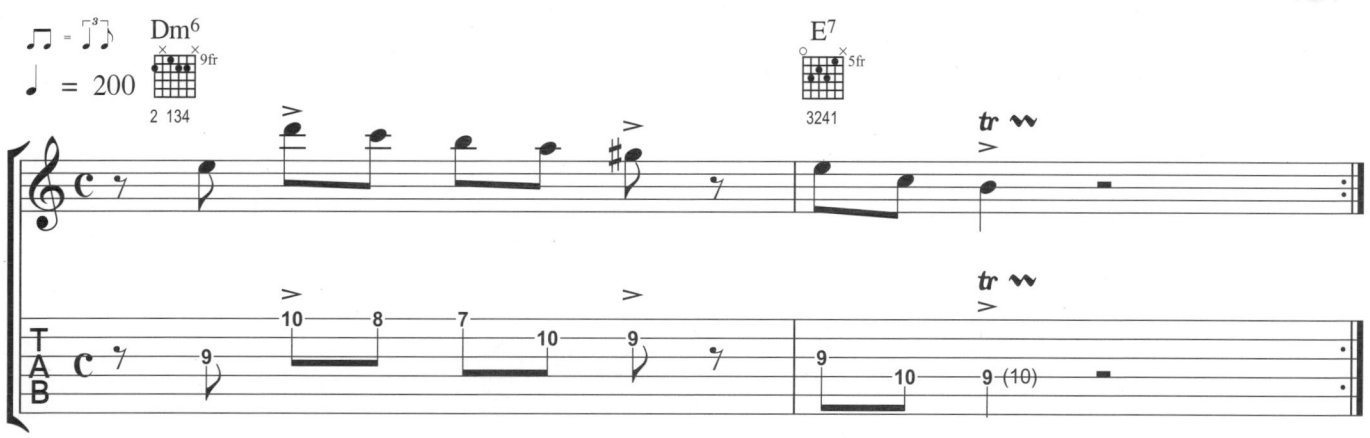

> *Tip 2:*
> *Learn to play as many songs as possible from memory (at first the rhythm and then the theme or melody).*
>
> *As a first step to learning new songs you can download many charts, TABs and transcriptions of Jazz and Gypsy Jazz songs on my website www.Jazzmanouche.de for free. Check it out!*

Lick 4/3

The third lick leads from the E major 7th chord (dominant) back to the root note (Tonic A) in Am6.

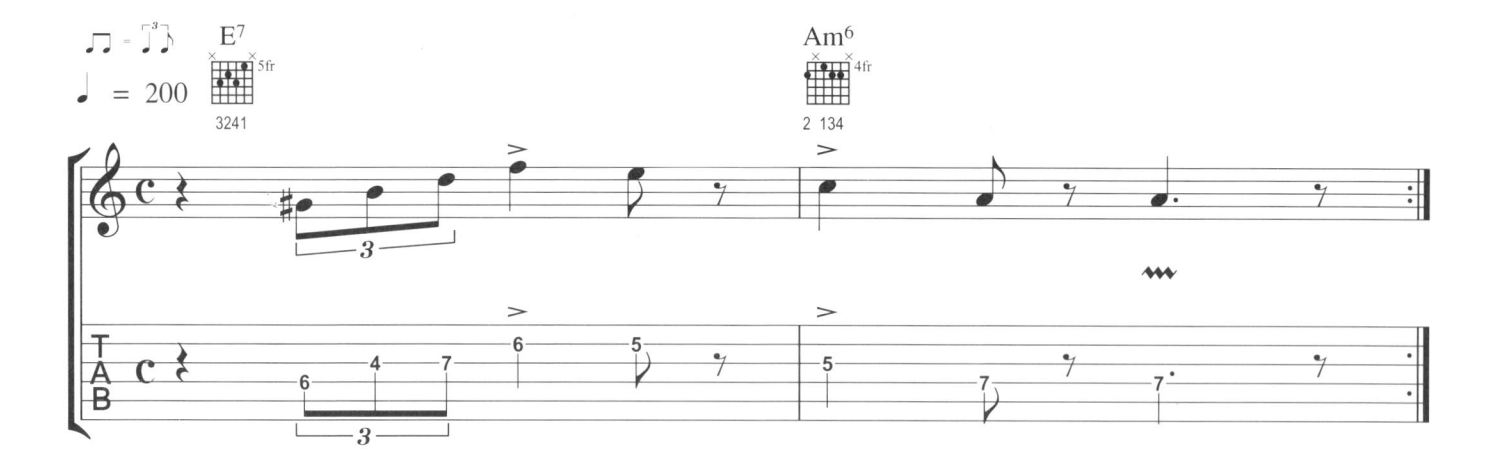

Lick 4/4

This lick illustrates the connection between the chords in great detail: from Am6 over to Dm6 and F7th back to the dominant E7th chord and again leading back to the root note (Tonic A) in Am6.

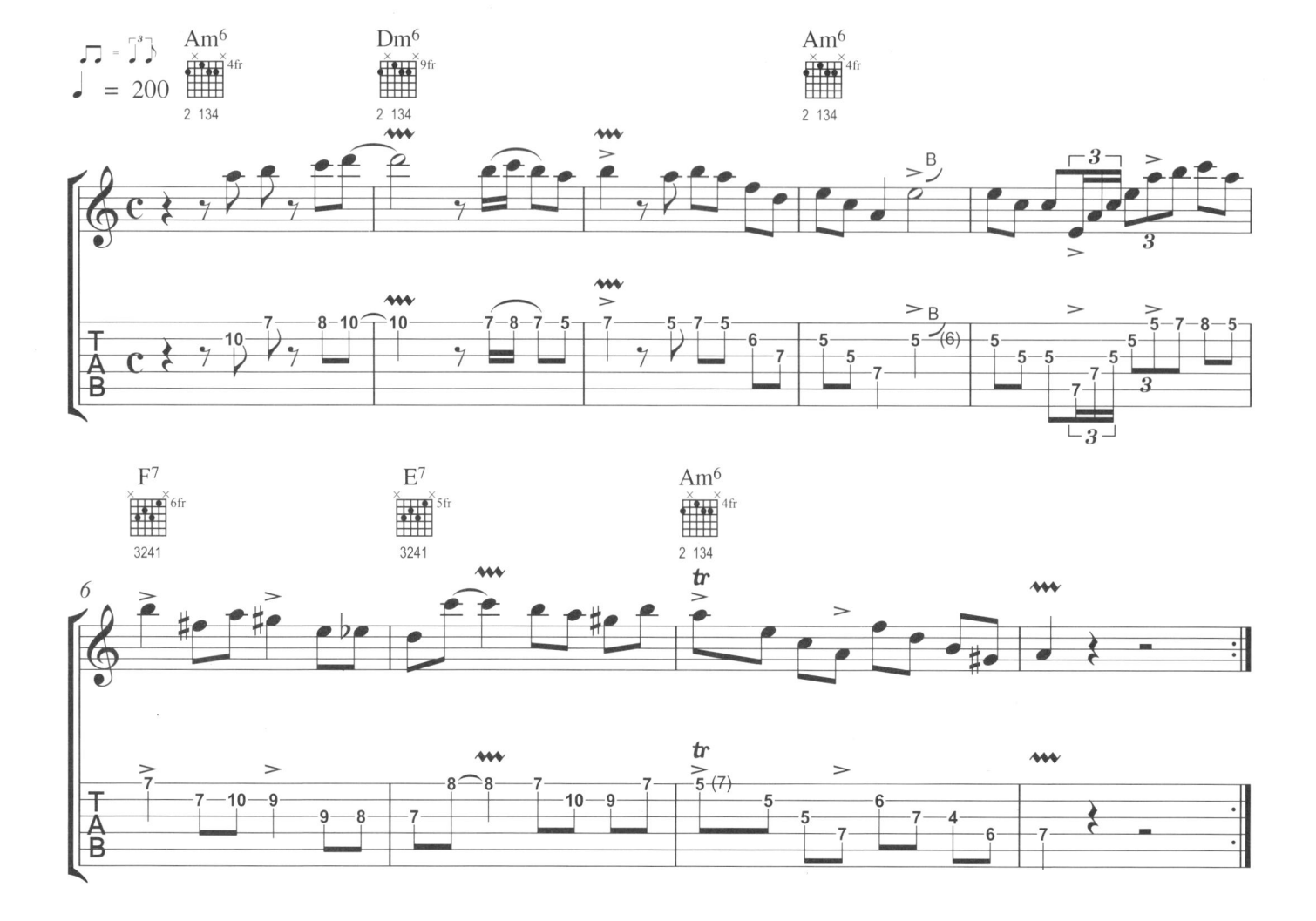

Part 2 – Solo Guitar

Lick 4/5

In the next four bars this lick connects the Am6 chord (root note) leading to the subdominant chord Dm6.

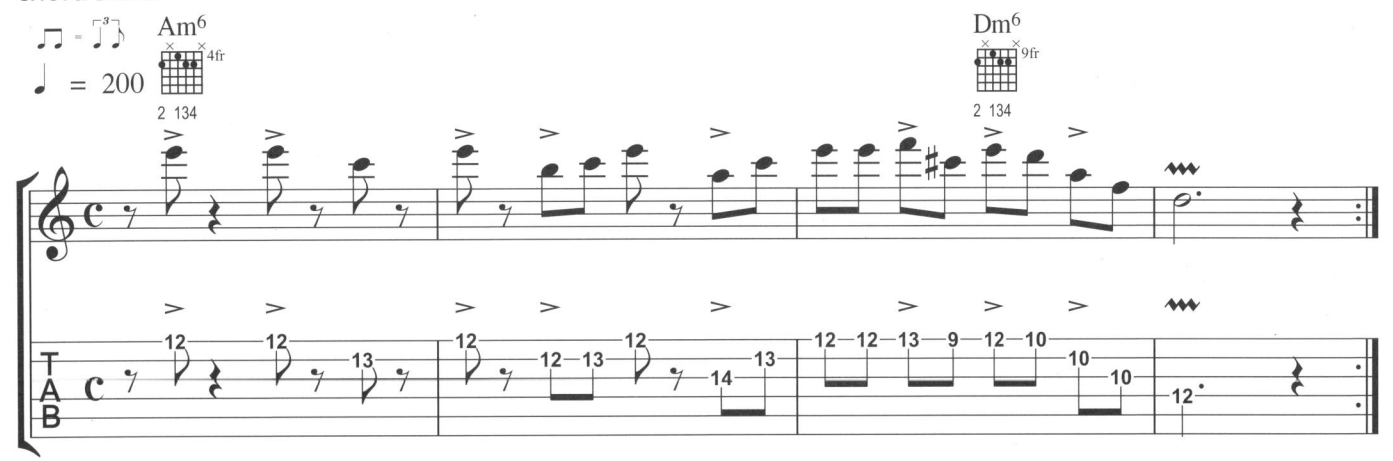

CD 48

Lick 4/6

Here are bars 11 to 14 of the solo, leading from the dominant E7 chord back to the root note (Tonic A) in Am6.

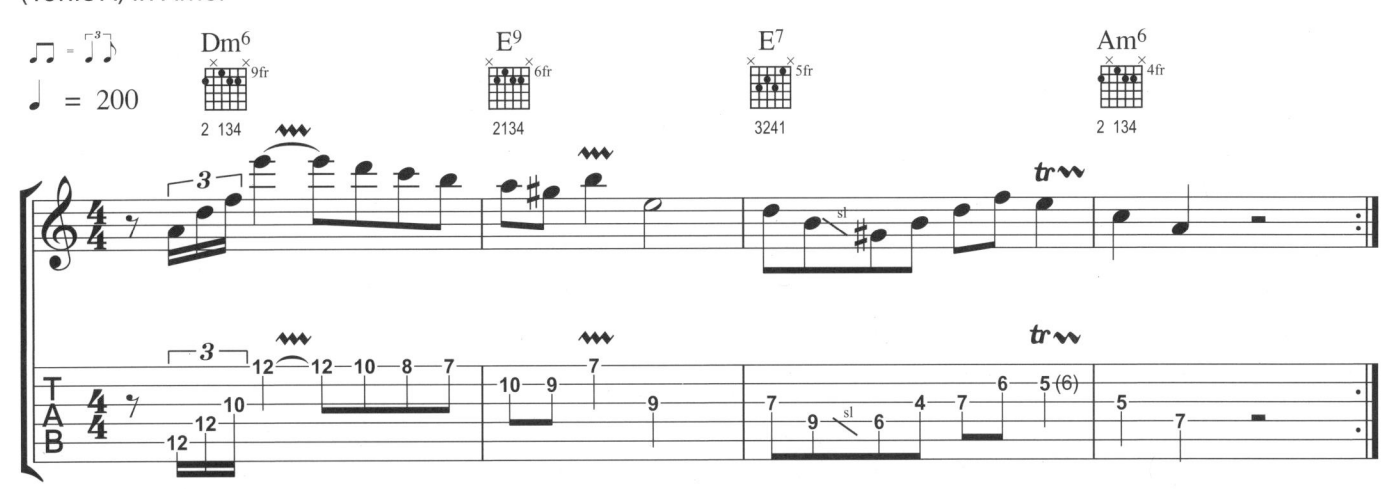

CD 49

Lick 4/7

Lick 7 again leads from the subdominant Dm6 chord back to the root note (Tonic A) in Am6.

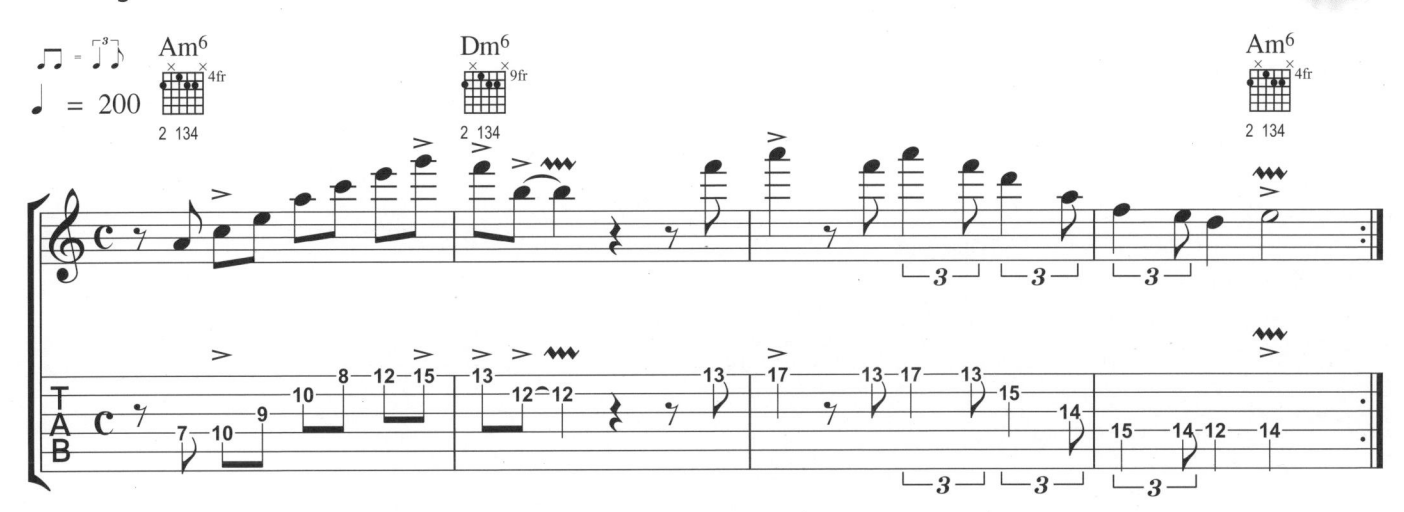

CD 50

Lick 4/8

This last lick, number eight, shows the dissolving of the dominant 7th chord change leading over from the F7th chord to E7 back to the root note in Am6 (Tonic A).

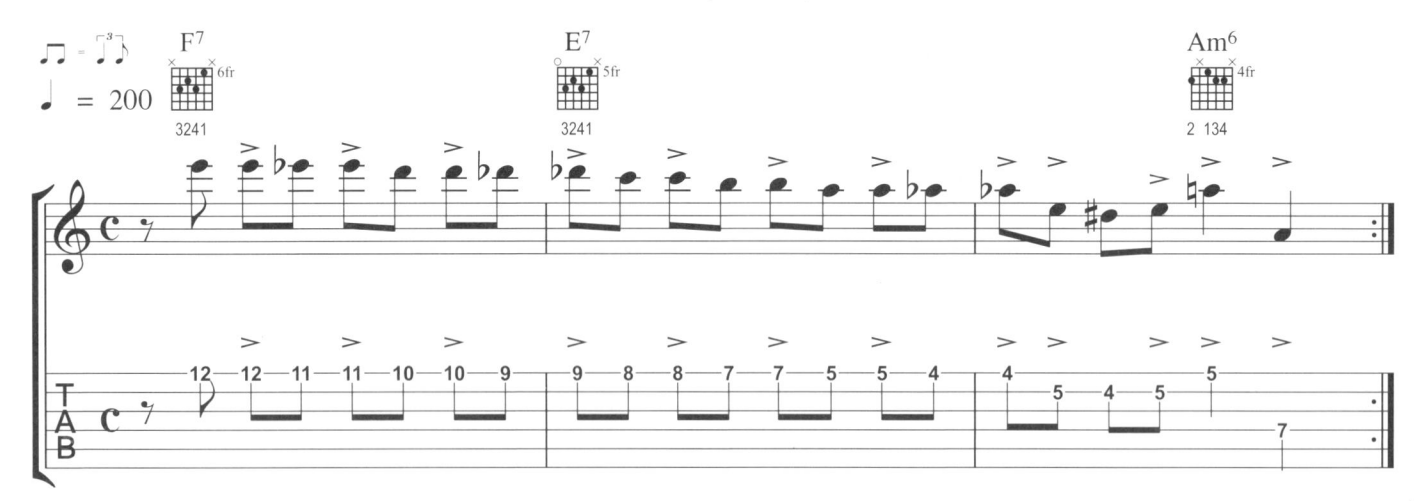

Solo transcriptions for practice

The following song transcriptions show many similarities in their structures to 'traditional' minor blues songs (the same as the licks in *Minor Swing*). These songs are intended to further help you practice your solo techniques. You will find the corresponding rhythm tracks for these songs in part one of *Rhythm Guitar* (page 40), as with the play along tracks on the included CD.

Excercise 4/9: Minor Swing (Reinhardt/Grapelli)

As the first solo example, here is the complete solo of *Minor Swing* from **Django Reinhardt's** 1937 recording. It is shown in standard notation and TAB.

All of the solo licks from *Minor Swing* that were shown in this chapter (page 85-87) can be transposed and used for soloing over the following songs:

4/10: Blues en mineur
(Reinhardt/Grapelli)
This is typical of standard minor blues in Gm and is very similar to *Minor Swing*.

4/11: Douce Ambiance
(Reinhardt/Grapelli)
A kind of minor blues due to its chord changes (almost identical to '*Blues en mineur*') but with a few very interesting chord additions and changes.

> **Tip:**
>
> *Try to use all of the techniques explained in this book (La Pompe rhythm, picking techniques, etc) with all new songs that you learn.*
>
> *By doing so you will gain a deeper understanding into the typical way of playing Gypsy Jazz and your own playing will develop. Another good idea is to take part in Gypsy swing jam sessions. This way you can practice all of your newly learned techniques as well as exchange knowledge with other musicians.*
>
> *For Gypsies (Sintis) this is a very important part of their traditions and rituals: whenever they meet somewhere, 'playing music together' is part of their every-day life and is used for sharing good times as well as strengthening the community.*

4/9 Minor Swing

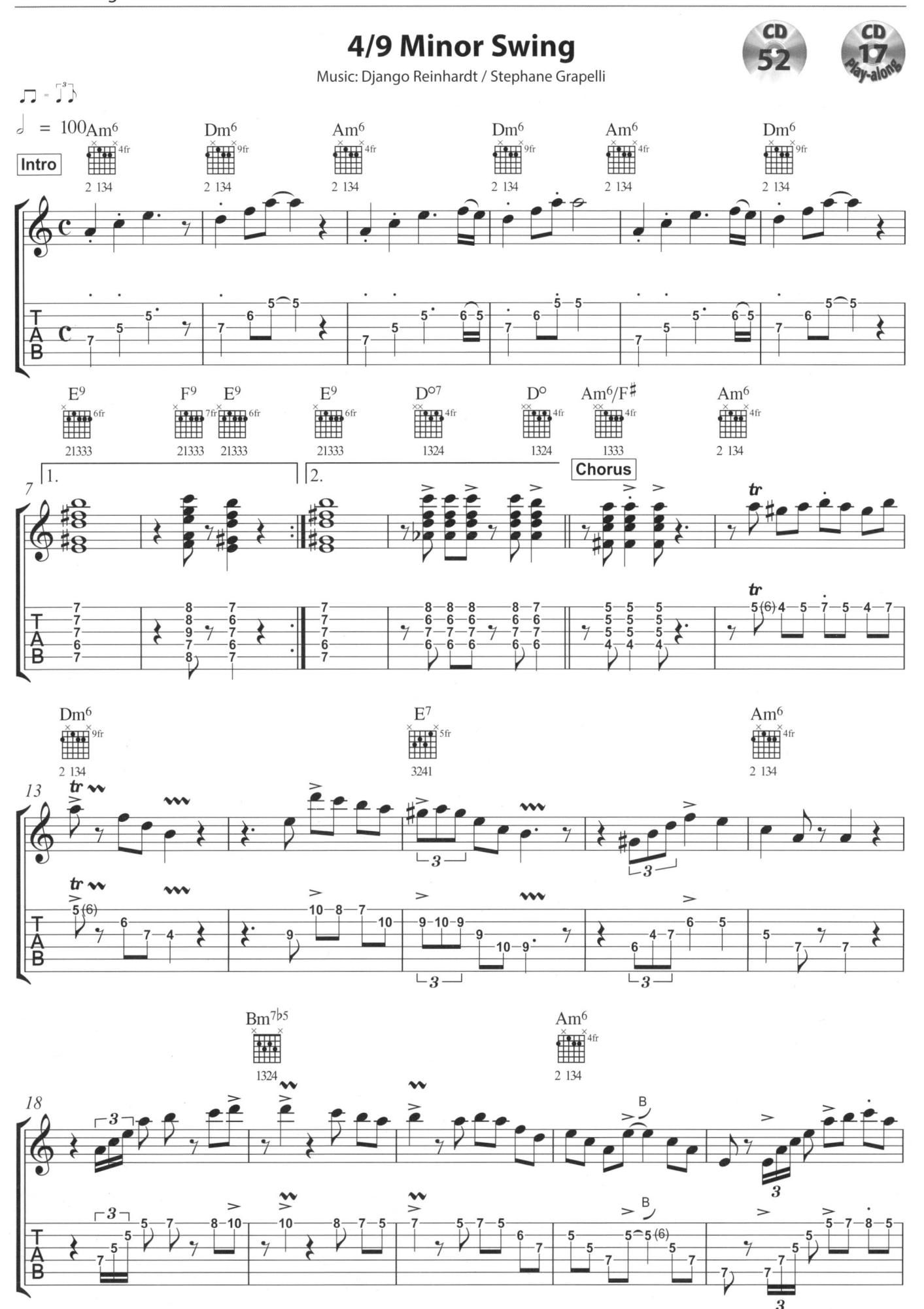

Music: Django Reinhardt / Stephane Grapelli

F7
6fr
3241
E7
5fr
3241
Am6
4fr
2 134
23
TAB
Dm6
9fr
2 134
E7
5fr
3241
28
Am6
4fr
2 134
A7
5fr
1 243
Dm6
9fr
2 134
Am6
4fr
2 134
33
F7
6fr
3241
E7
5fr
3241
Am6
4fr
2 134
38

Minor Swing – Solo Guitar

Dm6/B
Cm6/A
Gm6/E
F♯m6/D♯
Fm6/D
Em6/C♯
D♯m6/C
C♯m6/A♯
Bm6/G♯
Am6/F♯
1333
61
sl
Gm6/E
E7
3241
62
let ring
Am6
2 134
Dm6
65
tr
B
Am6
F7
69

Minor Swing – Solo Guitar

"Talent works, genius creates ..."

(Robert Schumann)

4/10 Blues en mineur

Music: Django Reinhardt / Stephane Grapelli

E♭9
21333
D9
21333
Gm6
2 134
D7♯9
2134
17
let ring
TAB
Gm6
2 134
21
(Harm.)
Cm6
2 134
Gm6
2 134
25
E♭7
3241
D7
3241
Gm6
2 134
D9
21333
D7
3241
29

Blues en mineur – Solo Guitar

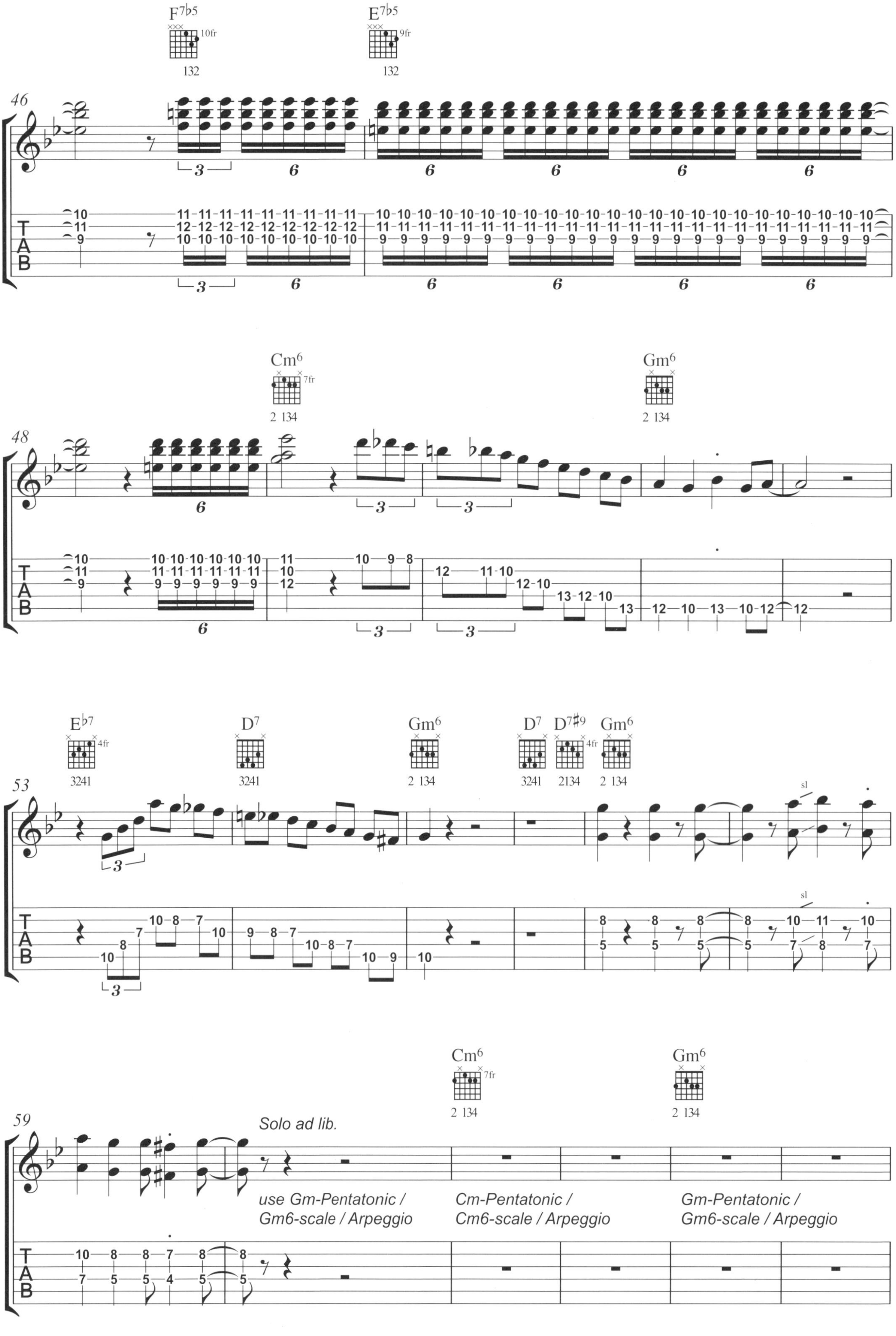
F7♭5
E7♭5
Cm6
Gm6
E♭7
D7
Gm6
D7
D7♯9
Gm6
Solo ad lib.
Cm6
Gm6
use Gm-Pentatonic / Gm6-scale / Arpeggio
Cm-Pentatonic / Cm6-scale / Arpeggio
Gm-Pentatonic / Gm6-scale / Arpeggio

Blues en mineur – Solo Guitar

4/11 Douce Ambiance

Music: Django Reinhardt

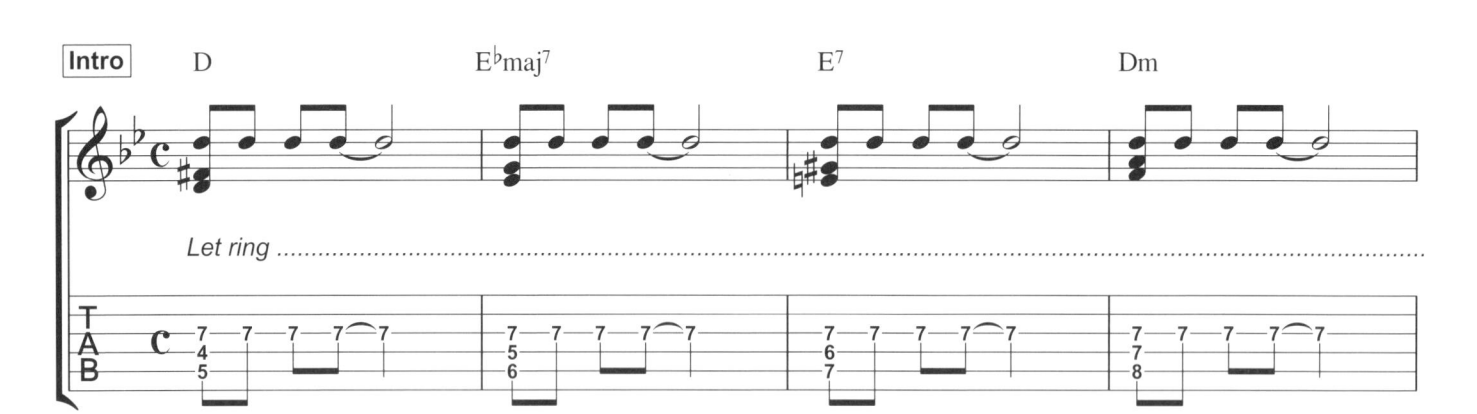

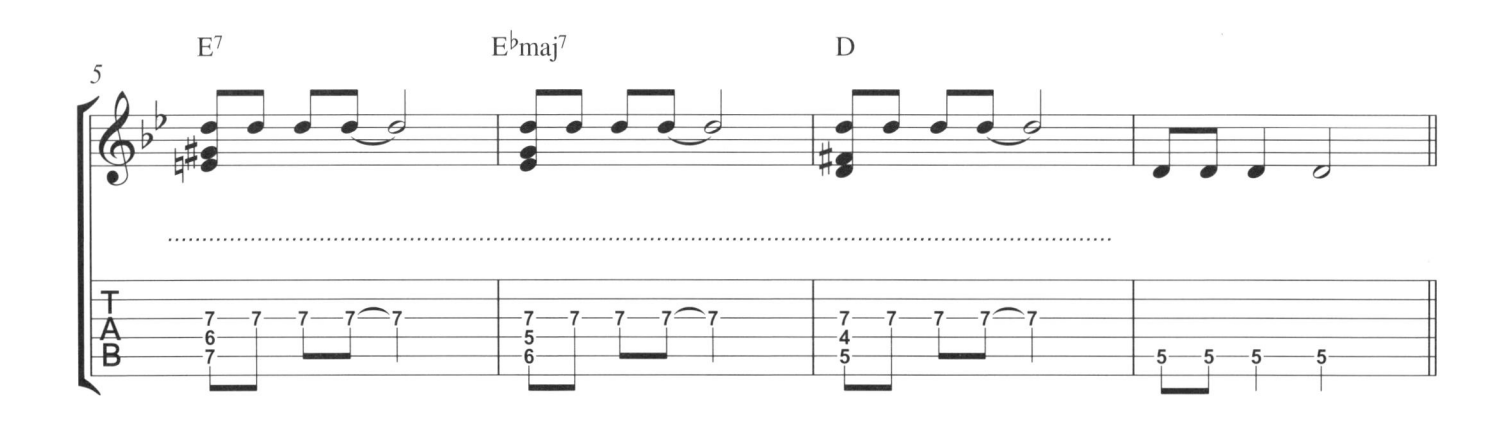

♩ = 100

Douce Ambiance – Solo Guitar

Gypsy Jazz Guitar

Part A (m. 33)

Chords: Gm6 | Gm6 | Gm6 | Gm6

(m. 37) Cm6 | Gm6 | Eb7 D7 | Gm6

Solo (m. 41)

Gm6 | | | Cm6 Gm6 | Eb9 D9

Solo ad lib. - use Gm-Pentatonic / Gm6-scale / Cm-Pentatonic / Cm6-Scale / F# dim.-scale / A dim.-scale

(m. 49) Gm6 | | | Cm6 Gm6 | Eb7 D7 Gm6

use arpeggios over Gm6 / Cm-Pentatonic / Eb7 / D7

(m. 57) Abm6 | | | Am6 | Ebo E9 Dbo Db9 D9

use Lick 5/2, 5/3, 5/5 (transposed)

Douce Ambiance – Solo Guitar

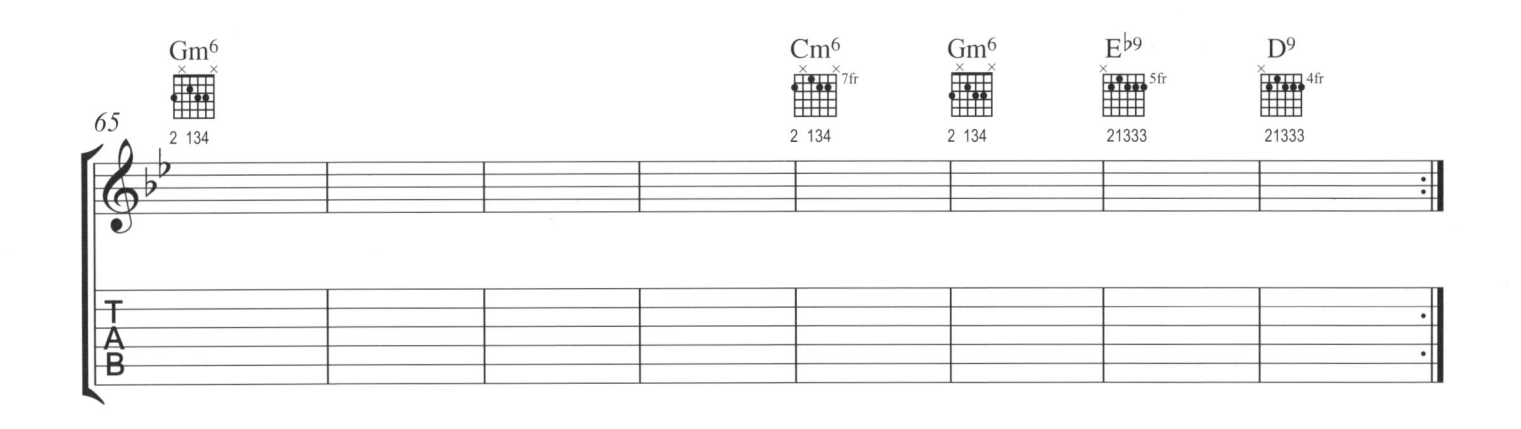

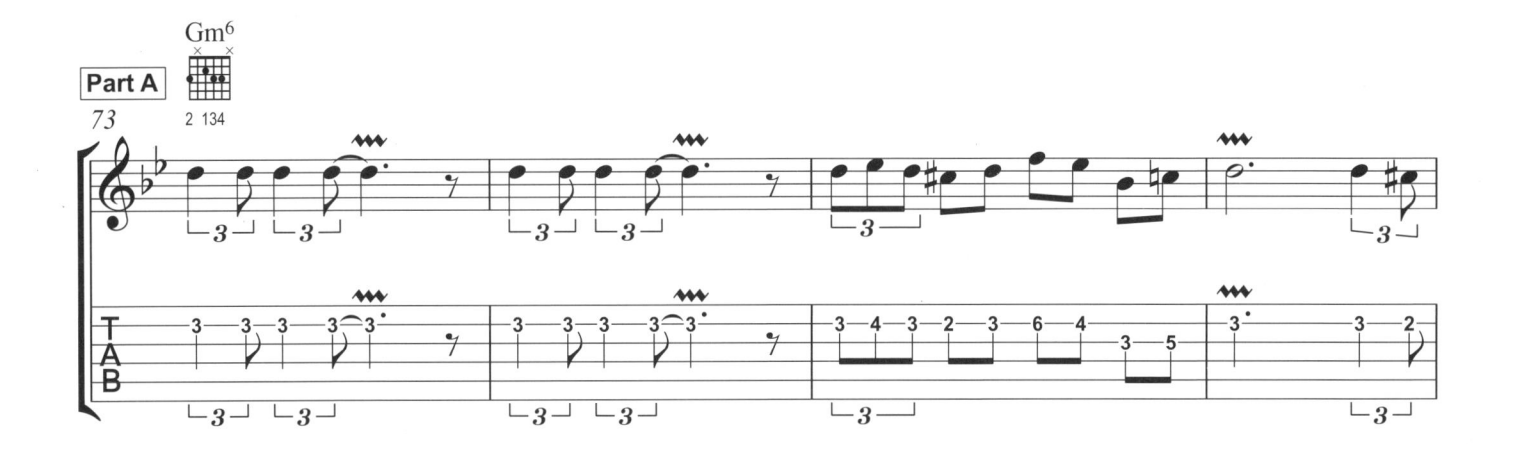

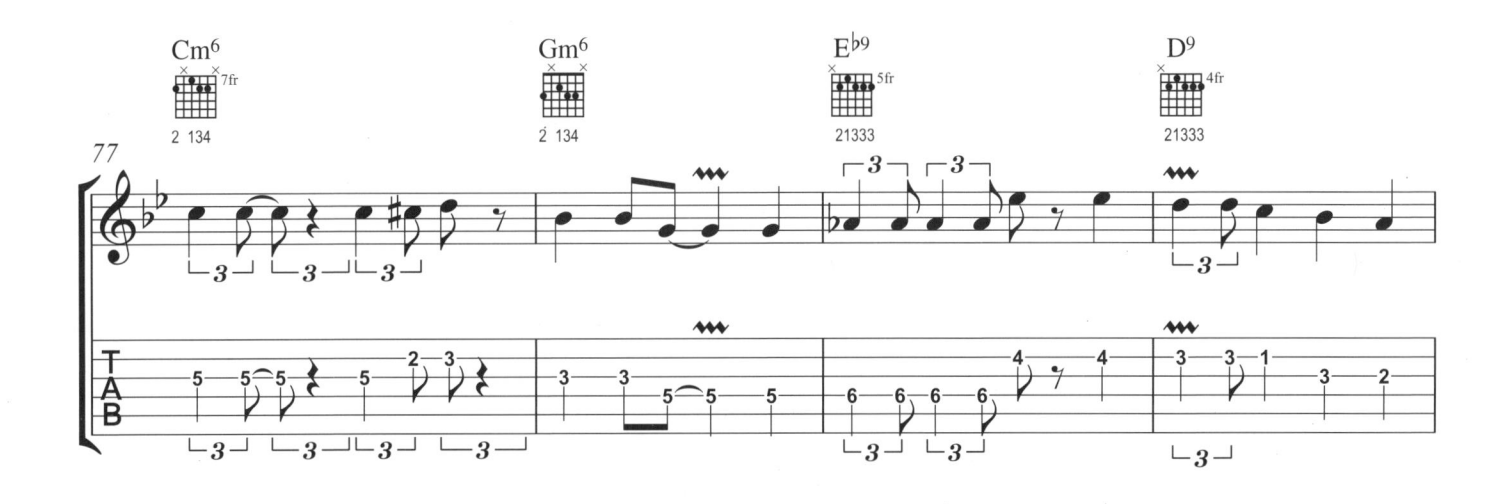

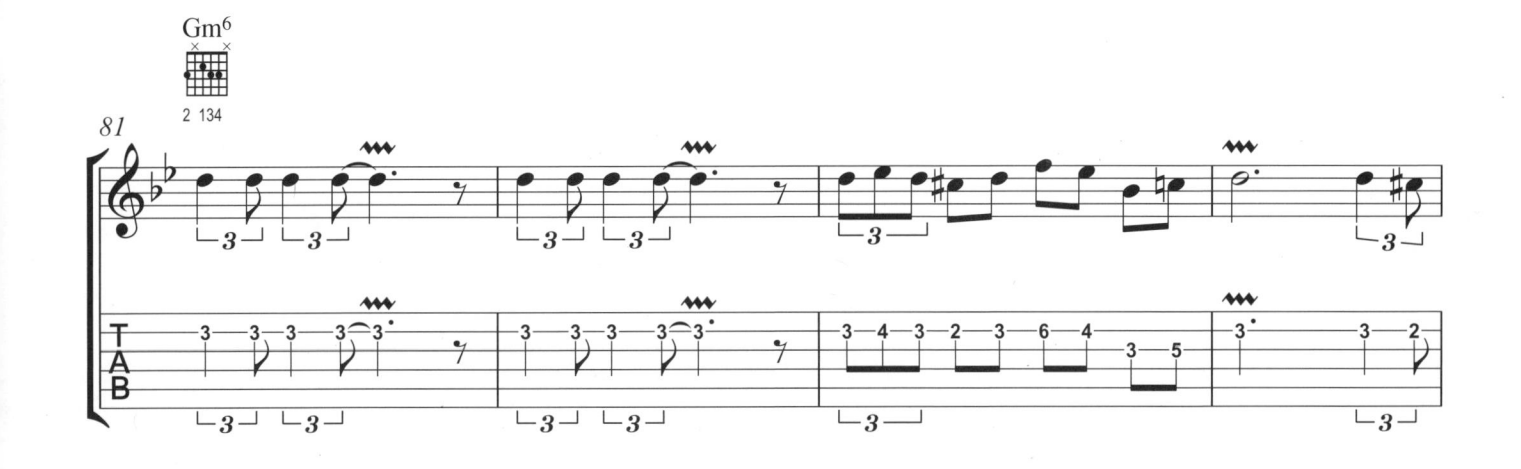

Cm6
Gm6
E♭7
D7
Gm6
E♭9
D9
Gm6
gliss.
E♭9
D9
Gm6
gliss.
Outro
D
E♭maj7
E7
Dm
Let ring
E7
E♭maj7
D
Gm

Part 2 – Solo Guitar

5. Tips & Tricks

In this part of Introducing Solo Guitar, I'm going to show you some useful tricks, scales and arpeggios that are often used in *Gypsy Jazz*.

> *Tip:*
>
> *All the tricks, arpeggios and scales used in chapter 5 can (of course!) be transposed and used in all the other keys that exist!*
>
> *Always learn to play licks and scales in ALL the keys there are as you will never know which key or song you will need them in whilst improvising!*
>
> *If you wish to learn more I would recommend my LIVE Masterclass for Gypsy Jazz Guitar. In this workshop I show many more of these techniques, focus more intensely on them and can personally advise you.*
>
> *More information can be found at www.gypsyJazzworkshop.net (see Workshops)*

Lick 5/1

This lick shows a kind of '*trill*' effect. It is a very common technique and is often used in *Gypsy Jazz* to play 'around' certain notes, often the root-note. This trick really belongs in the standard repertoire of any *Gypsy Jazz* guitarist.

CD 55

Lick 5/2

This one shows an arpeggio in Am. This lick is often added to the end of a phrase, mostly when returning to the root-note of a solo (in this case the root-note A).

CD 56

Lick 5/3

This is another arpeggio in Am with the typical surrounding of the root-note used in *Gypsy Jazz*.

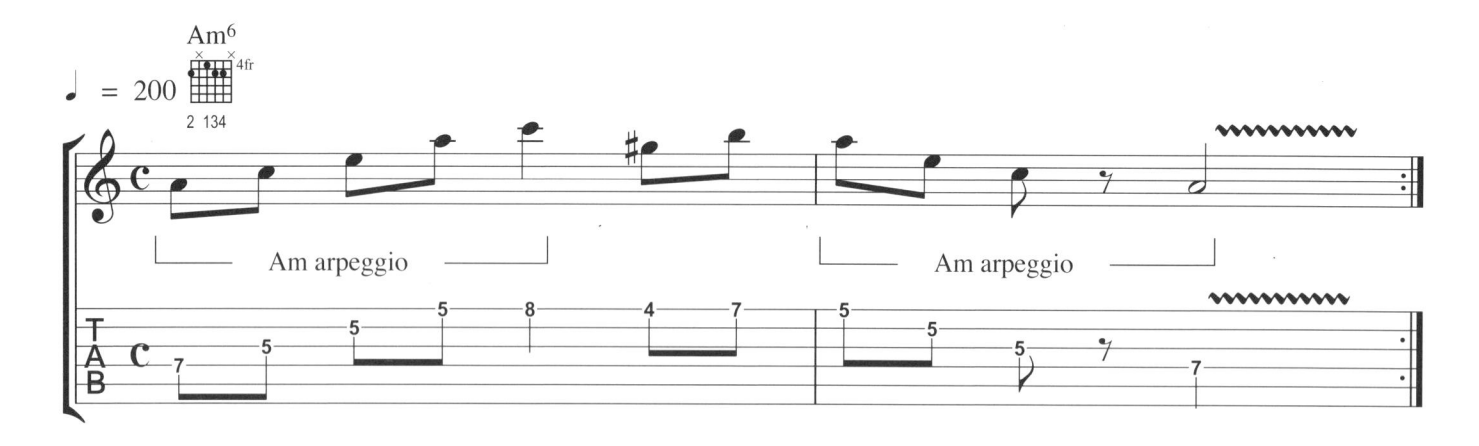

Lick 5/4

This shows a lick in Gm6 but played over a C7add-9 chord. It is very common in *Gypsy Jazz* to play any minor 6 arpeggio or lick over any related dominant seventh or ninth chord.

Lick 5/5

This shows an ascending lick in D harmonic minor with an added D minor arpeggio over two octaves.

Part 2 – Solo Guitar

Lick 5/6

This is an example of how to use a harmonic minor scale (Dm) played over a seventh chord (A7).
Be sure to end on the triad! This is another trick that any *Gypsy Jazz* guitarist should have in their repertoire.

Lick 5/7

This is another lick with a trill surrounding effect, similar to the one in example 5/1.

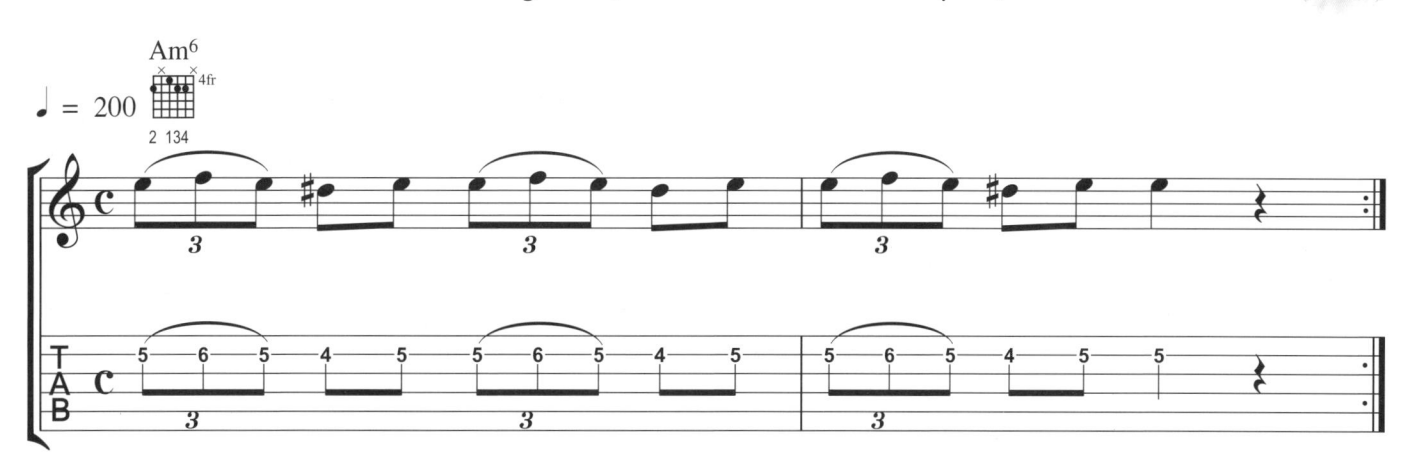

"You don't need any brains to listen to music"

(Luciano Pavarotti)

6. Scales – Part 2

As mentioned earlier in the book, scales are the basic connections between keys in almost any kind of music ('*Introducing Solo Guitar Lesson One*', page 79). Because of this it is vital for every musician to gain as much knowledge about them as possible and to practice them regularly. Some of you may already know the following scales, particularly if you have regularly played blues guitar (if this is the case you could leave out the following exercises).

An important feature of the blues scales (generally used in standard blues as well as Jazz) which will be shown next, is the addition into a regular pentatonic scale of added half tone steps (flatted fifth = b5) between the fourth and fifth note, also called 'Blue Note'. The scales shown will be used in this way in *Gypsy Jazz*.

Tip:

Blue notes are certain tones that create the typical blues character of melodies. These are: the minor third note, the seventh and/or the diminished fifth note of a scale.

The intonation of the notes separates from the typical sound of the western sound system.

Normally the third note (triad) is intonated by major or minor third, the seventh note with major or minor seventh and the fifth note between diminished and clear fifth notes (on the guitar often also played with the bending technique).

Important note: When improvising with these scales, it is very important to play them with the very swing-sounding triplet accents! To use the scales on one of the song examples (e.g. Play-Along tracks on the audio CD) you should be able to play them at a medium tempo of 120-150 BPM fluently forwards and backwards.

Scale 6/1 Minor pentatonic scale in C minor

This example shows a standard pentatonic scale in C minor. This scale, often known from blues, is reduced to five tones (*penta* = Greek, meaning '*five*'). Pentatonic scales may be used as short connections between other scales or arpeggios in *Gypsy Jazz*. The main benefit of this scale is that it is easily playable and besides that, as it is reduced to five tones by leaving off the regular half tone steps of usual major and minor scales, it may be used on both major and minor chords making it a very useful scale in any key.

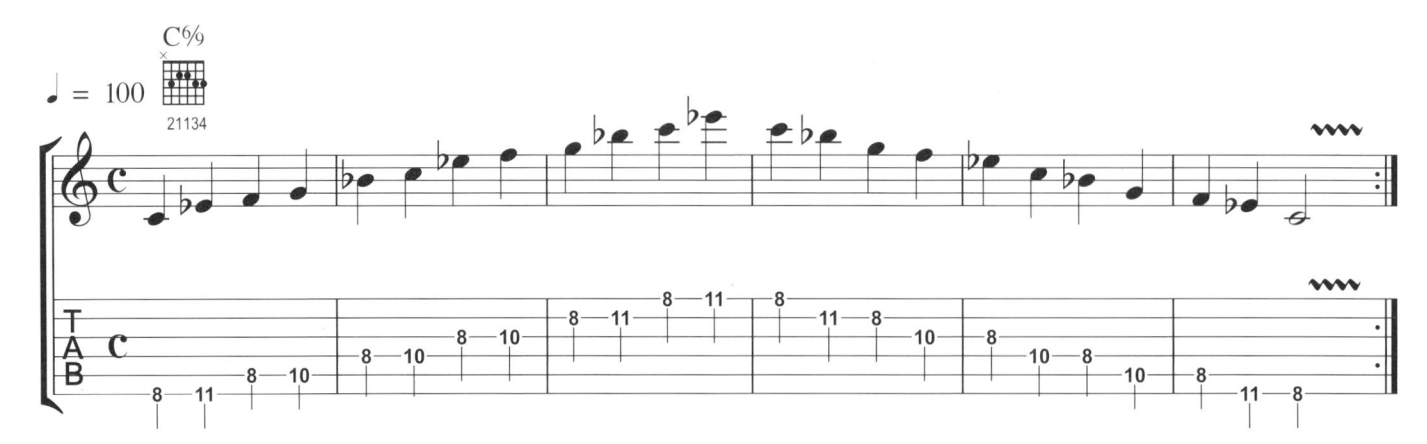

Scale 6/2 Minor-Pentatonic-scale in C with added *Blue Note* (add♭5)

In this example you can see an extended pentatonic scale (from 6/1) with an added blue note (B.N) between the fourth and fifth note (= add b5).

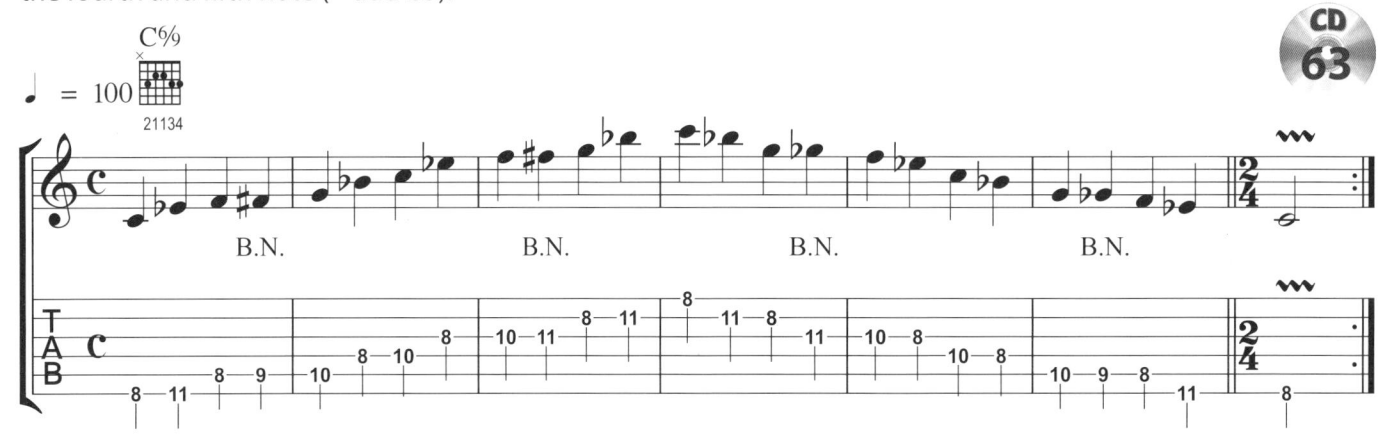

Part 2 – Solo Guitar 109

Scale 6/3 Minor pentatonic scale in C (over three octaves)

The following example extends the standard pentatonic scale about three more added positions (octaves) over the fretboard.

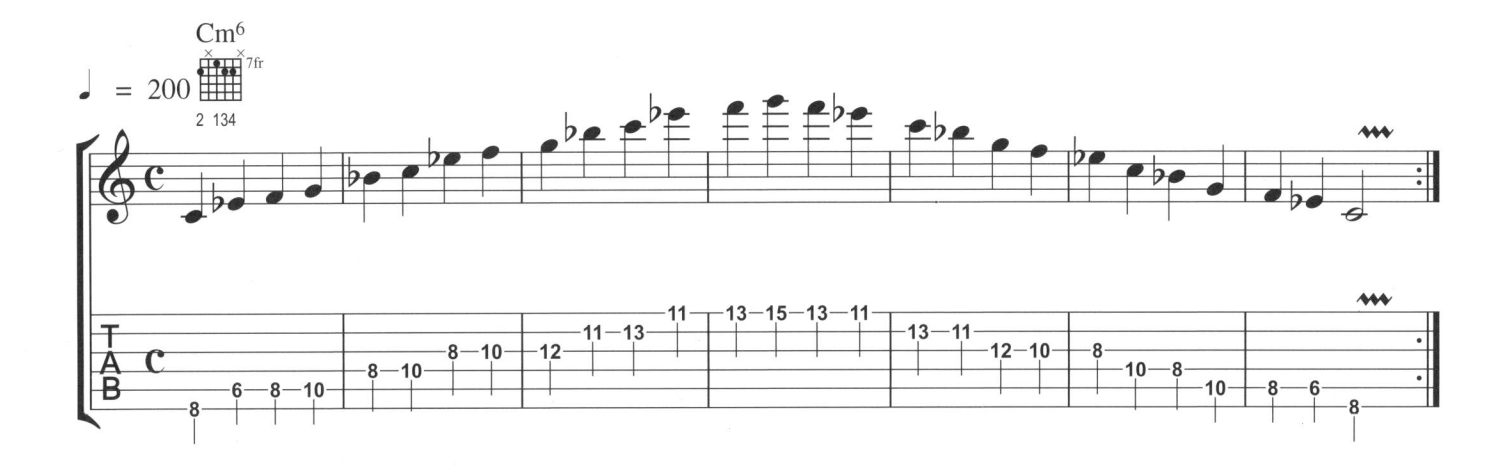

CD 64

Scale 6/4 The blues scale in C

This example (also known as the 'blues scale') is, in principle, the same scale as the one shown in example 6/3 as an extended standard pentatonic scale, but this time with added blue notes (B.N).

CD 65

Scale 6/5 The harmonic minor scale in A

As a last example for scales that are typically used in *Gypsy Jazz*, here is a harmonic minor scale in A minor. The harmonic minor scale is one of the most used scales in *Gypsy Jazz*. The major seventh note (maj7 = G# instead of G) inside of a regular minor scale creates this kind of slightly 'oriental' sound, which is very typical of *Jazz-Manouche* (see *Lick 5/6*, page 107).

7. The Use of Scales and Arpeggios in Gypsy Jazz

As we have seen in the previous chapters, scales and arpeggios are cornerstones for solo playing in *Gypsy Jazz*.

In this chapter, and for finishing the section on Introducing Solo Guitar, I will show you some more practical examples of how scales and arpeggios are typically used by *Gypsy Jazz* guitarists today and in the past by musicians such as **Django Reinhardt, Romane, Lollo Meier** or **Stochelo Rosenberg**.

These examples are very useful for practicing your solo technique as well as improvising over all of the Play-Along songs in this book and on the audio CD.

Tip:

In Gypsy-Jazz different scales are being used depending on the way of playing the style (modern, bebop, swing): minor 6 scales, diminished scales, major 7th scales, major 9th scales as well as regular pentatonic scales with or without added blue notes, whole tone scales or a mix of it all – the Gypsy Jazz repertoire is particularly full and rich – so really creativity rules!

As well as the scales, arpeggios have a great deal of importance in Gypsy Jazz, particularly those invented by Django Reinhardt with his outstanding way of playing certain voicings. Nowadays, some Gypsy Jazz guitarists play the style in a more contemporary way – they use 'modal' Jazz playing. Modal playing uses changed steps of scales and arpeggios of the basic C major scale, for example, playing a Dm arpeggio over a C major 7th chord.

The truth is Gypsy Jazz is at the highest technical level of guitar playing, using almost all of the guitar techniques that are known and commonly used today.

Part 2 – *Solo Guitar*

Example 7/1 Cm6 arpeggio in Django style

The first example shows a C minor6 arpeggio (over a C minor6 chord) like you can hear in
Django Reinhardt's interpretation of the song *'Blues en mineur'* (bar 5-7 of his solo).
Django often used this kind of minor6 arpeggios especially in a substituted way – as over major chords.

Example 7/2 Gm scale in Django style

The following example of a trill with an added G minor scale was used by *Django* in *'Douce Ambiance'*.
He surrounds the fifth note (D) and then ends his lick in Gm.

The technique of surrounding notes is very typical of *Gypsy Jazz* (see *Lick 5/1* in *Tips and Tricks*, page 105).

Example 7/3 Dm6 arpeggio in Django style

This example shows a chromatic surrounding of the note (E) at the beginning of the lick, something that
Django used very often in his solos (here in *'Anniversary Song'*). The lick then extends into a bidirectional
Dm6 arpeggio which *Django* at first played upwards and then downwards to finally end with a short Am arpeggio.
This changing of direction within a solo is also very typical of *Gypsy Jazz*.

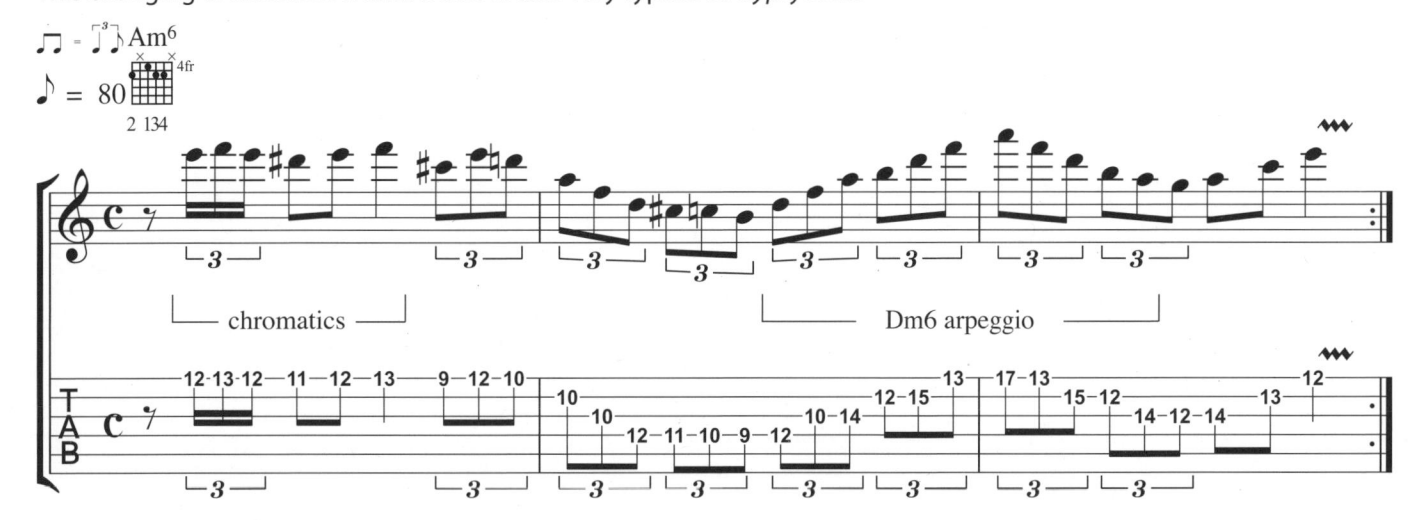

Example 7/4 Dm arpeggio in Lollo Meier style

Here is an example in the style of the Dutch Gypsy guitarist **Lollo Meier** as you can hear in his solo from '*Some of these Days*' (on his album '*Rosas*'). He begins with a typical surrounding, adding a chromatic scale downwards, ending the lick with a typical minor arpeggio over D-minor (see *Arpeggios, Lesson 3/7*, page 84).

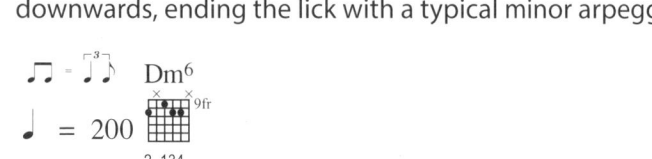

Example 7/5 Diminished scale in Lollo Meier style

In his solos, **Lollo Meier** often likes to use the following typical diminished scale that, in this example, he ends into a straight D minor arpeggio (excerpt is from '*Some of these Days*').

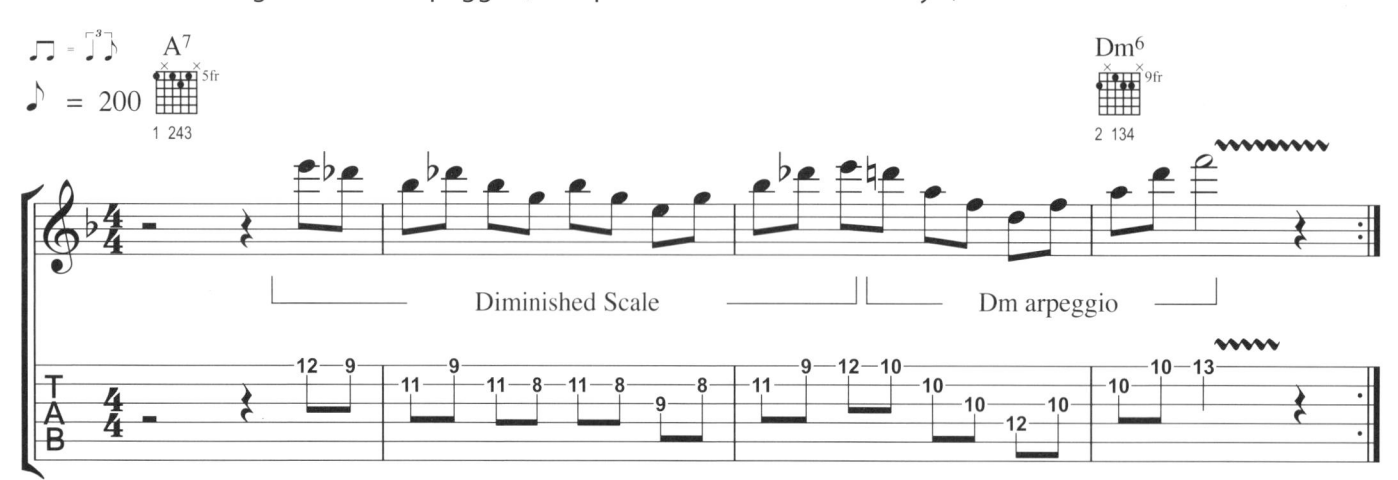

Example 7/6 Harmonic minor in Django style

You can hear very typical examples of connecting scales and arpeggios with solos in many of **Django Reinhardt's** solos (in this example, '*Swing 48*'). He starts off this solo with a chromatic scale, transforms it into a harmonic minor scale in Gm before the second bar and then again changed his lick into a Gm arpeggio to finally end with a diminished arpeggio in A over the Gm6 chord in the third bar.

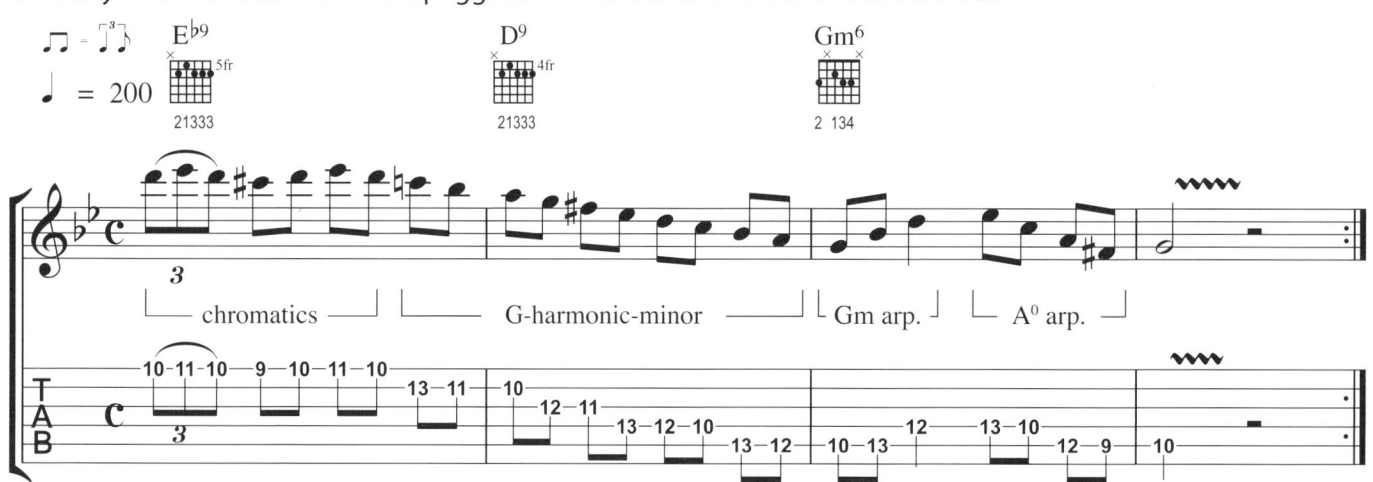

Part 2 – Solo Guitar

Example 7/7 C major arpeggio in Django style

CD 73

A typical C major arpeggio (C shape) in the style of *Django Reinhardt's* interpretation of *Duke Ellington's* 'It Don't Mean A Thing'.

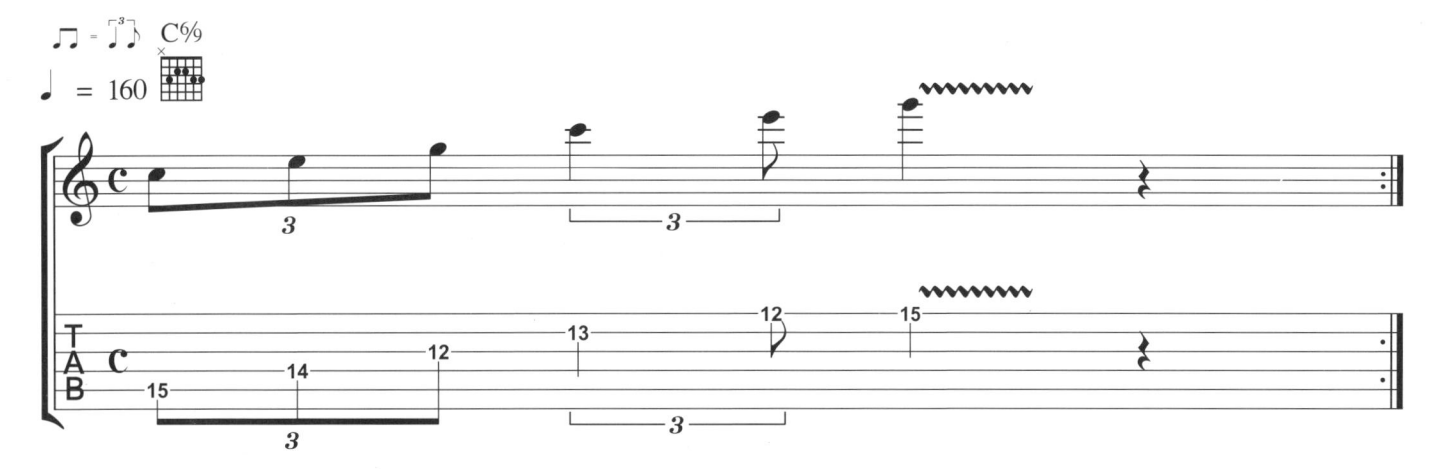

Example 7/8 Arpeggio Repetitions in Django style

CD 74

This is a good example of how *Django* used to play arpeggios: he would connect repetitions of arpeggios one after another. This example is a Dm arpeggio (excerpt from '*Blue Drag*').

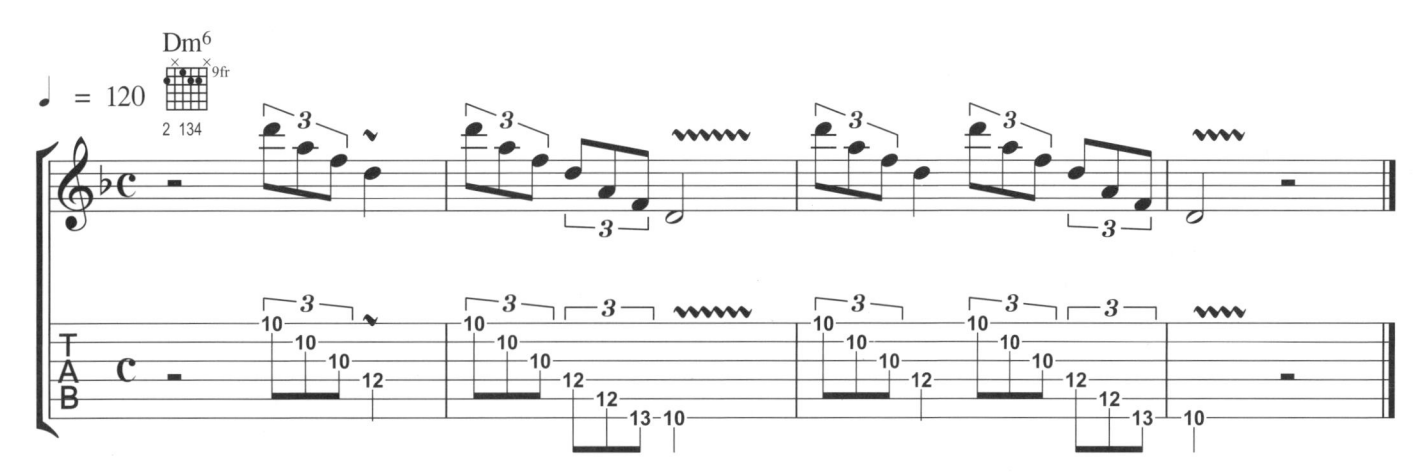

Example 7/9 Chord Substitution in Django style

CD 75

This is an example of a very typical solo substitution in *Gypsy Jazz*: a D minor6 arpeggio will be played over a G major7 add9 chord. As in the example before, *Django* repeats the figure a few times to end it on the sixth note of the song (to hear in *Django Reinhardt's* version of the song '*Undecided*').

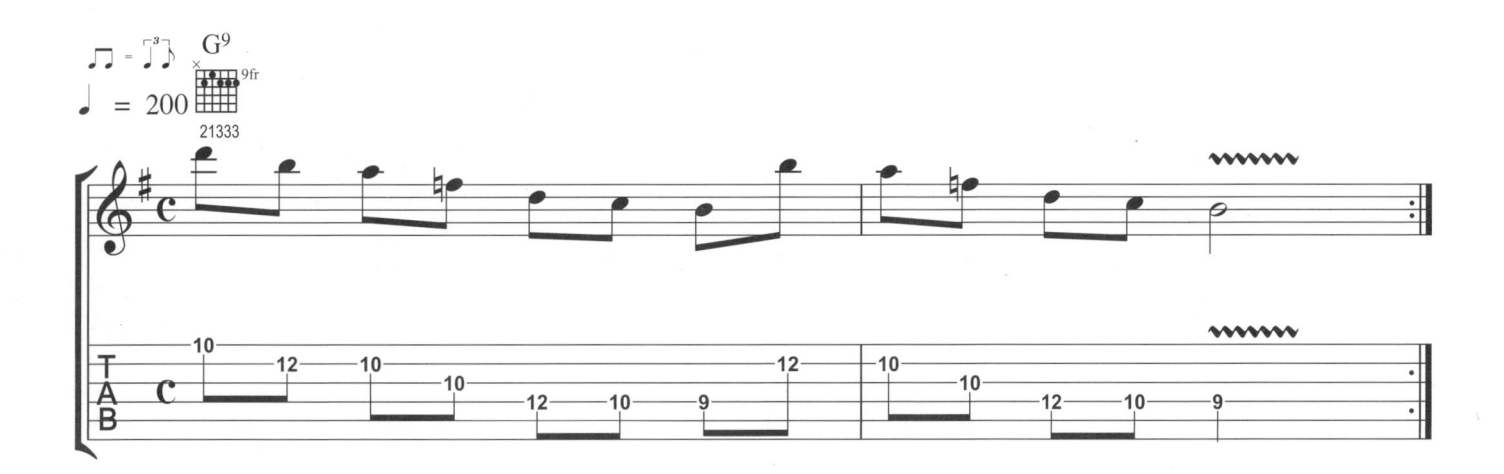

Example 7/10 Arpeggio sequences in Romane style

This example illustrates well the connecting of different arpeggios. In this example the connecting of the chords Dm6 and Am6, like the French *Gypsy Jazz* guitar maestro **Romane** played in his version of the French waltz *'Passion'* on his album *'Swingin' in Nashville'*.

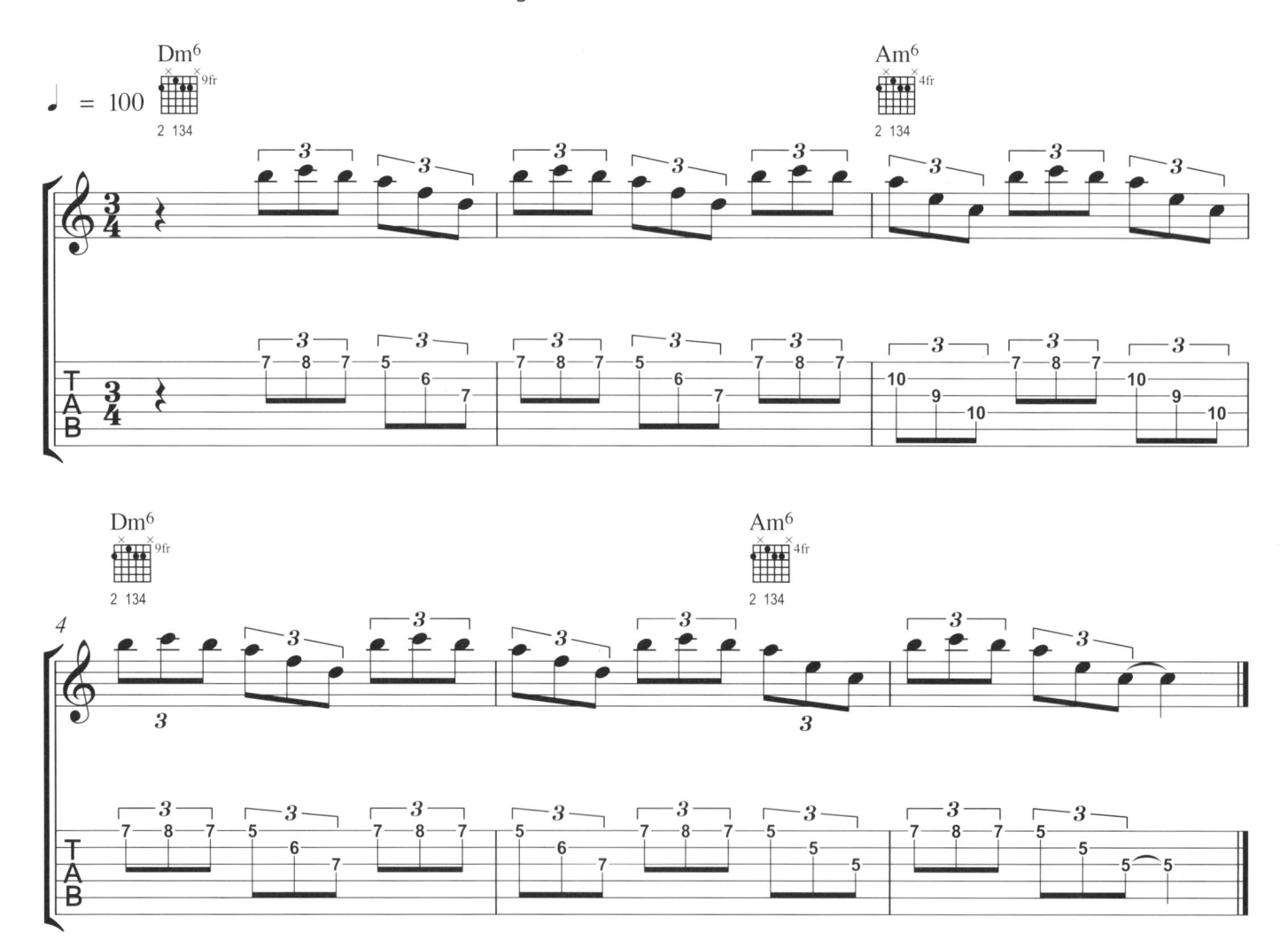

Example 7/11 Combination of scales and arpeggios in Lollo Meier style

Again, another example of connecting scales and arpeggios as **Lollo Meier** played in his solo from *'What's this thing called love?'* After a chromatic surrounding in the beginning of the lick, he adds a diminished scale in E° to again change this one into an F minor6 arpeggio at the end of the second bar.

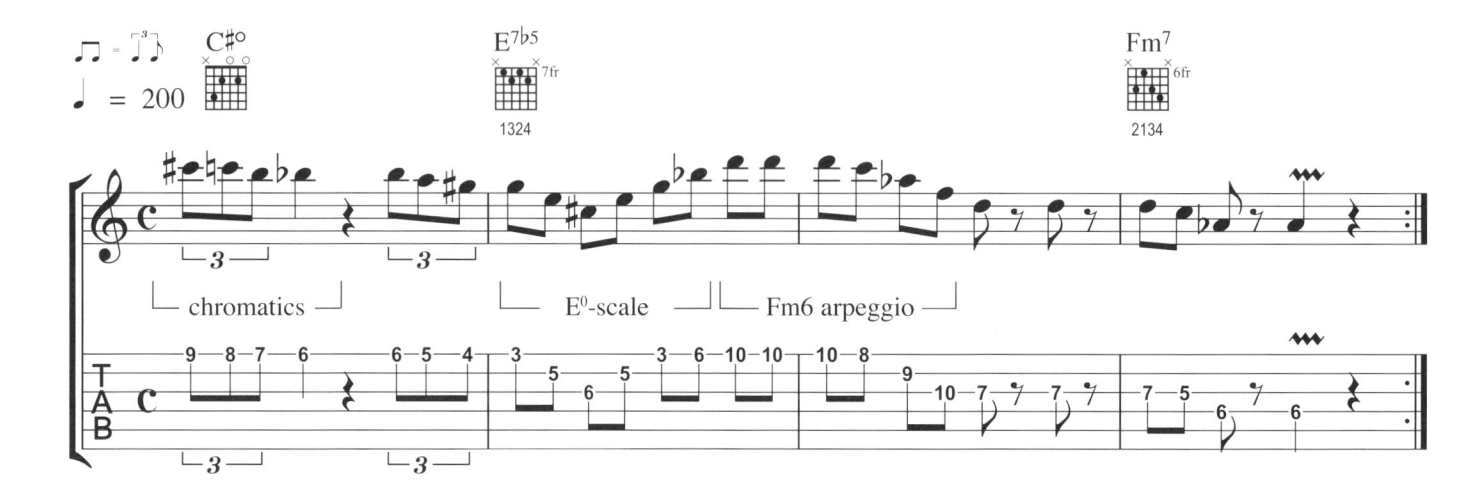

Part 2 – Solo Guitar 115

Example 7/12 Diminished scales in Stochelo Rosenberg style

This example shows the extensive use and connecting of different diminished scales in *Gypsy Jazz*. **Stochelo Rosenberg's** solo in **Reinhardt's** *'Song D'Automne'* is a good example of this.

Stochelo begins with a typical diminished scale in A°, changes it (at the end of the second bar) into a diminished scale in B°, then in bar four starts again with a short chromatic scale into another diminished scale in G°, which the then ends by surrounding the root note of the following F minor7 chord. These 'repeated changes' and surrounding notes are very common in *Gypsy Jazz*.

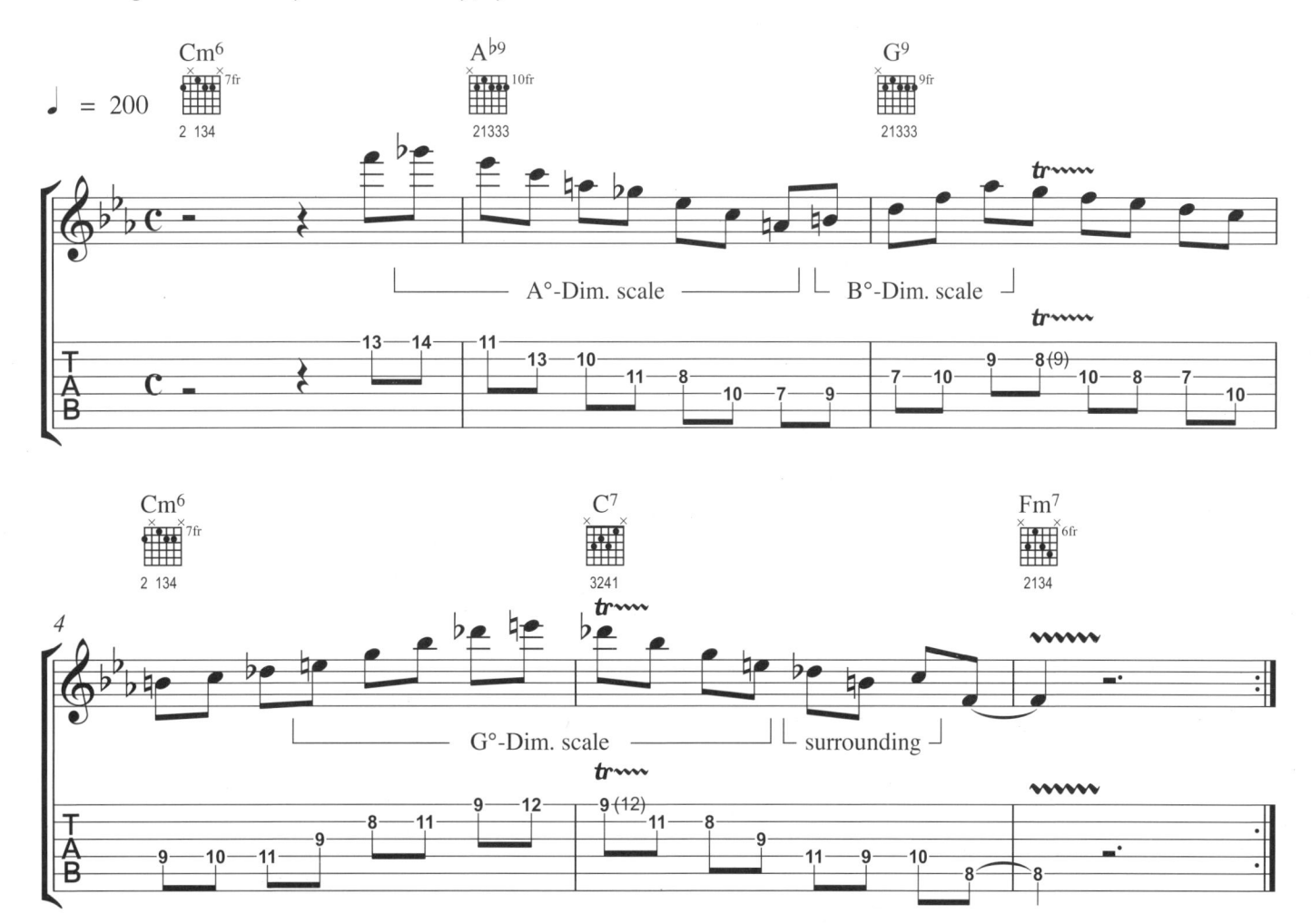

Example 7/13 Cm6 arpeggio in Django style

This last example shows a simple C minor6 arpeggio which was typical for **Django** and which many other *Gypsy Jazz* guitarists often like to use. Stochelo Rosenberg plays such a simple arpeggio exactly in the way **Django** did, in his own version of *'Song D'Automne'*.

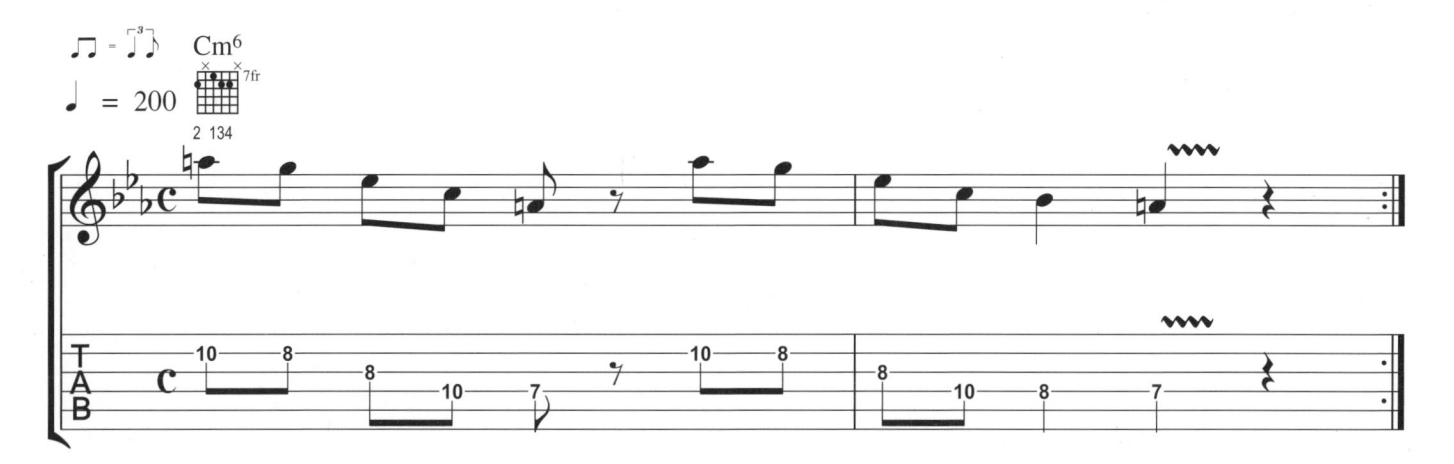

Solo Transcriptions for Practice (2)

As we have now included more arpeggios, tricks and scales (in chapters 4-7, 'Tips and Tricks', 'Scales Part 2' and 'Use of Scales and Arpeggios in *Gypsy Jazz*') into our solo technique, I'd like to give you some more song exercises for practice. This time two of the songs have a close relation to traditional major blues and one with classical minor blues. You'll also see a typical Gypsy-Waltz written by myself.

You will find all the notated songs on the Play-Along CD to practice with.
Keep up the swing!

8/1: Blues Clair (Django Reinhardt)
This is a good example of a typical II-V-I blues from the *roaring twenties*.
For improvisation you can use the pentatonic blues scale in C, major arpeggios in C, regular minor scales as well as minor 6 scales or arpeggios in C major.

8/2: Good Times (Schukar ziro) (Bertino Rodmann)
This slow ballad, written by myself, is an example of a song with a typical major II-V-I structure. The transcribed solo contains the theme and is intended to give you some inspiration for your own solos.

8/3: Valse à Bertino (Le grand escalier)
(Bertino Rodmann)
This waltz demonstrates the extensive use of minor and major arpeggios with added diminished melodic minor and major scales.
Important: to begin with, practice the transcribed solo very slowly so that you can master fluent playing of the nested and connected arpeggios.

> *Tip 1:*
> *Gypsy (-Jazz) waltzes are great for studying the style of Jazz-Manouche or Gypsy Jazz because the melodies and themes often use typical scales and arpeggios. Try to learn a couple of well-known waltzes such as 'La Gitana', 'Valse á Django' or 'Passion' for your repertoire.*

8/4: Swing 48 (Django Reinhardt)
This song could be called the 'fast brother' of the song '*Blues en mineur*'. This is because the chords are very similar, as are the improvising possibilities. However, for most of the time this song is played very fast (+/- 200 BPM) in comparison to '*Blues en mineur*'. You can use pentatonic minor scales, melodic minor scales, diminished scales and, of course, arpeggios in all keys for improvising.

> *Tip 2:*
> *To being with, practice all of the solos <u>very slowly</u>. Then once you can play them fluently in the correct tempo, you can start to try improvising and adding your own licks, scales and tricks from the examples in this book. Once you can improvise on the solo, then you can start trying to play faster.*
>
> *Remember to always play all the examples given (rhythms or solos) with a metronome!*

8/1 Blues Clair

Music: Django Reinhardt

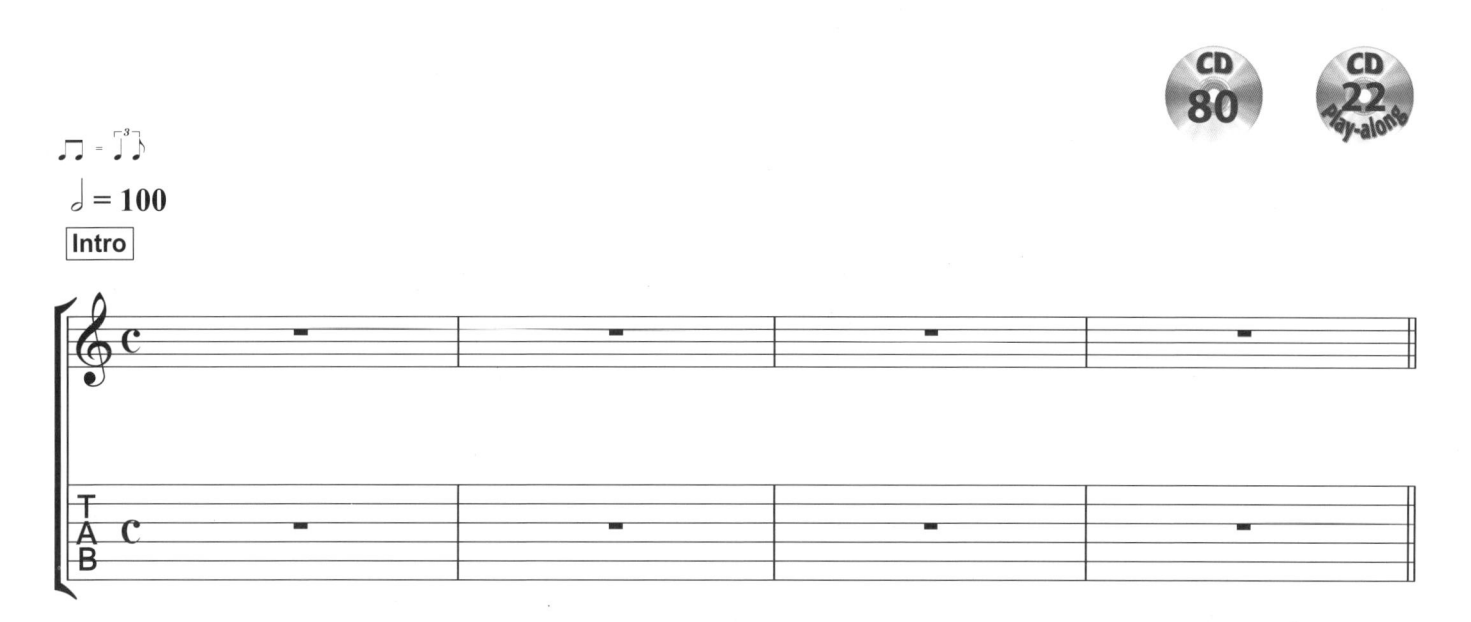

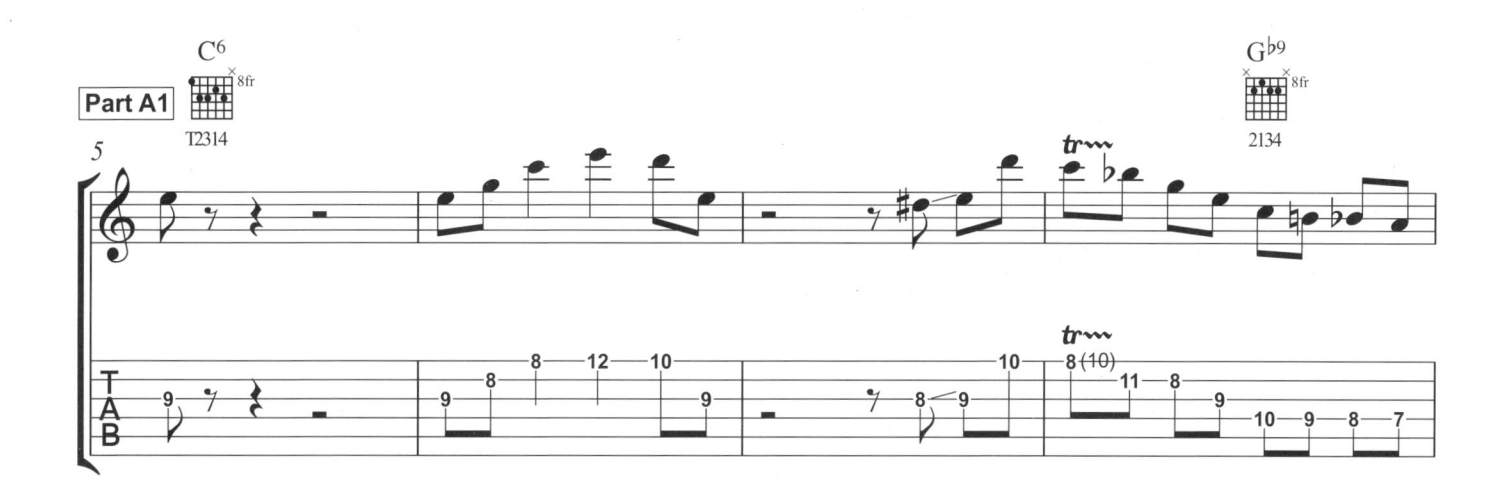

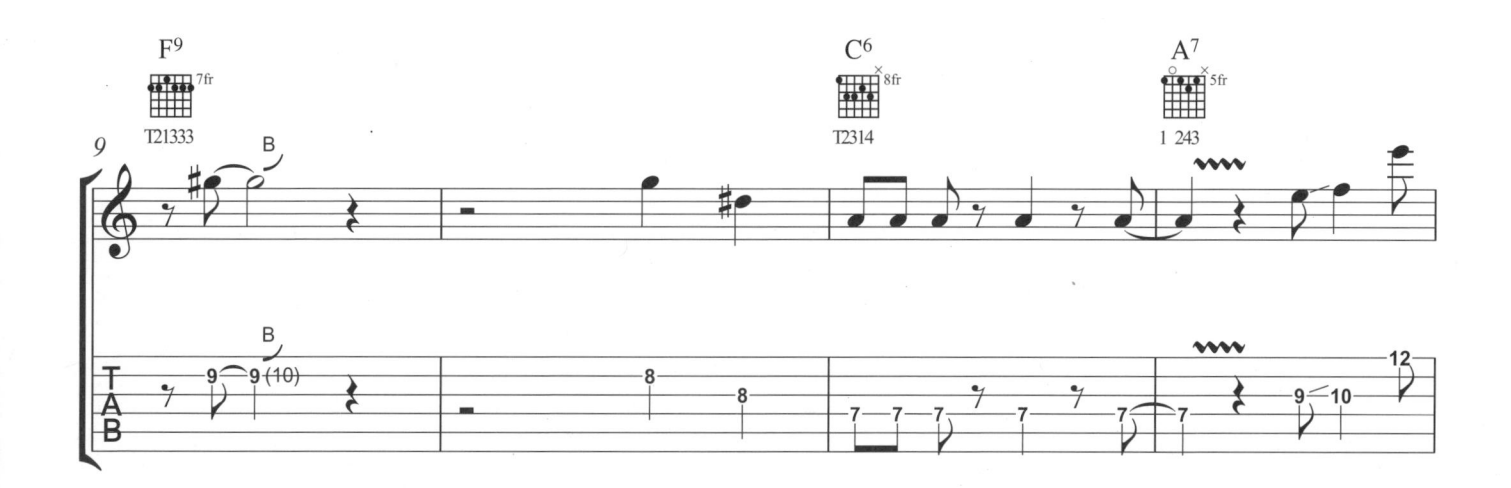

Solo ad lib.

use C-major-scale / C7-scale / G7-scale / A7-scale / F- and C-Arpeggios / Cm-Pentatonic / Cm6-scale

Blues Clair – Solo Guitar

8/2 Good Times (Schukar ziro)

Music: Bertino Rodmann

Good Times (Schukar ziro) – Solo Guitar

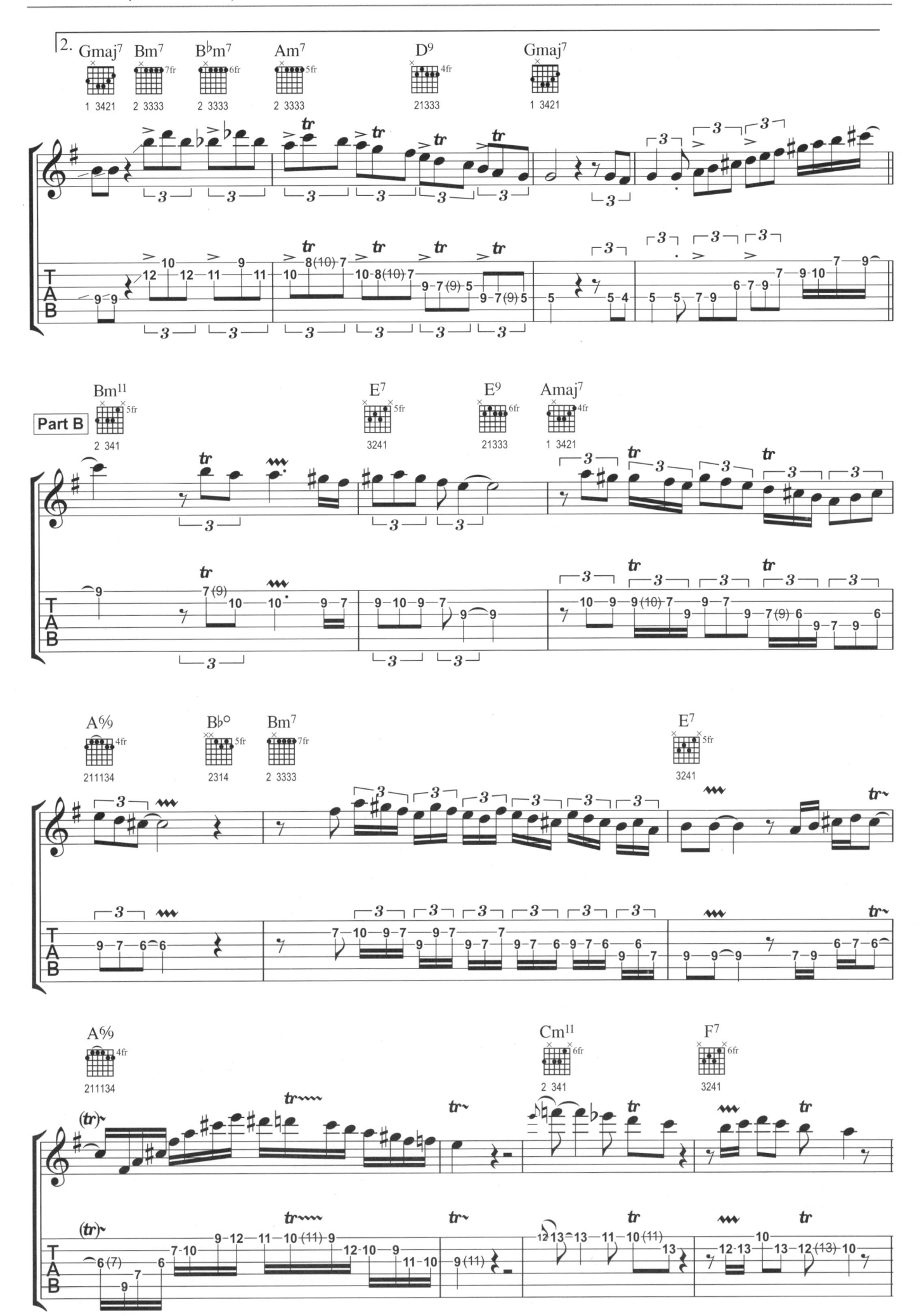

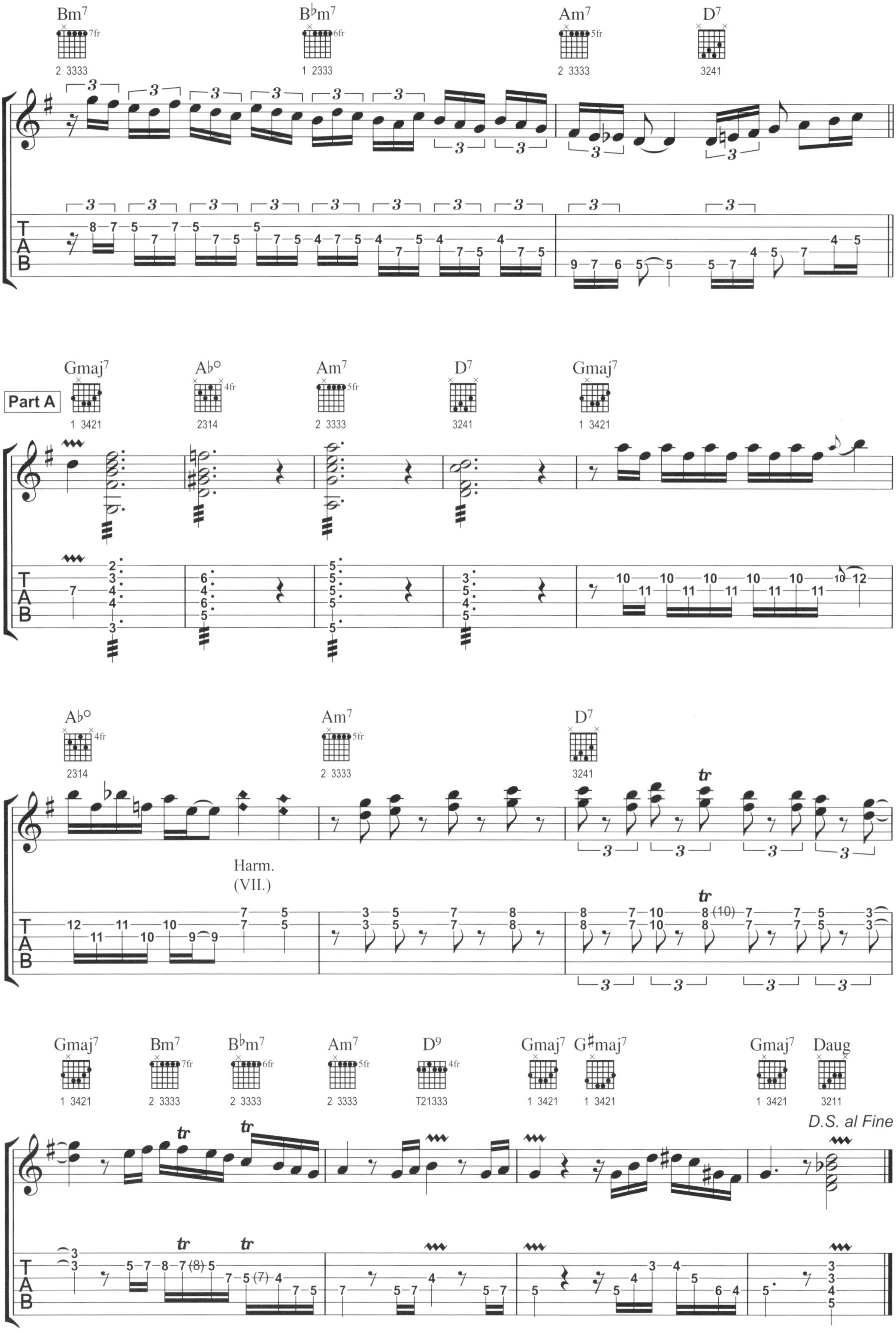
Bm7
B♭m7
Am7
D7
Part A
Gmaj7
A♭°
Am7
D7
Gmaj7
A♭°
Am7
D7
Harm.
(VII.)
Gmaj7
Bm7
B♭m7
Am7
D9
Gmaj7
G♯maj7
Gmaj7
Daug
D.S. al Fine

8/3 Valse à Bertino (Le grand escalier)

Music: Bertino Rodmann
© 2011 by Alfred Music Publishing GmbH

Intro

$\quad$ = 208

Gm6 — B♭m6 — Am7 — D7♭9

Gm6 — B♭m6 — Am7 — A♭13

Part A

Gm7 — Gm6 — Gm7 — Gm6

A7

B♭°
2314
E°
1324
D9
21333
D7
3241
Gm6
2 134
B♭m6
2 134
Am7
2 3333
D7
3241
Part A
Gm7
2 3333
Gm6
2 134
Gm7
2 3333
Gm6
2 134
A7
1 243

Valse à Bertino (Le grand escalier) – Solo Guitar

Am11 D7 Gm7 Gm6
49
Am7 D7 Gm7 D7 Gm6
53
Part C
Gmaj7 C7 Gmaj7 G6
57
Gmaj7 B♭m6 Am6 D9
61

Valse à Bertino (Le grand escalier) – Solo Guitar

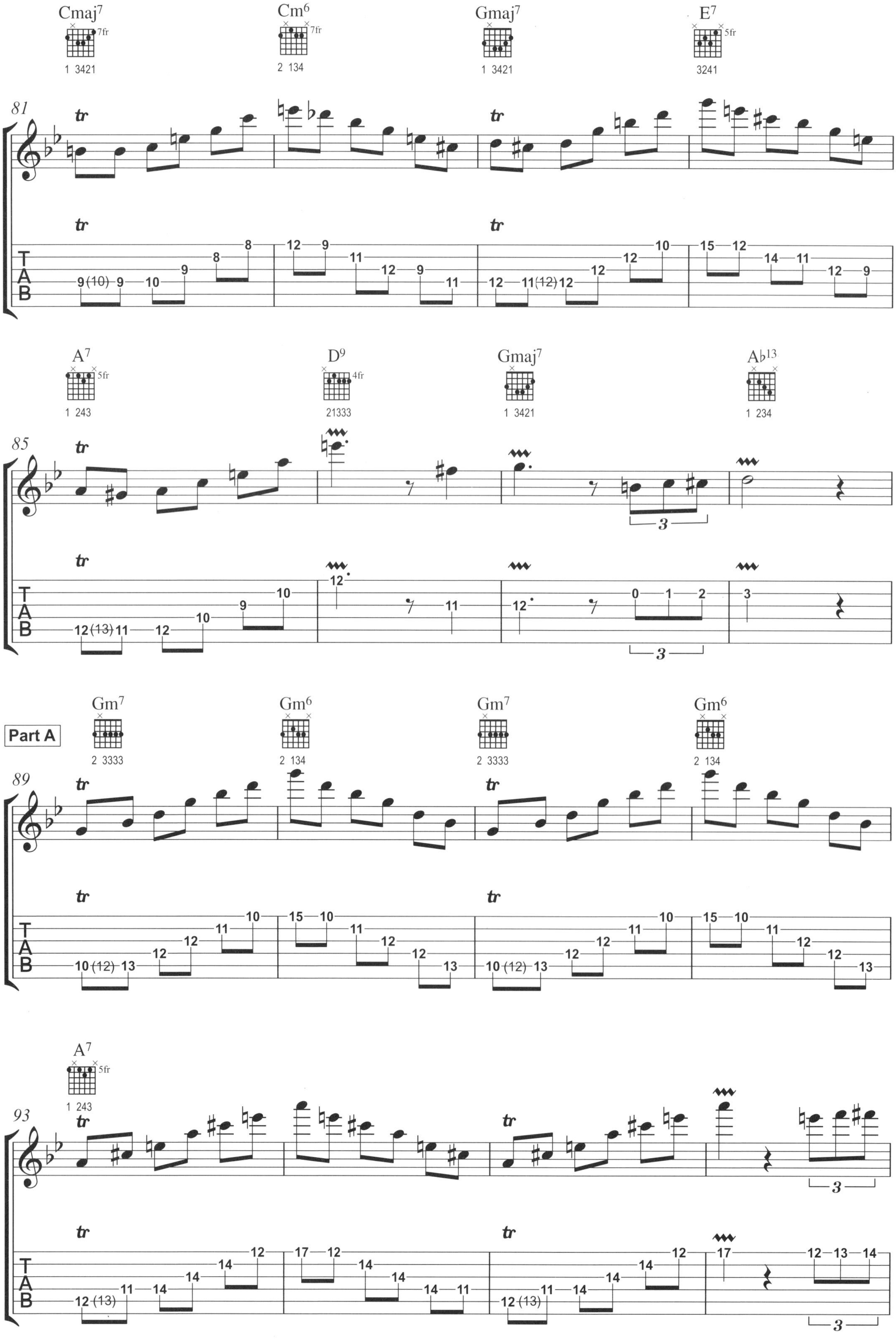
Cmaj7
Cm6
Gmaj7
E7
A7
D9
Gmaj7
A♭13
Part A
Gm7
Gm6
Gm7
Gm6
A7

Valse à Bertino (Le grand escalier) – Solo Guitar

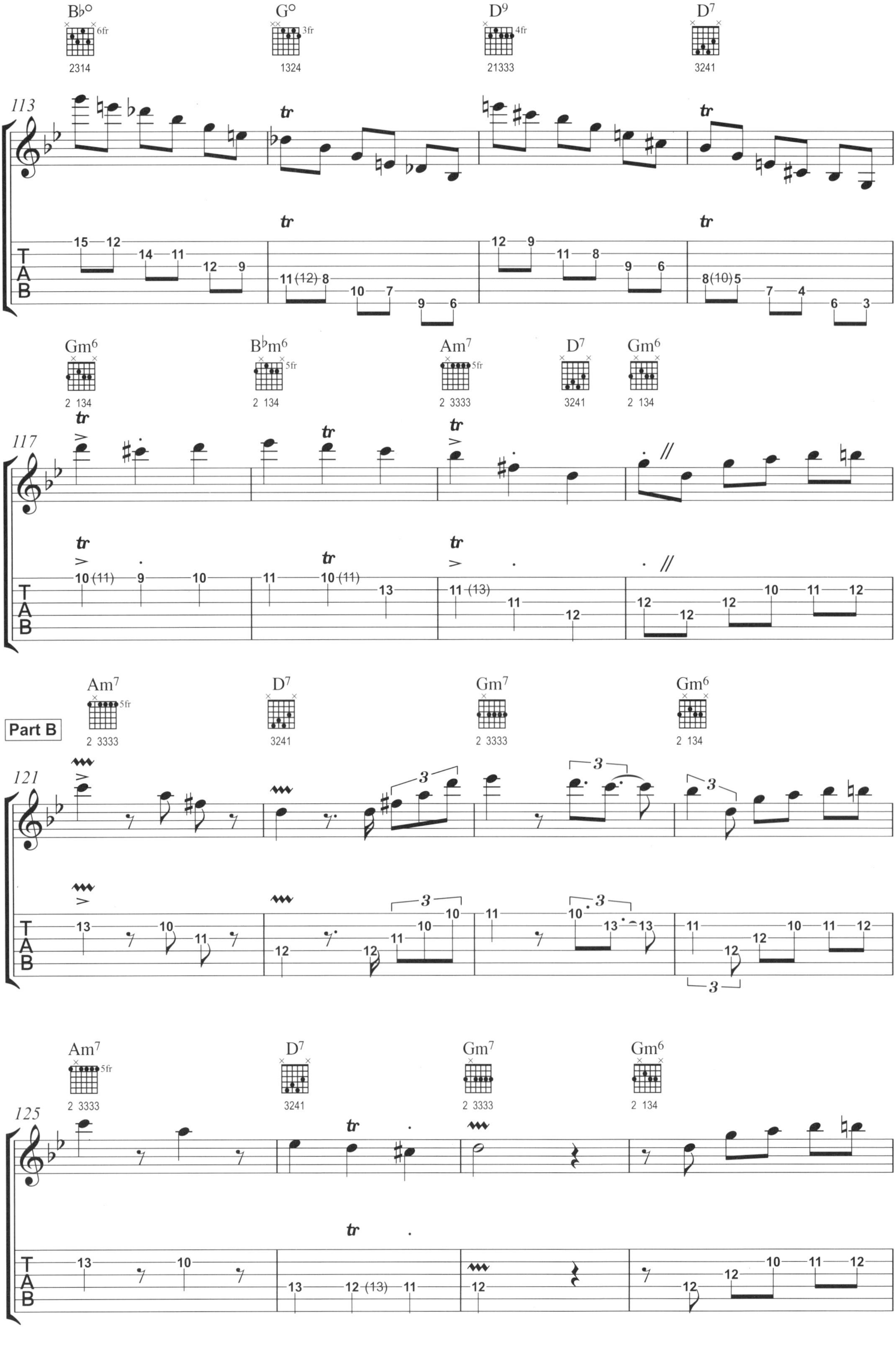

B♭°
G°
D9
D7
Gm6
B♭m6
Am7
D7
Gm6
Part B
Am7
D7
Gm7
Gm6
Am7
D7
Gm7
Gm6

Valse à Bertino (Le grand escalier) – Solo Guitar

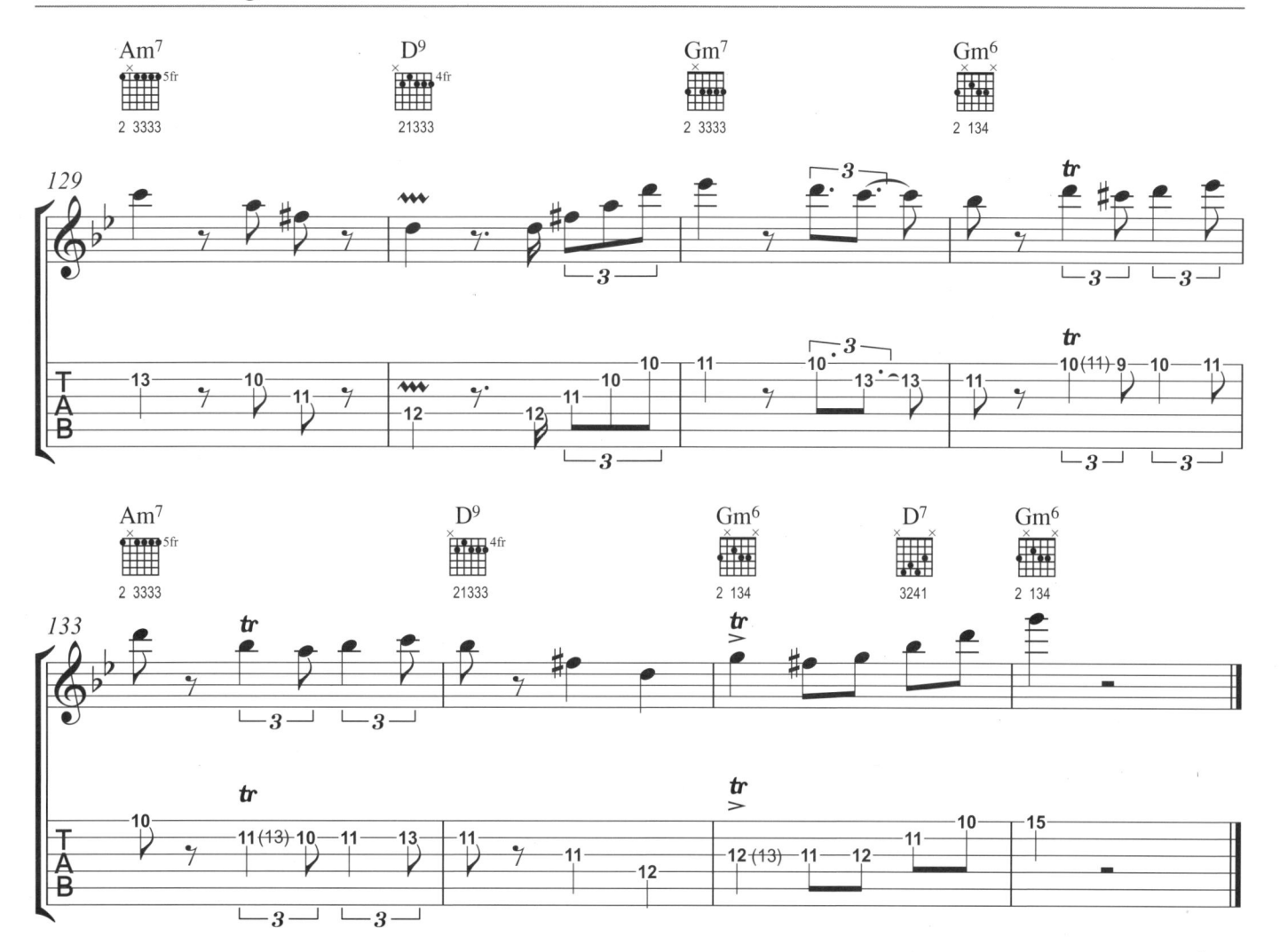

8/4 Swing 48

Music: Django Reinhardt

Swing 48 – Solo Guitar

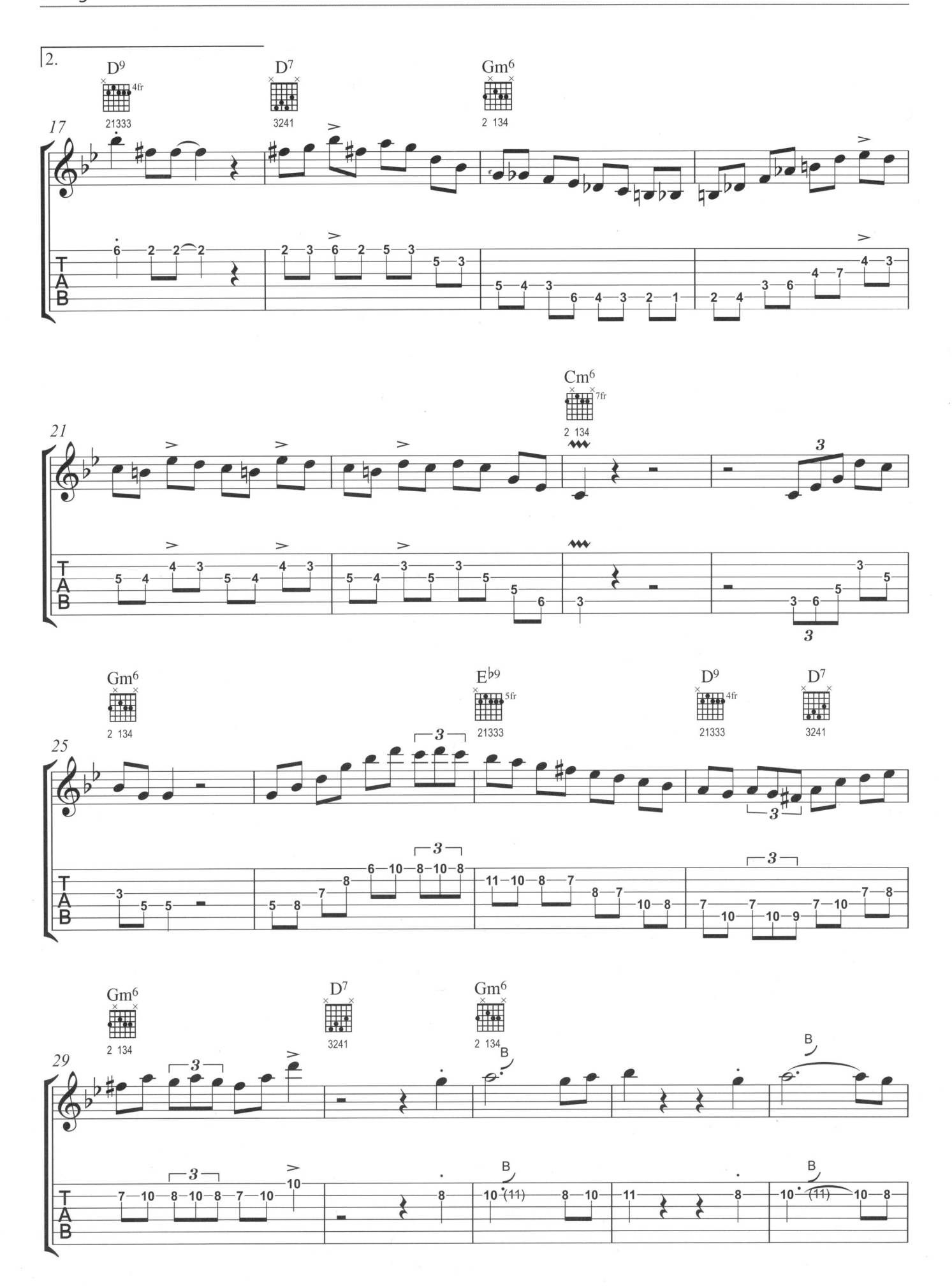

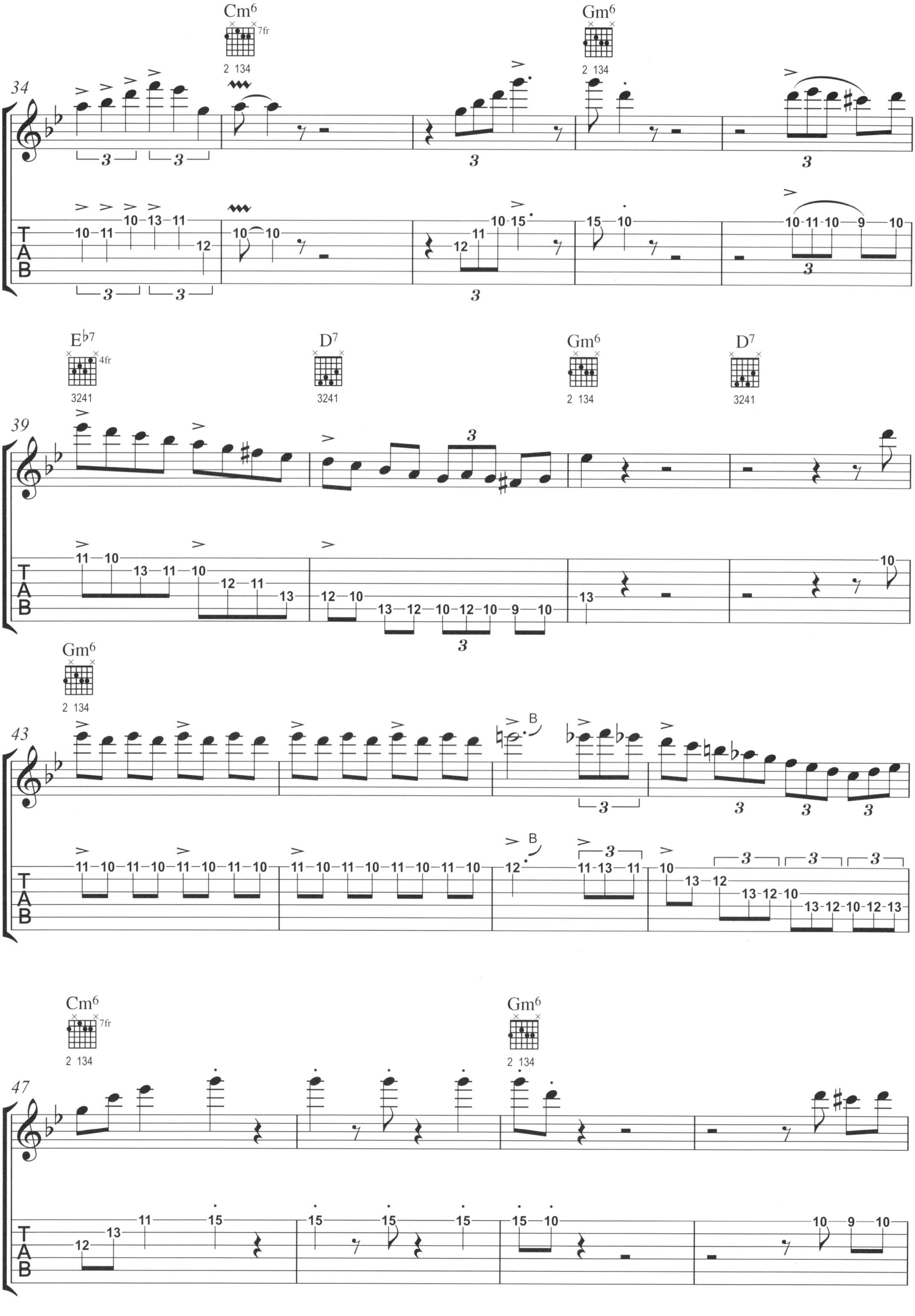
Cm6
7fr
Gm6
34
TAB
Eb7
4fr
D7
Gm6
D7
39
Gm6
43
B
Cm6
7fr
Gm6
47

E♭7
4fr
3241
D7
3241
Gm6
2 134
D7
3241
51
Gm6
2 134
G7
1 243
55
Cm6
7fr
2 134
Gm6
2 134
59
E♭9
5fr
21333
D9
4fr
21333
D7
3241
Gm6
2 134
D7
3241
63
Harm..............................

Gm6 — Solo ad lib.

use Gm6-scale / Gm6-arpeggio / Gm-Pentatonic / Cm6-scale / Cm6-arpeggio / Cm-Pentatonic /

Cm6 ... **Gm6**

Eb7- and D7-arpeggios and -scales / Lick 5/1 through 5/8 and exercise 7/1 through 7/13 (transposed)

E♭9 | **D7** | **Gm6** | **E♭9** | **D7**

Gm6

Swing 48 – Solo Guitar

"If music be the food of love, play on..."

(Shakespeare, Twelfth Night)

Epilogue
Respect and Tolerance, Tradition and Understanding

Well, I know that today *respect* can be a sensitive issue. Oftentimes, people do not have any respect for anything, whether it be for other people, animals or nature. That being said, I don't wish to offend anyone by reprimanding with a raised finger! But when it comes to *Gypsy Jazz* I feel it is necessary to remind everyone that respect and mutual understanding are important – and that's why I want to talk about this in some depth.

For many centuries, Gypsy musicians have been well known for their musical ability and have therefore always been invited with pleasure – but only for their playing. Often the hosts would not wish to have any personal contact with them after they were done playing. The musicians were expected to pack up and leave as soon as they had finished playing, once again taking to the road. Many people thought this way and, regrettably, many still do today.

To be honest, it took me a very long time to decide to write this book about Gypsy Jazz. Why?

Well, firstly it was because of the great respect that I feel for **Django Reinhardt** as well as the other *Sinti* Jazz musicians. But also for the respect I have for their culture!

So after long discussions with **Denni** (one of my masterclass students and a German *Sinto* himself) he finally convinced me that if I wrote this book it would help to share this wonderful music with others. In this way it would be possible to spread the fascination of the guitar-style of Django and all the other Sinti-musicians, as well as to create more respect and admiration for the old *Sinti* culture. So I wrote this book in the hope that those who use it for their own studies will, in their hearts, understand and respect this culture the same as I do!

In the early 1980s I had my first contact with the *Sintis*. It was with some direct relatives of the **Reinhardt** family in southern Germany and my band and I played a lot for them. At this time I (like many others) really had no knowledge about the traditions and rules in *Sinti* life.

Yet, through many experiences with them my respect and appreciation of their customs, rules and behaviour grew. I had many scepticisms and prejudices about *Sinti* and *Roma* culture but over time this changed to a bigger understanding and knowledge about a culture that has been marked by persecution, expulsion and rejection for centuries.

As a *Gadjo* (Romanes for '*non-Gypsy*') I am not comfortable with some of the negative sides of their culture that I still don't understand or sometimes, don't want to understand. And yes (regrettably!), I have also had some negative experiences with some *Sintis in the past*.

But there are good and bad people in all countries and cultures – there is a lot of bad in my own German culture too! But what really counts in the end is the individual, not the tribe, skin colour or nationality!

I strongly believe that anyone who wishes to play *Jazz-Manouche* or *Gypsy Jazz*, the music of the *Sintis* old culture, should have enough knowledge to be able to respect and uphold the traditions, customs and behaviours of the *Sinti* and *Roma* (at least to a certain extent).

Again, I don't want to offend anybody with my pointed finger, but I do want to encourage some important points: **mutual respect and tolerance!**
Much of the lack of understanding and mutual rejection of our two peoples has to do with the fact that mutual respect and tolerance is often not maintained.

Regrettably, many *Gadjos* that wish to play *Gypsy Jazz* or *Jazz-Manouche* seem to be completely uninterested in the Gypsy traditions nor do they have any respect for them – they don't seem to care about it at all. Nevertheless, I am sure (and this is my deepest belief!), that one can only play this music well (authentically) if you understand and respect how *Sintis* live, in the past as well as today.

Only once you understand how the culture and the music are connected, can you develop and understand why certain techniques are played the way they are and not differently!

This is true of the rhythm of *Gypsy Jazz*. Many *Gadjos* think it is just a little 'boom-chick' betraying their ignorance of this culture and music. Actually, it is not so simple – in fact it is much more subtle than you may think.
This is also true when playing solo – many scales, arpeggios, melodies and patterns show their origin of Arabic, Balkanian or other musical influences.

These influences together with the European musical traditions such as czárdás, French chanson and musette waltzes flamenco and Jazz make up the melange that is *Jazz-Manouche*. If you do not appreciate these traditions at all, or if you believe that you could play like **Django** just by 'copying it a bit', then you will fail. It will be a mere 'pastiche' and never sound authentic.

It may be that one day, things that you play will sound 'close to *Gypsy Jazz*' – you will surely be able to learn some pieces that sound a bit like it – or almost. But to be able to play the style and sound really authentic is something completely different and depends upon a much deeper understanding about the culture and the music – of this I am sure!

You can prove what I am saying by listening closely to one of the many *Gadjo Jazz-Manouche* bands that are around today, and comparing them with real Gypsy bands. The bands that sound genuine are the ones that are aware of the traditions of the *Sinti* and *Roma*, or even learned directly from them. A very good example of one of these bands is the French group '*Selmer #607*' which also has in it members of the *Reinhardt family* (*Noe Reinhardt*) as well as some 'gadjo'-musicians like **Richard Manetti** or **Adrien Moignard.**

To this end, I would recommend to anyone that wants to play *Gypsy Jazz* to first take a close look at the culture of the *Roma* and *Sinti*. However, always conduct this research with the necessary respect and from a suitable distance, as a civilised person. To impose oneself or to behave inappropriately is impertinent and not wanted in our own society – nor is it with the *Sintis*. I have always found that *Sinti* and *Roma* are very friendly and hospitable people but it always depends on your own behaviour. **So please, give them some respect!**

To speed or not to speed?
I would now like to spend some time talking about speed in music in general as well as in *Gypsy Jazz*.

Today, many guitarists copy the sound of *Gypsy Jazz* players such as **Bireli Lagrene, Stochelo Rosenberg, Andreas Öberg, Adrien Moignard** and other high class guitar players – but the sound gets transformed from original *Gypsy Jazz* to a kind of high-speed swing.

This is very sad as it doesn't have anything to do with the real art of *Jazz-Manouche*. Remember that swing Jazz was dance music at that time!

You can hear this if you listen to some old recordings of the 1920-30s. A good example of this is the song '*Charleston*' recorded by **Django Reinhardt** in 1936 with the **QDHDF**.

I must admit that I really appreciate the guitarists mentioned above – they are all high class players of this genre and others.

Sadly, it seems today that speed has become the most important element to establishing oneself as a guitarist in this style. But to be honest, the speed at which these guitarists are playing may be fascinating but it is not everything! It is much more important to have something to say with their instruments.

Django Reinhardt, Tschan-Tschou Vidal or *Baro Ferret* always had something to say with their guitars!

It can be fascinating to listen to these fast players and admire their ability. But at the same we must ask the question – '*What does speed deliver as a musical expression?*' What is it? Aggression or sadness? Happiness or passion?

I can see none of these attributes in speed. And if speed be 'everything' in music then it means nothing.

Also, have you ever tried to dance with your partner at a speed of 250 BPMs? *C'est impossible!*

When you listen closely to **Django Reinhardt's** playing you may be captivated by the incredible speed at which he sometimes played, especially knowing that he only had two healthy fingers! But at the same time you can realise that he used speed only as a vehicle when musically appropriate. It was never to 'show how good he was' as a guitarist or mere flamboyance but as a musical necessity.

So this is something that I would like you to keep in mind when playing: treat speed with respect and yes, be fascinated. But don't idolise so it becomes the only important part of your playing, especially not in *Gypsy Jazz*!

Never forget that speed is something that comes automatically once you have really understood something and practiced it slowly many times. Control is the key!

What is important when playing is the meaning of your music, to communicate and give something to the audience. It's about what you want to convey in your music and it coming through to the ears of your listeners. How fast you can play this or that lick, scale or trick doesn't really matter, playing with your heart is much more important.

If sometimes you don't know how to move on with your playing, just go back to the source of it all and listen to some original recordings of **Django Reinhardt**, or other *Gypsy Jazz* masters like **Fapy Lafertin, Angelo DeBarre** or **Romane**.

Maybe you will then be able to feel the same as I do and you will be able to get new inspiration, you'll find a new understanding and your horizon will widen and become more enlightened. Maybe then you will also start to understand what has been discussed above.

For now, I wish you lots of fun and good luck with playing *Gypsy Jazz* – so go ahead to learn now!

Keep up the swing,
Bertino Rodmann

About the Author

Alexander Bertino Rodmann was born in 1958 into an artistic family. His mother was a painter and artist and his grand-uncle worked as a violist in southern France. *Bertino* has played the guitar since the age of thirteen.

Growing up surrounded by the blues, rock and pop music of the 1970s, he began playing the guitar auto-didactically just by listening to 33 inch vinyl records and trying to copy, learn and play what he heard.

After many musical experiences in countless bands and with projects and studio recordings in different styles, he started to get interested in Jazz especially in swing and Jazz-manouche in the early 1980s.

He was introduced to the style of *Gypsy Jazz* at a friend's house by listening to a record of **Django Reinhardt & the Quintette du Hotclub de France** which overwhelmed him. In the following years, *Bertino* became almost 'infected' with this music and this forced him to once again learn by ear what he heard on those records.

In the many hours of his self-study he listened to the licks, tricks and solos of **Django Reinhardt, Hännsche Weiss, Angelo DeBarre, Fapy Lafertin** and many others of today's *Sinti* guitarists, trying to learn and incorporate their musical language into his own style of playing.

To expand his knowledge of *Gypsy Jazz* and to learn more from the source, *Bertino* took part in several masterclasses starting in 2006 with **Romane** (in Lyon, France), in 2007 with **Stochelo Rosenberg** (in Augsburg, Germany), and in 2012 with **Angelo DeBarre** (in Samois, France).

Bertino has worked as a musician and guitar teacher for many years. He has worked for several music schools in and around Frankfurt (Germany) and today gives mostly private lessons.

Due to the large number of student enquiries that he received about lessons on *Gypsy Jazz* for guitar, he started his own workshop **'Masterclass for Gypsy Jazz Guitar'** in 2007. In the autumn of 2011 he released his first guitar method book 'Gypsy Jazz Guitar'. Today he plays *Jazz-Manouche*, Jazz, swing, bossa and more, with his own band '**Coeur du Bois**'.

Bertino has several websites about *Gypsy Jazz* that offer lots of information and news about *Gypsy Jazz* as well as online registration for his masterclasses:
www.Jazzmanouche.de
www.gypsyJazzworkshop.net

" Music should strike fire from the heart of man and bring tears from the eyes of woman ..."

(Ludwig Van Beethoven)

Glossary

Alternate Picking
Every beat is always played up and down (up and down strokes) with the pick. The direction is never changed no matter what string is being played (see chapter *Introducing Solo Guitar*, page 77).

Apoyando
Apoyando (IPA: [a p o ˈja n d o], Spanish for 'locked on' or 'lean on') is a picking technique for the guitar that originally comes from classical guitar playing. Whilst playing apoyando the finger gets laid (locked) onto the next following string, resting there until the next beat.

Arpeggio
Arpeggio (Pl.: Arpeggios) is the musical name for a chord where the notes are played one after another, not all together at once. It is also known as a *broken chord*.

Chords
A chord is any set of two or more notes that are played at once. For example, if you play three notes beginning from the root note of a major scale in steps of triads at the same time, this will be 'root chord' or a 'major chord'. And can be described as a triad of major quality built upon the root note.

Example: a C major chord contains the notes C E G – these are the 1st, 3rd and 5th notes of the major scale.

It is common in jazz to have 'altered chords' used. These are chords with four, five or even six notes, mostly as one, two or more notes added to a basic triad. Chords and their symbols often vary in music notation. The same chord can be marked with different labels.

Example: the chord G major 7 can be noted as G-major7 or Gmaj7 or GM7 or GΔ7 or even as Gj7. In this book I use the following terminology for the chords (all examples in C):

C	-major chords (C= C-E-G = step: 1-3-5)
C7	-major 7th chords (major triad + add. minor seventh, step: 1-3-5-b7)
C7/9	-major 7th/9th chords (major triad + add. minor seventh and ninth, step: 1-3-5-b7-9)
Cmaj7	-major 7th chords (major triad + add. major seventh, step: 1-3-5-7)
Cm	-minor chords (minor triad, Cm = C-Eb-G, step: 1-b3-5)
Cm6	-minor 6th chords (minor triad + add. sixth, step: 1-b3-5-6)
Cm7	-minor 7th chords (minor seventh, step: 1-b3-5-b7)
Cm11	-minor 11th chords (minor triad + eleventh, step: 1-b3-5-11)
Cm7b5	-half diminished chords (root, minor third, flatted fifth, flat seventh, step: 1-b3-b5-b7)
C° (dim)	-diminished chords (root, minor third, flatted fifth, step: 1-b3-b5-(6))

Be aware of the different chord voicings and fingerings in Gypsy-jazz with identical chord names (see chapter *Chord Substitution*, page 30).

Chord Substitution
The exchanging of chords with tonal relatives e.g. other substituted chords is called chord substitution in jazz harmony.

Example: in a jazz chord sequence it would be possible to play 'Dm7 – Db9 – Cmaj7' instead of the chords 'Dm7 – G7 – Cmaj7', where Db = the tritone of G.

Generally, in jazz, all chords can possibly be exchanged while improvising. Substitutions of minor or major parallels doesn't affect the sound much whereas, substitutions of dominant chords can lead to complete harmonic chaos.

Gypsy Jazz Guitar – Glossary

Czárdás

This is the music of the Hungarian gypsies, often wrongly called 'gypsy music'. Czardas (also Csárdás, Csárdá, Czárdász (pronounced 'tschardasch') from the Hungarian word csárda which means guesthouse) is the Hungarian national dance. It is a long, slow 'pathetic' circular dance of men in 2/4 rhythm (lassú) in the minor key followed by a wild major key dance of men and women pairs called 'friss'.

There are different theories about where this dance came from. Some say its origins are an ancient dance of the Haiduks (an old Hungarian tribe) whereas others believe it has connections to the 'verbunkos' (advertising dances), a dance from the 18th century that the Hungarian gypsies used to exhibit soldiers for the Habsburgian army.

Today, czardas are played by most Hungarian gypsy ensembles. They also have a role in classical music through the compositions of Hungarian composer Franz Liszt. He composed several czardas for piano, his most famous being the 'Czardas Macabre'.

Hot Club de France

The *'Hot Club de France' (HCDF)* was a group of Jazzfans from France, founded by **Charles Delauney**, the man who 'discovered' **Django Reinhardt** in the early 1920s. He later went on to become his mentor and manager for a while.

The *HCDF* organised jazz concerts, published a French jazz club newspaper and was involved in many of the later recordings of *'Django Reinhardt & the Quintette du Hot Club de France' (QHCDF)*. **Charles Delauney** also organised tours across France for many famous American jazz musicians such as **Duke Ellington, Louis 'Satchmo' Armstrong** and **Benny Goodman**. As well as the tours he organised meetings between these musicians and **Django Reinhardt**.

Jazz-Manouche

French term for *Gypsy Jazz*, Jazz music played by *Sinti* or *Manouche*.

La Pompe

The rhythm *La Pompe* (*pompe* = French for *'to pump'*) is the swing Jazz rhythm that was made famous by the **Quintette du Hot Club de France** and **Django Reinhardt** although it was mostly influenced by the playing of **Django's** younger brother **Joseph 'Nin-Nin' Reinhardt** and the other rhythm guitar players of the **QHCDF** e.g. **Roger Chaput, Marcel Biancci** and others.

Maccaferri, Mario

Mario Maccaferri was born in Cento near Bologna in 1900 and died in Paris in 1993. He was a well-known classical guitarist and student of the famous classical guitar maestro **Andrés Segovia**. **Maccaferri** was also a guitar maker and developed the legendary D- and O-hole **Selmer guitars** (acoustic jazz guitars), the model 'Orchestre' and model 'Jazz'. He worked for **Selmer** in Paris from 1932 to 1936. Later, he became the developer of the plastic mouthpieces for saxophones and in the early 1950s built another legendary guitar: the 'Plastic Maccaferri Guitar', a guitar that was completely made out of plastic.

Reinhardt, Django

Jean Baptiste 'Django' Reinhardt (*23rd January 1910 in Liberchies, Belgium; †16th May 1953 in Samois-sur-Seine near Paris) was a guitarist, composer and bandleader and marked as the founder of European jazz.

More information can be found at ***www.jazzmanouche.de*** (*'Django and Guitars'*).

Joseph 'Nin-Nin' Reinhardt, the younger brother of the famous guitarist *Jean Baptiste 'Django' Reinhardt*, was *Django's* steady companion and was also a rhythm guitarist.

For most of his life, *Joseph* was cast in the shadow of his famous brother. Whilst being a very respected and talented guitarist he lacked the genius and brilliant creativity of his older sibling. In the 1960s he released some unsuccessful records as a solo artist.

Reststroke

The reststroke (English for Apoyando = to rest) comes from classical guitar playing and is a picking technique for the right hand (see chapter 'Introducing Solo Guitar', page 77).

Selmer

A French company that were a maker of saxophones and clarinets in the early 1900s. Later on they were the maker and distributor of the famous D- and O-hole guitars, the model 'Orchestre' and model 'Jazz' (acoustic jazz guitars without pickups) that were designed and developed by *Mario Maccaferri* and made famous by *Django Reinhardt* who played them until his death in 1952.

Between 1932 and 1952 only about 1000 of these guitars were built. Selmer later specialised in building saxophones and clarinets after the guitar production ceased in 1959.

More information on Selmer can be found at www.jazzmanouche.de (see Django & Guitars – Selmer guitars).

Sweptstroke

To sweep means that several strings should be played one after another without the pick leaving the strings.

Swing (rhythm)

Swing is a flowing 'swinging' rhythm particularly played in jazz but also used in other musical styles such as country music.

The swinging effect has three basic elements:

- the shuffle – this is the ternary interpretation of a 'binary rhythm' (the interpretation between subtle delays of notes on the counting time 'and' leading up to the real ternary, triplet extreme).
- the offbeat – on the emphasis between beat and basic pulse (on the counting time 'and').
- the backbeat – also the emphasis of the 'weak' counts (which on a 4/4 beat are the '2' and '4').

This rhythm is one of the more important elements in jazz. In 'new classical music' (such as by Igor Stravinsky) this rhythm is used, particularly in some tangos. A good early historical example of this is 'Notes inégales' in French baroque music of the 17th and 18th centuries.

Tritone (Tritonus)

A tritone is a musical interval which contains three (tri) whole tones (tonus). The diminished fifth-position (from the root note) would be one. Example: G, tritone = Db

Up until the late middle ages, the triton was known as the 'devils interval' or 'the devil in music' (Lat. 'diabolus in musica') because of its harmonic difficulties in singing and playing.

Sources:

Paul Hohstetter – The Story of Selmer – http://www.lutherie.net/selmindx.html

Michael Horowitz – Gypsy Picking, 2003, published at: DjangoBooks.com, USA

The History of the Roma – http://www.romahistory.com

Thanks

This book is dedicated to my beloved wife Gina. She has always supported me regardless of what has been happening to us in all of those years. She has always brought love and warmth into my life and has patience and understanding for my love of music. *Merci mon amour!*

Once again, I would like to thank **Django Reinhardt**, the guitar genius and greatest player of all, and also to all the *Sinti* guitarists of today and the past for the great inspiration, depth and emotion in their music.

A special thank you goes to **Romane** and his sons **Richard** and **Pierre Manetti** for all their shared knowledge, inspiration and patience.

Many thanks also to my band 'Coeur du Bois': Titi Bamberger (guitar), Jonas Lohse (bass), Matthias Hampel (guitar) for his rhythmic support on the recordings. Thanks to the recording studio 'King 54' and the sound engineers Michael Laven and Krys Kozlowski for the great sound of the CD recordings. Also to Leo Eimers and Maurice Dupont for their wonderful guitars and their help and support of this book.

Last but not least, I would like to thank you, all the interested guitarists who have bought this book and who will, by learning and playing its contents respectfully, help to keep the wonderful music of *Gypsy Jazz* alive!

Keep up the swing!

Tracklist – CD

Track-#	Title	Length	Tempo (BPM)	Time
1	Tuning	00:28	---	---
2	Finger Exercise 1 with chromatics	02:29	200	4/4
3	Finger Excercise 2	00:47	200	4/4
4	Rhythm Guitar Excercise 1, Lesson 1	00:22	100	4/4
5	Rhythm Guitar Excercise 2, Lesson 1	00:22	100	8/8
6	Rhythm Guitar Excercise 3, Lesson 1	00:17	100	8/8
7	Rhythm Guitar Excercise 1/1, Lesson 1	00:21	100	4/4
8	Rhythm Guitar Excercise 1/2, Lesson 1	00:28	100	3/4
9	Rhythm Guitar Excercise 1/3, Lesson 1	00:22	100	4/4
10	Rhythm Guitar Excercise 1/4, Lesson 1	00:19	200	8/8
11	Rhythm Guitar Excercise 1/5, Lesson 1	00:19	200	8/8
12	Rhythm Guitar Excercise 2/1, Lesson 2 'La Pompe'	01:32	100	4/4
13	Rhythm Guitar Excercise 2/2, Lesson 2, Chord-Substitution	00:53	200	4/4
14	Rhythm Guitar Excercise – Gypsychords	02:27	---	---
15	Rhythm Guitar Excercise 2/3, Lesson 2, Chord-Substitution	00:52	200	8/8
16	Rhythm Guitar Excercise 2/4, Lesson 2, Chord-Substitution	00:52	200	8/8
17	Rhythm Guitar Excercise 3/1, Lesson 3 *Minor Swing*	02:13	100	4/4
18	Rhythm Guitar Excercise 3/2, Lesson 3 *Douce Ambiance*	02:57	100	4/4
19	Rhythm Guitar Excercise 3/3, Lesson 3 *Good Times – Schukar ziro*	03:53	75	4/4
20	Rhythm Guitar Excercise 3/4, Lesson 3 *Blues en mineur*	02:39	70	4/4
21	Rhythm Guitar Excercise 3/5, Lesson 3 *Valse à Bertino*	02:16	208	3/4
22	Rhythm Guitar Excercise 3/6, Lesson 3 *Blues Clair*	02:08	100	4/4
23	Rhythm Guitar Excercise 3/7, Lesson 3 *Swing 48*	02:27	112	4/4
24	Solo Guitar 1, Picking Technique 1/1 Reststroke Picking	00:45	100	4/4
25	Solo Guitar 1, Picking Technique 1/2 Up-/Down-Reststroke Picking	00:45	100	4/4
26	Solo Guitar 1, Picking Technique 1/3 Sweptstroke Picking	00:23	200	8/8
27	Solo Guitar 1, Picking Technique 1/4 Arpeggio Picking	00:32	200	8/8
28	Solo Guitar 2, Scales – Part 1, 2/1 Simple Pentatonic in Am	00:29	200	4/4
29	Solo Guitar 2, Scales – Part 1, 2/2 Am Pentatonic + 6th	00:34	200	4/4
30	Solo Guitar 2, Scales – Part 1, 2/3 Am6 scale	00:29	200	8/8
31	Solo Guitar 2, Scales – Part 1, 2/4 D major scale	00:34	200	8/8
32	Solo Guitar 2, Scales – Part 1, 2/5 Seventh scale E7	00:36	200	8/8
33	Solo Guitar 2, Scales – Part 1, 2/6 E7 diminished scale	00:35	200	8/8
34	Solo Guitar 2, Scales – Part 1, 2/7 Seventh scale A7	00:38	200	8/8
35	Solo Guitar 2, Scales – Part 1, 2/8 Gmaj7 scale	00:44	200	8/8
36	Solo Guitar 2, Scales – Part 1, 2/9 G major scale (Django style)	00:36	200	8/8
37	Solo Guitar 3, Arpeggios, 3/1 Am arpeggio	00:45	100	4/4
38	Solo Guitar 3, Arpeggios, 3/2 Am6 arpeggio	00:52	100	4/4
39	Solo Guitar 3, Arpeggios, 3/3 Am6 arpeggio (Variation)	00:34	200	8/8
40	Solo Guitar 3, Arpeggios, 3/4 G-Major arpeggio	00:40	100	4/4
41	Solo Guitar 3, Arpeggios, 3/5 G-Major arpeggio (Variation)	00:35	200	4/4
42	Solo Guitar 3, Arpeggios, 3/6 G-Major arpeggio (D-Shape)	00:41	100	4/4
43	Solo Guitar 3, Arpeggios, 3/7 Cm arpeggio	00:43	100	4/4

Gypsy Jazz Guitar – CD-Tracklist

Track-#	Title	Length	Tempo (BPM)	Time
44	Solo Guitar 4, Solo Lick 4/1 ('*Minor Swing*')	00:18	200	8/8
45	Solo Guitar 4, Solo Lick 4/2 ('*Minor Swing*')	00:17	200	8/8
46	Solo Guitar 4, Solo Lick 4/3 ('*Minor Swing*')	00:19	200	8/8
47	Solo Guitar 4, Solo Lick 4/4 ('*Minor Swing*')	00:23	200	8/8
48	Solo Guitar 4, Solo Lick 4/5 ('*Minor Swing*')	00:22	200	8/8
49	Solo Guitar 4, Solo Lick 4/6 ('*Minor Swing*')	00:23	200	8/8
50	Solo Guitar 4, Solo Lick 4/7 ('*Minor Swing*')	00:23	200	8/8
51	Solo Guitar 4, Solo Lick 4/8 ('*Minor Swing*')	00:21	200	8/8
52	Solo Guitar 4, 4/9, Solo '*Minor Swing*'	02:15	100	4/4
53	Solo Guitar 4, 4/10, Solo '*Blues en mineur*'	02:39	70	4/4
54	Solo Guitar 4, 4/11, Solo '*Douce Ambiance*'	02:56	100	4/4
55	Solo Guitar 5, Tips & Tricks, Lick 5/1	00:19	200	8/8
56	Solo Guitar 5, Tips & Tricks, Lick 5/2	00:17	200	8/8
57	Solo Guitar 5, Tips & Tricks, Lick 5/3	00:18	200	8/8
58	Solo Guitar 5, Tips & Tricks, Lick 5/4	00:20	200	8/8
59	Solo Guitar 5, Tips & Tricks, Lick 5/5	00:20	200	8/8
60	Solo Guitar 5, Tips & Tricks, Lick 5/6	00:21	200	4/4
61	Solo Guitar 5, Tips & Tricks, Lick 5/7	00:16	200	4/4
62	Solo Guitar 6, Scales – Part 2, 6/1 Cm pentatonic	00:57	100	4/4
63	Solo Guitar 6, Scales – Part 2, 6/2 Cm pentatonic + 6th	01:02	100	4/4
64	Solo Guitar 6, Scales – Part 2, 6/3 Cm pentatonic over 3 octaves	00:39	200	4/4
65	Solo Guitar 6, Scales – Part 2, 6/4 Blues scale in C	00:45	200	4/4
66	Solo Guitar 6, Scales – Part 2, 6/5 Harmonic minor scale in A	00:43	200	4/4
67	Solo Guitar 7, The use of scales & Arpeggios, Example 7/1	00:20	200	4/4
68	Solo Guitar 7, The use of scales & Arpeggios, Example 7/2	00:15	200	4/4
69	Solo Guitar 7, The use of scales & Arpeggios, Example 7/3	00:24	80	4/4
70	Solo Guitar 7, The use of scales & Arpeggios, Example 7/4	00:15	200	4/4
71	Solo Guitar 7, The use of scales & Arpeggios, Example 7/5	00:19	200	4/4
72	Solo Guitar 7, The use of scales & Arpeggios, Example 7/6	00:20	200	4/4
73	Solo Guitar 7, The use of scales & Arpeggios, Example 7/7	00:15	160	4/4
74	Solo Guitar 7, The use of scales & Arpeggios, Example 7/8	00:19	120	4/4
75	Solo Guitar 7, The use of scales & Arpeggios, Example 7/9	00:15	200	4/4
76	Solo Guitar 7, The use of scales & Arpeggios, Example 7/10	00:24	100	4/4
77	Solo Guitar 7, The use of scales & Arpeggios, Example 7/11	00:22	200	4/4
78	Solo Guitar 7, The use of scales & Arpeggios, Example 7/12	00:24	200	4/4
79	Solo Guitar 7, The use of scales & Arpeggios, Example 7/13	00:15	200	4/4
80	Solo Guitar 8, 8/1, Solo '*Blues Clair*'	02:07	100	4/4
81	Solo Guitar 8, 8/2, Solo '*Good Times – Schukar ziro*'	03:53	75	4/4
82	Solo Guitar 8, 8/3, Solo '*Valse à Bertino*'	02:15	208	3/4
83	Solo Guitar 8, 8/4, Solo '*Swing 48*'	02:28	112	4/4